Land of Our Lady Series

Volume I — Founders of Freedom

Volume II — Bearers of Freedom

Volume III — Leaders of Freedom

Volume IV — Challenge of Freedom

Volume V — Guardian of Freedom

THE NEUMANN PRESS

Mary's Immaculate Conception

HISTORY. The Patroness of the United States is Mary Immaculate. The choice of Mary Immaculate as the principal Patron of the United States was decreed by the First Council of Baltimore, on February 7, 1847.

The dedication of our country under the spiritual banner of Mary Immaculate represents the united appeal of American Catholics for Mary's intercession. It not only gives honor to her, but enlists her help in making our country spiritually strong. This means that our country looks upon Mary as its special protector. Through her intercession, we hope to obtain special favors and blessings from God. The feast-day of the Immaculate Conception is December 8.

BELIEF. Catholics believe that Our Lady was preserved from all stain of original sin from the moment when her soul was united to her body— the Immaculate Conception. This special privilege was granted to Mary by Almighty God, through the merits of Jesus Christ.

Prayer

O GOD, who by the Immaculate Conception of the Virgin didst make ready a fitting habitation for Thy Son, we beseech Thee that Thou who didst keep her clean from all stain by the precious death of the same Thy Son, foreseen by Thee, mayest grant unto us in like manner to be made clean through her intercession and so attain unto Thee. Through the same Christ Our Lord. Amen.

An indulgence of three years: Plenary on the usual conditions, if this prayer is recited daily for a month (See "The Raccolta," the official book of indulgenced prayers, page 266).

DOGMA. The Immaculate Conception is a dogma (a truth solemnly declared by the Church to be an article of Catholic faith), and was defined by Pope Pius IX on December 8, 1854. It is one of five great truths pertaining to Mary. The other four are: Her Assumption, her Divine Motherhood, her Perpetual Virginity, and her Plenitude of Grace.

Courtesy of Rev. J. B. Carol, O. F. M.

Land of Our Lady Series

Founders of Freedom
by
Sister M. Benedict Joseph, S.H.N.
Los Angeles, Calif.

Bearers of Freedom
by
Sister M. Veronica, S.P.B.V.
Central Falls, R. I.

Leaders of Freedom
by
Sister M. Clarita, O.P.
Watertown, Mass.

Challenge of Freedom
by
Sister M. Theresine, S.N.D.
Cleveland, Ohio

Guardian of Freedom
by
Sister M. Augusta, H.H.M.
Akron, Ohio

Land of Our Lady Series

Guardian
of
Freedom

by Sister M. Augusta, H.H.M.

EDITOR-IN-CHIEF:
Rev. Timothy F. O'Leary, Ph.D.
Assistant Superintendent of Schools
Archdiocese of Boston

ASSISTANT EDITOR-IN-CHIEF:
Sister M. Veronica, S.P.B.V.

CO-EDITORS:
Rt. Rev. Clarence E. Elwell, Ph.D.
Superintendent of Schools
Diocese of Cleveland

Rev. Patrick J. Roche, Ph.D.
Assistant Superintendent of Schools
Archdiocese of Los Angeles

REPUBLISHED BY
THE NEUMANN PRESS
LONG PRAIRIE, MINNESOTA

BY SPECIAL ARRANGEMENT WITH
BENZIGER PUBLISHING COMPANY
NEW YORK, CINCINNATI, CHICAGO, BOSTON, SAN FRANCISCO

Nihil Obstat:

JOHN M. A. FEARNS, S.T.D.,
Censor Librorum.

Imprimatur:

† FRANCIS CARDINAL SPELLMAN,
Archbishop of New York.

January 15, 1953.

The Nihil Obstat and Imprimatur are official declarations that a book is free from doctrinal or moral error. No implication is contained therein that those who have granted the Nihil Obstat and Imprimatur agree with the contents, opinions or stateents expressed.

ISBN 0-911845-57-7
THIS 1997 EDITION IS PUBLISHED THROUGH SPECIAL ARRANGEMENT WITH BENZIGER PUBLISHING COMPANY BY THE NEUMANN PRESS LONG PRAIRIE, MINNESOTA

EDITORS' INTRODUCTION

UNLIKE its past record of isolationism, the history of the United States in the twentieth century embraces the story of the world from the vantage point of American interest and leadership. The problems of this century are encumbered with social implications never before known in this Land of Our Lady.

A retrospective glance at the mid-century milestone reveals a story of strife for social justice, social security, and world peace caused by the impact of scientific and human forces at work in an ever-shrinking world. Many of these problems of modern history are constantly recurring under various new aspects but remain for the most part unsolved. Through such a background, eighth grade pupils strengthen their concepts of history as a record of the accomplishments of mankind.

History should be a real and vital factor, a dynamic force in the lives of children so that they will become conscientious, intelligent and active citizens of America and of the world. This text helps pupils to understand the relationships of history to their everyday lives. The author has brought into Christian focus such pressing problems of current history as labor, industry and agriculture, the changing foreign policy of the United States, the implications of the New Deal, and the establishment of the United Nations Organization.

Only those with sound convictions, based on a Christian philosophy of life, can make a lasting contribution to the welfare of mankind. It is highly desirable, therefore, that Catholic boys and girls be clearly informed of the contributions of the Catholic Church to our American democracy and the leadership which the Church is giving towards the solution of the vital problems of modern life.

The organization and interpretation of the historical content which embraces the twentieth century can be intelligibly presented to pupils only by weaving the content around large movements or elements. These movements are the subjects of the six Units of the text. Fundamental Christian social principles are related to the content, when necessary, to show their positive or negative application. The subject matter is told in simple, narrative style, with a vocabulary geared to the comprehension level of eighth grade pupils.

To enlist the pupils' understanding of each phase of history, the text is replete with ample study activities at the end of each chapter. Additional material and mastery tests are found at the end of each Unit.

The present text, *Guardian of Freedom,* fulfills the need for an accurate and Christian explanation of the basic movements at work in the present century. It tells how a comparatively young nation grew in power, influence, and leadership to take its place today as a tower of strength — a *guardian of freedom.* It is fitting that a nation dedicated to Mary, Our Hope, should itself become a beacon of light and a true hope of the world.

THE EDITORS

CONTENTS

UNIT ONE

THE UNITED STATES — A GIANT AMONG NATIONS

UNIT TWO

THE AMERICAN BUSINESS WORLD — OWNERS, MANAGERS, AND WORKERS

Part One — The Owners and Managers

Part Two — American Workers

UNIT THREE

THE FARMER — AN INDISPENSABLE MEMBER OF THE AMERICAN NATION

UNIT FOUR

AMERICA'S MARCH OF PROGRESS

UNIT FIVE

THE UNITED STATES AND THE STRUGGLE FOR WORLD SUPREMACY

Part One—The First World War

Part Two—The World Goes to War a Second Time

UNIT SIX

THE PRESERVATION OF OUR AMERICAN HERITAGE

LIST OF MAPS

FOREWORD

THE publication of the "Land of Our Lady" Series marks a notable advancement in the field of history textbooks for Catholic elementary schools. The Series fulfills very effectively the need for history textbooks that are devoid of secularistic and materialistic tendencies and based on the sound principles of Christianity and therefore, a Christian philosophy of history.

This Series includes not only the factual data that comprise the history of America as a nation, but it incorporates also those elements of American Catholic history that can be assimilated by pupils of the elementary school level. The growth and development of the Catholic Church in the United States parallels the content of American history in each textbook of the Series.

The greatest contribution of these texts to the training and schooling of young American Catholic boys and girls is the manner in which Christian social principles are woven in the texts. As the various events of history are taken up for study, the textbooks point out the positive or negative correlation of the factual data to the principles of Christian social living.

We are grateful to the firm of Benziger Brothers, and to the competent Board of Editors and Authors for the task they have successfully accomplished in producing this American Catholic Series, "Land of Our Lady."

RT. REV. FREDERICK G. HOCHWALT, PH.D.
SECRETARY GENERAL, N.C.E.A.

UNIT ONE

THE UNITED STATES—A GIANT AMONG NATIONS

12

UNIT ONE

THE UNITED STATES—A GIANT AMONG NATIONS

PICTURE to yourself the changing civilization in this land which we are so proud to call our own. Can you see those early days when generous-hearted missionaries carried Christ's banner in the wilderness? Perhaps you also catch a glimpse of the time when men were so distressed because our nation was at the point of being divided. Can you recall the reason? Men refused to live in accordance with the principle that we are all brothers in Christ and made to His image and likeness. We know that slavery finally led to secession. It took a long war between the North and the South to save the Union. Do you think this war would have been prevented if men had respected the law of God and the Bill of Rights? Are you determined always to keep that law and to treasure those rights by carrying out the duties which they impose?

One more view of the past is necessary before stepping into the drama which represents the rest of the history of our land. It was not only the descendants of the early American colonists who helped our country to become great. A tide of immigrants from the Old World brought not only the will to learn and work, but hearts which quickly filled with loyalty for their new country. They contributed greatly to the development of this *Land of Our Lady.*

The first act in this year's historical drama takes us outside the boundaries of the United States. We shall see how the ideas of the founding fathers regarding the place of the United States in world affairs gradually came to be changed. These ideas had to change because our country was growing. In fact, it was becoming a "giant" as the title of this unit tells. This giant reached out and acquired such lands as Alaska, the Hawaiian Islands, the Philippines, Cuba, and Panama.

CHAPTER I

THE UNITED STATES EXPANDS ITS BOUNDARIES

Points to learn about. You understand that when we speak about our "founding fathers," we mean those fearless men like George Washington, Thomas Jefferson, and the others who established our country. If these men were to return to the United States today, they would find many changes. They would see trains, airplanes, radio, and television. There are other changes, too, which would be evident to one who had lived in the early days of our country.

In the first place, after the United States became a new nation, its leaders settled down to the task of developing that nation. They thought that since they were now free of European nations, they could concentrate on their own. For a short time they were right, but no nation can be entirely independent.

Secondly, the Americans began acquiring territory of their own, just as the European nations acquired colonies in the sixteenth and seventeenth centuries. In doing this, the United States had to come into contact with foreign nations. These new contacts had a decided effect on American foreign relations.

As we read this chapter, let us keep in mind the following points: (1) Our Changing Policy in World Affairs, (2) the Purchase of Alaska, and (3) the Annexation of Samoa and the Hawaiian Islands.

1. Our Changing Policy in World Affairs

On several occasions, our founding fathers made clear their ideas regarding our relationship to world affairs. They believed that America was to be for the Americans. When President Washington gave his farewell address in 1796, he said: "Steer clear of permanent alliances with any portion of the foreign world." John Adams declared that if foreign nations wished to "cut one another's throats," they could, but they would have to do so without any help from the United States. Thomas Jefferson believed that the United States should cultivate "peace, commerce, and honest friendship with all nations" but make "entangling alliances with none."

Many other early American leaders made similar statements. They wanted the United States, a new nation, to be allowed to develop in its own way, without becoming involved in any European quarrels. This policy is one of isolation, that is, attending to our business and letting other nations attend to theirs.

Reviewing the Monroe Doctrine. The United States, having gained its freedom from England, was watching some South American countries in 1810 trying to free themselves from Spain. Our country sympathized with its South American neighbors and realized that in order to insure our own safety, Latin American republics had to be made safe also. President Monroe, after a consultation with two former Presidents, Jefferson and Madison, and his Secretary of State, John Quincy Adams, sent a statement to Congress in 1823.

This statement was broad and bold, and was directed at all European nations. It warned them on two points: (1) that no European nation would be permitted to acquire land or colonize in either North or South America, (2) that any attempt on the part of a European nation to interfere with any existing governments in the Western Hemisphere would be considered an "unfriendly act."

The United States expected its position to be recognized by European countries because it determined to refrain from interfering in European problems. This "Monroe Doctrine" was never a law or a treaty, but it was respected largely because England, which then

Bettmann Archive

James Monroe, Author of the Monroe Doctrine.

controlled the Atlantic, supported it for her own reasons. In the course of this unit, we shall see how the doctrine has been applied when problems arose.

Isolationism—an impossibility in the modern world. We can readily understand how the early founders of our nation wished to follow the "hands-off" policy of isolation. But conditions changed. As the nineteenth century drew to a close, American investments and commerce spread across all oceans. Today, modern means of transportation and communication have made each country the neighbor of every other one. Because of the airplane, no country, regardless of how well surrounded by barriers, is safe from invasion by an enemy. Isolation from modern ideas or propaganda is even less possible.

The result is that the United States can no longer live completely by itself. Because it desires peaceful relations with all countries, it finds itself necessarily drawn into an effort with other nations to establish world peace. It can not idly watch a strong nation unjustly gain control of a weaker one. In other words, our attempt at isolation has definitely and necessarily been abandoned.

2. Alaska—Our First Territory Outside the Homeland

Nineteenth-century Americans looked upon Alaska as nothing more than an enormous iceberg. They thought it was too close to the North Pole to be comfortable. But it has since proved to be America's treasure house in the North.

A Russian Territory. In 1728, Captain Vitus Bering, an officer in the Russian navy, sailed the sea which now bears his name and discovered Alaska. However, not until his first visit to the mainland of Alaska in 1741, did Russia claim the land. When the Russians entered Alaska, they carelessly wasted the animal and sea life which abounded there. They hunted for riches, but soon became tired, because of the difficulties encountered in what seemed to be nothing but wasteland and frozen wilderness. Eventually, they returned home.

A doubtful bargain. However, the Russians did not forget about Alaska. Frequently, Russian boats could be seen as far south as the Canadian shores. The Monroe Doctrine proved satisfactory in keeping friendly relations between Russia and the United States. Besides, Russia had been in sympathy with the North at the time the slaves were freed in the United States.

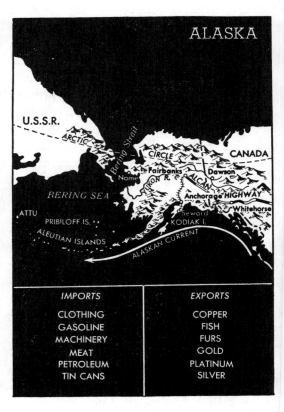

In 1867, when Russia needed money, the American Secretary of State, William Seward, offered to buy Alaska. Russia gratefully accepted the $7,200,000 which we paid her. Most Americans scoffed at paying Russia this amount of money for what they called a "giant icebox," "Seward's Folly," and "President Johnson's polar-bear garden." Seward believed he had made a rare bargain, and he proved to be right. Critics realized it when gold was discovered there in 1896. Overnight, the icebox became a treasure chest.

A view of Alaska. Alaska is about one-fifth the size of the United States. A large part of it lies north of the Arctic Circle. This northern region is covered with Arctic grasslands, where large herds of reindeer, caribou, and musk-ox graze. The winter in this part of Alaska is very long, with few hours of sunlight during the day.

The climate along the coast of southern Alaska is more like that of our own. The waters of the warm Alaska current flow in this direction, making even the winters mild. Here can be found many fine harbors and hundreds of very valuable small islands.

Inland, red and Alaska cedars bend over streams that some day may furnish the power that will crush them into paper. Here, also, abound many kinds of wild life, such as foxes, wolves, and coyotes. The furs obtained from these animals have brought much wealth to the United States.

The mineral resources of Alaska are vast. In 1896, gold was discovered in the Klondike, a small tributary of the Yukon River. The excitement of the gold rush in Alaska was as wild as that in California in the days of the "forty-niners." This sudden spurt of enthusiasm died down as quickly as it had appeared. The gold which seemed so abundant soon became scarce. Many Americans gave up their search for the precious metal and settled down to fishing and fur trading.

The most important mineral found in Alaska is copper. The output of copper usually exceeds the gold output. The total yield of gold, copper, silver, and other metals has more than paid for Seward's "snow-farm."

Sea wealth in the waters of Alaska. Fishing is the most important industry in Alaska. In its icy waters lurks a wealth of plump salmon and glistening seals. The United States Coast Guard escorts hunters to the points where seal-fishing is permitted. If the United States did not guard the seal-fisheries by permitting fishing only at certain times and in certain places, there would soon be no seals left. The next few paragraphs will explain why guards are stationed at the seal-fisheries.

Dispute over Bering Sea. The question of seal-fishing became an important one early in President Cleveland's second administration (1893-1897). Bering Sea, as you can see on the map on page 16, lies in the north of the Pacific Ocean and is cut off from it by the long line of the Aleutian (al-you'-shun) Islands. These islands are the homeland of seals. Each spring the seals go to the Pribilof (pree-bil-off') Islands, which are just a little north of the Aleutians, for their young to be born. They remain on these islands all summer,

By Ewing Galloway, N. Y.

The homeland of seals. On the Pribilof Islands seals swarm all summer long, teaching their young to care for themselves.

teaching their young how to care for themselves.

When the seals returned to the Aleutian Islands, ships from all nations of Europe would be waiting for them. Frequently, many very young ones would be killed.

While Russia owned this territory, she tried to save the seals by declaring that Bering Sea was a *closed sea,* that is, not open to vessels of other nations. The United States disregarded this claim, as did the other countries.

When the United States acquired the territory, however, and made the same claim, other nations likewise refused to regard it. She tried to use force to make the other countries abide by her demand. Great Britain protested vigorously when some of her fishermen were seized. As a result, a conference was called at Paris in 1893 to settle the dispute. The case was brought before a court of *arbitration.* Arbitration means the attempt at the peaceful settling of a dispute. This court decided that the United States government had no right to regulate fishing beyond three miles from shore, which is according to international law. Great Britain was given a payment for the seizure of her fishermen.

By 1911, seal-breeding on the Pribilof Islands had declined so much that the nations of the world realized the United States was right in trying to regulate seal-fishing. An international agreement was made to protect seals for the future.

This agreement forbade seal-hunting for five years, in order to give the seals a chance to increase in numbers. After that, hunting was permitted only on land, and only a limited number of seals could be killed each year.

Government of Alaska. From 1867 to 1877, Alaska was governed by the United States Army. After that time, it was neglected. Five thousand miles from Washington seemed too far away. However, when gold was discovered, Alaska

A farm in Alaska. This scene shows that Alaska is not the "Giant Icebox" that Americans first thought it.

By Burton Holmes, from Ewing Galloway

Alaska Railroad.

came into notice again. Today, the President of the United States appoints a Governor for Alaska. The country is permitted to send a delegate to attend the sessions of Congress in Washington, but he may not vote. Congress, too, has reserved to itself the right to decide on important questions regarding Alaska. For many years, Alaska has applied for statehood, but as yet its application has not been accepted.

Present-day Alaska. Alaska is bidding for settlers. It is not all a cold wilderness. While farming is not too important an industry at present, experts say that Alaska's farmland could feed 10,000,000 people. Fertile interior valleys can be reached by the government-owned Alaska Railroad. Modern highways have replaced the rugged trails over which dog sleds toiled in the "gold rush" days. The famous Alcan Highway connects Alaska with the United States.

Thriving towns have their own airports where mail and passenger planes come in from all parts of the world. Since there are few railroads because of sparse population and the difficulties involved in laying tracks, the airplane has become of major importance. In 1941, there were more landing fields in Alaska than in any state of the Union, except Texas. These, plus the radio and cable, bring news of the world to places otherwise isolated for many months of the year.

Missionaries in Alaska. The first priests to enter Alaska were sent by the Greek Orthodox Church of Russia. After the United States purchased the territory in 1867, it was not long until American priests were there. The Oblates of Mary Immaculate were the first American missionary priests to enter Alaska, but they did not remain long. They made a noble beginning which the Jesuits were to continue.

The Jesuits began their missionary work in Alaska in 1882. Their work was hard and challenging. They had to be men of iron will to fight the strange epidemics which occurred among the Eskimos. The priests had to change native superstitious practices, which persisted in spite of early Christianization.

The first Bishop of Alaska. Father

Joseph Crimont (cree-mon'), a Jesuit, went to Alaska in 1894 as a young priest. He had been in frail health, but had always felt the desire to be a missionary. His health improved in spite of the hardships of the North. He became the first Bishop to be in charge of Alaska. Missionary progress increased under his guidance, and, no doubt, through the Queen and Patroness of Alaska, St. Thérèse of the Child Jesus.

The Glacier Priest. Probably one of the most popular names connected with the Alaska missions in the twentieth century is that of Father Bernard Hubbard, a Jesuit. He is not only an explorer, but a lecturer and a photographer. Through these means, he has done much to make Alaska's missions known throughout the United States.

Father Hubbard's scientific contributions are many. He has made studies of the Alaskan glaciers. He has studied plant life in the Arctic region, and has made a collection of rocks and important specimens of plants. During the Second World War, his knowledge of weather conditions in the Arctic was a source of priceless information to the Army.

Father Hubbard has risked his life on many occasions to secure valuable scientific information for the United States. His illustrated lectures throughout the country have resulted in financial assistance for the Alaskan missions.

Value to the United States. Be-

Brown Brothers

Bishop Joseph Crimont, S. J.

The Glacier Priest. Father Bernard
Hubbard, S. J.

Brown Brothers

sides furnishing untold wealth to the United States in minerals, sea and wild life, Alaska has been a worthwhile investment for other reasons. Until the Second World War, Americans were inclined to regard it as a land too far in the North to be concerned about. The war has impressed upon them that the Aleutian Islands form stepping-stones which shorten considerably the distance between the United States and Japan. Then, too, Bering Strait is scarcely more than fifty miles of water separating Alaska from Russia. Alaska's nearness to both of these countries thus makes it very important as a means of defense for the Western Hemisphere. Can you see how valuable and necessary are the many Alaskan airports about which you have previously read?

3. The Annexation of Samoa and Hawaii

For several hundred years, trade had been going on between the United States and the Orient. In order to increase and protect this commerce, the United States desired to secure possession of some of the islands in the Pacific.

We have learned that Balboa discovered the Pacific Ocean early in the sixteenth century. But he did nothing more in the way of exploring it. What lay in that great expanse of water? Had not Magellan spent ninety-eight days sailing over it without so much as a sight of land? No one knew there were hundreds of islands scattered over its surface.

Samoa, land of sunshine. One group of islands, known as the Samoan Islands, lies northeast of Australia. Here one finds a winterless land of sunshine and warm winds. In spring, terrific hurricanes frequently sweep the islands.

After the Bering Sea controversy, the United States was more than ever concerned about her affairs in the Pacific. One of her interests lay on Tutuila (too-too-ee'-la) Island, in the Samoan group. As far back as 1872, a native chieftain of Tutuila had ceded the best port of that island to the United States. This port, Pagopago (pang'-o pang'-o), has since then been used by our Navy as a supply station for ships crossing the Pacific.

Nature helps to settle a quarrel. Two other countries, Germany and Great Britain, were also interested in these islands. On one occasion when the American flag was torn down by some German sailors, American and German warships prepared for battle. England also favored the Germans. Before the two fleets could do any actual fighting, one of the spring hurricanes wrecked their vessels. This sobered the countries involved, and they made an agreement for joint control of the islands. The agreement lasted about ten years, amid almost constant friction.

Finally, in 1899, while President McKinley was in office, Great Britain gave up her claim in return for some territory in Africa. Germany remained in Samoa until after the First World War, when

Pagopago. This important naval base was ceded to the United States in 1872.

her portion of Samoa was given to New Zealand.

The natives of Samoa. The people for the most part are olive-skinned Polynesians. They are often called the "supermen" of the Pacific Islands because of their height and strength. They have not intermarried with other races, and so have retained their pure Polynesian characteristics. They are simple, honorable, and hospitable.

Catholic, Protestant, and Mormon missionaries have worked among the Samoans, but since the Protestant missionaries reached the islands before the Catholics, they have more converts. Of the fifteen thousand people living there, only about one tenth are Catholics.

A poet's delight. Perhaps you will be surprised to know that Robert Louis Stevenson, the famous author of *Treasure Island*, spent the last four years of his life in Samoa. When his health failed, he took his family with him to the warm islands in the hope of recuperating. During these few years, Stevenson did a great deal towards introducing

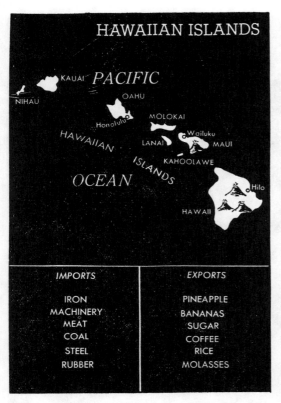

HAWAIIAN ISLANDS

PACIFIC

KAUAI

NIHAU

OAHU

Honolulu

MOLOKAI

HAWAIIAN

LANAI

Wailuku

MAUI

KAHOOLAWE

ISLANDS

OCEAN

Hilo

HAWAII

IMPORTS	EXPORTS
IRON	PINEAPPLE
MACHINERY	BANANAS
MEAT	SUGAR
COAL	COFFEE
STEEL	RICE
RUBBER	MOLASSES

western civilization into the islands. He loved this land of cocoa palms and giant ferns so much that he requested to be buried on the summit of one of its mountains.

Hawaii — the crossroads of the Pacific. The Hawaiian Islands are at once a playground, a source of important food products, and an outpost of defense for the United States. The gentle springlike climate, green forests and fields surrounded by the blue sea, and the charming atmosphere of these islands have earned for them the name of the "Paradise of the Pacific." Their natural situation in the center of the Pacific Ocean has also made them known as the "Crossroads of the Pacific."

The Hawaiian Islands stretch out about twelve hundred miles, but only eight of the islands are inhabited. The others are game grounds for hunters and fishermen. A dozen different nations have contributed to the permanent population of these islands. The native Hawaiians probably came from Samoa centuries ago, but they are now in the minority and are largely mixed with other peoples. The Hawaiians are hospitable to visitors and have the pleasing custom of decorating them with garlands of gay flowers called *leis* (lays).

Discovery of Hawaiian Islands. The English explorer, Captain James Cook, on one of his Pacific Ocean voyages, discovered this group of picturesque islands in 1778. He named them the Sandwich Islands for his English friend, the Earl of Sandwich. Later, their name was changed to the native one, Hawaii.

In the early nineteenth century, American whaling vessels in the Pacific used Hawaii as a convenient supply and repair port. Soon, Protestant missionaries went from New England to introduce Christianity into the islands. The people, led by the example of their King, accepted the new faith. It was through these missionaries that American influence was extended throughout the islands.

American influence in the islands. There were several reasons why America was interested in Hawaii. Many of our business men had invested money in the large sugar

Hawaii at work.

Hawaii at play.

plantations which had developed there. When other nations also attempted to extend their influence on the islands, President Tyler declared that the Monroe Doctrine included these islands.

The native King was glad to accept the "protection" of the United States, in which country he placed the most confidence. This was in 1876. Soon railroads, telegraph lines, and irrigation systems were established. A thriving business was developing under American control, but the native Hawaiians were not accustomed to hard work. As a result, many Chinese, Japanese, Koreans, Filipinos, and Portuguese were brought into the islands.

These different peoples often intermarried with one another and with the native Hawaiians. Some people expected that such racial mixtures would produce an inferior type of person. On the contrary, it has produced a vigorous and hard-working people who have adopted many of our ways and are intensely loyal to the United States. During World War II, even those of Japanese origin worked for American victory.

A Queen is deposed. When conflicts arose between the various races and the American land-owners, it was frequently necessary to bring in the United States Marines to restore order. In 1891, a Queen came to the throne in Hawaii. She was Queen Liliuokalani (lee-lee-oo-owe-kah-lah'-nee). She disliked the interference of foreigners and was determined that she would work for her own people. A revolution broke out against the Queen's rule. Since the Americans also opposed her, the Marines were called in, and she was unjustly deposed. In 1893, the American flag was raised over the government building and the Hawaiian Republic was formed with Sanford Dole, an American, as its first President. The Queen appealed to the President of the United States for help, but before he could act in the matter a new President, Grover Cleveland, took office.

Cleveland attempts to restore peace. President Cleveland sent a commission to the Hawaiian Islands to investigate the affair. After due consideration, he concluded that the revolution was encouraged by American planters. He learned that the Hawaiians themselves did not desire annexation to the United States.

Cleveland withdrew the Marines, and ordered the American flag to be taken down from the government building. He promised to restore the throne to Queen Lil, as she is often called, provided that she would pardon the revolutionists. When she refused to do this, Cleveland recognized the provisional government, which Sanford Dole had set up during the revolution.

Hawaii becomes an American territory. When William McKinley became President in 1897, he considered it necessary that the United States should control Hawaii. Our commerce in the Pacific had grown. In order to protect it, American power was to be firmly established. As a result, in 1898, Hawaii was annexed to the United States. Two years later, Congress made it a colonial territory, and all inhabitants of the islands became American citizens. English is the official language of the islands.

Like Alaska, Hawaii has often expressed its desire to be represented by a star in the American flag, but its application for statehood has just as often met defeat when it reached the Senate. Perhaps the future may bring statehood to this group of valuable islands in spite of their distance from the United States.

Twentieth century Hawaii. The Hawaiian Islands are an important food-producing region for the United States. Sugar from Hawaii contributes to our own insufficient supply. Pineapples are raised and exported to various countries. Schools have been established, good roads have been built, and thousands of tourists visit the islands to enjoy the delightful climate and see the volcanoes there.

On the island of Oahu (owe-ah'-hoo) is the naval station of Pearl Harbor. The United States has made extensive improvements at this station. It is the principal center of defense in the middle Pacific Ocean. It was here that the Japanese dropped bombs on our warships on December 7, 1941. You will read about that incident later when you study the Second World War.

The Naval Base at Pearl Harbor. The ships in the harbor are gathering prior to the first Atomic Bomb test at Bikini.

The Catholic religion in Hawaii. There are about five hundred thousand inhabitants in the Hawaiian Islands. Of this number, about one hundred twenty thousand are Catholic. Most of the Chinese and Japanese still cling to their pagan religions. The practicing Catholics are principally the native Hawaiians and the Americans.

Catholic missionaries have been in Hawaii since 1833. Colleges, academies, parish schools, and asylums provide a full Catholic influence on the islands.

Molokai. One of the islands which has attracted the interest of people throughout the world is Molokai (moe′-low-kye), which has been a leper colony since 1873. It was hoped that the spread of leprosy could be checked by keeping lepers together in one place, away from other people. Formerly, when a victim entered the colony, he never returned to his former home. Today, through the untiring efforts of priests, Sisters, and doctors, some victims become well enough to leave the island.

Father Damien, friend of the leper. Father Damien was born in Belgium and joined the order of the Sacred Hearts of Jesus and Mary. He was sent, along with others of his Order, to Hawaii as a missionary. In 1873, he asked to become chaplain at the leper colony on Molokai.

Father Damien worked zealously to make the poor living conditions in the leper colony more comfortable. He improved housing, food and water supply. He founded schools and built churches. He was doctor, nurse, teacher, and spiritual guide.

Because of the fear of leprosy, government officials did not visit the island and knew nothing of the miserable conditions under which the lepers lived. Can you understand why it was difficult for Father Damien to make them understand his pleas for assistance?

Father Damien was never to see the American flag raised over the islands. He was with his lepers for sixteen years, and contracted the disease himself about four years before he died. If he could return there today, he would see modern hospitals where special studies to control leprosy are made. And he

Father Damien.

Father Damien's church.

would be happy to find that the island is under the spiritual guidance of the Catholic Church.

Brave women. The Sisters who care for the lepers on Molokai are a group of devoted and faithful women. These Sisters of the Third Order of St. Francis came from the United States in 1883, with Mother Marianne as Superior, to help Father Damien. They found they would have to care for the lepers by scrubbing and cleaning the floors, walls, beds, linen, and furniture. They made dresses for the women and girls and encouraged the lepers to help each other.

Soon their efforts met with success. The civil authorities realized the good work they were doing, and placed greater confidence in them. Shortly after the Sisters' arrival, Father Damien died, and they increased their labors.

In the many years that the Sisters have worked among the lepers, none of them has ever contracted the disease. In the early days, one of the Sisters feared that she might succumb to it.

One day she confided her fears to Mother Marianne, who told her: "You will never become a leper, nor will any of the Sisters. God has called us to this work, and if we are prudent and observe the rules of sanitation, none of us will be afflicted."

Do you know the meaning of these?

"founding fathers"	propaganda
permanent alliances	isolation
entangling alliances	persisted
characteristics	hospitable
international law	closed sea
interference	leis

Some questions to think about and discuss:

1. Explain this statement: "Neither the United States nor any other country is completely self-sufficient."
2. Discuss the value of the work of Father Hubbard.
3. How has Alaska paid for itself in the years since we purchased it?
4. Why was the United States interested in Samoa?
5. What evidences of American influence can be seen in Hawaii today?

Test your knowledge

Copy the words under Column B on a piece of paper. After each word or group of words, place the number from Column A which is related to it. You will need to use several numbers after some words.

Column A		Column B
1. Annexation	9. Bering Sea	Founding fathers
2. Leper Colony	10. Pagopago	Pearl Harbor
3. Isolationism	11. Captain Cook	Alaska
4. Leis	12. Aleutian Islands	Hawaii
5. Father Hubbard	13. Pineapples and sugar cane	Molokai
6. William Seward	14. Crossroads of the Pacific	Seal-fishing
7. Father Damien	15. President McKinley	Closed sea
8. Oahu		Samoa

CHAPTER II

SPANISH CONTROL CEASES IN AMERICA

Setting the stage for a new act. You recall that Spaniards were among the first to colonize in America. In this chapter, we shall learn that they were the last foreign nation to leave our territory. All Spanish claims to the mainland of North America had been given up by the end of the nineteenth century, but Spain still held some of the islands near it.

Through revolution, some of Spain's colonies in South America had broken away from her. The island of Cuba, long discontent with Spanish rule, decided to follow their example. We aided in that revolution.

In the Pacific, far to the west of the United States was another group of islands known as the Philippines. They, too, were owned by Spain. The war, which is known as the Spanish-American War, took us as far as these islands.

Justice-loving Americans wondered whether or not the United States had a right to interfere in the government of these territories. Were we imposing our way of living upon people who wanted to be free, even as we wanted to be free when

we revolted against England during the American Revolution?

To solve some of these problems, we shall study the following points in this chapter: (1) The American Attitude towards Cuba, (2) Unsuccessful Efforts to Prevent War, (3) Results of the Spanish-American War, and (4) The United States Manages the Philippines.

1. The American Attitude towards Cuba

It was the year 1896. At the conclusion of a bitter and exciting campaign for the presidency, William McKinley was elected. Business in the United States was flourishing, and a new supply of gold had been discovered in Alaska. The most outstanding incident during President McKinley's administration, however, was the war with Spain, which began with Cuba's desire for independence.

The United States keeps an eye on Cuba. Cuba was the last large Spanish-owned territory in the Western Hemisphere. Since Cuba possessed vast natural resources, and was very close to Florida, the United States tried to purchase it from Spain in 1848. The offer was rejected. When, year after year, revolts against alleged Spanish cruelties occurred, the United States declared that if ever her own peace were endangered, she would be justified in seizing Cuba. The United States based her attitude on the principles set forth in the Monroe Doctrine.

Incidents which preceded the Spanish-American War. For many years, American citizens had been leaving the United States to settle in Cuba. There they invested money in sugar and tobacco plantations.

On September 16, 1895, a band of Cuban guerillas proclaimed the island independent. To show their dislike of the Spanish government, these guerillas traveled from the east to the west of the island, setting fire to plantations and destroying everyone who opposed them. The Spaniards themselves did not help matters. General Weyler, whose duty it was to hold the island for Spain, put into concentration camps all who were accused of participating in the revolution.

American sympathy aroused. Some of the newspapers in the United States, eager for sensational or exciting news, featured glaring headlines of the terrible conditions in the concentration camps in Cuba. They frequently carried accounts which were untrue. The American plantation owners stirred up sympathy, too, by reports of the damage done to their crops. But all events were brought to a climax with the sinking of an American battleship. Here is the story of that important incident.

"Remember the Maine!" At the request of the United States, Spain recalled General Weyler from Cuba in 1897. But that did not bring peace. The United States government then ordered a warship to Cuban waters to insure the safety of the American citizens on the island. The battleship *Maine* anchored at Havana, the largest harbor of the island, in January, 1898. After peacefully standing by for three weeks, a terrible explosion sent the warship to the bottom of the harbor. The American people, already aroused to anger, demanded war with the cry, "Remember the *Maine!*" They insisted that the Spanish government atone for the loss, since they believed that government to be responsible.

Was it an accident? Captain Sigsbee of the *Maine,* one of the survivors, immediately asked for an investigation before any blame would be placed. Although no evidence of neglect on the part of the crew could be found, Spain denied any responsibility in the matter and expressed her regrets.

The real cause of the explosion was never discovered, and war seemed imminent.

The disaster brought the atttention of the nation to Father John Chidwick, the chaplain of the *Maine*. He ignored danger in helping his shipmates after the explosion. It is interesting to know that he was the third Catholic chaplain in the history of the United States Navy, the first one having entered the service in 1888.

Destruction of the "Maine." While anchored in Havana harbor, a terrific explosion
sent this U. S. battleship to the bottom.

2. Unsuccessful Efforts to Prevent War

Within a month after the sinking of the *Maine*, Congress had voted $50,000,000 for war preparations.

Archbishop Ireland

Some American newspapers said that because Spain was a Catholic country, Catholics in the United States would cast their lot with Spain.

Attitude of the Church towards the war. Archbishop Ireland of St. Paul, Minnesota, lost no time in telling the nation that Spain's religion did not enter into the problem. He also assured the government that no true Catholic would even speak of aiding Spain against the United States in the event of war. He had long been an intimate friend of President McKinley, and together they set to work to make plans to avoid war.

On the other side of the Atlantic, Spain said she would be willing to abide by the decision of Pope Leo XIII in the matter. Many Americans were displeased because they did not desire the Holy Father to intervene in American affairs. Archbishop Martinelli, the Apostolic Delegate in Washington, assured the public that the Pope would not act unless both sides requested his services.

Before any agreement could be reached, war was declared by the United States on April 25, 1898. At the same time, Congress announced that the purpose of the President's intervention was to "establish by the free action of the people of Cuba a stable and independent government of their own in the island."

The Pacific battleground. The Spanish-American War was fought for the most part on water. Fighting occurred in both the Atlantic and the Pacific Oceans. When war was declared, Commodore George Dewey was in command of an American fleet in the Pacific Ocean. He was loading supplies at Hong Kong, off the southern coast of China. Word came to him that he was to go immediately to the Phil-

The Battle of Manila Bay. Dewey's fleet has destroyed the Spanish vessels in the background, and is steaming victoriously into Manila harbor.

Brown Brothers

The Rough Riders

ippine Islands, where a revolt against Spain was in progress. He surprised the Spanish fleet in Manila Bay on May 1, and within six hours destroyed it entirely.

Manila under siege. Because Dewey had no army of occupation, he did not attempt to take Manila. He merely held the harbor, thus cutting off all supplies from the city.

When the United States' army of occupation arrived, the Army and Navy together attacked Manila, the capital of the Philippines, and captured the city.

Even before the army of occupation arrived the Filipinos banded together under the leadership of Emilio Aguinaldo (ah-ge-nahl'-doe), who had joined with the Americans against the Spanish. He believed that, when the war was

over, the United States would recognize the independence of the Philippines.

When Aguinaldo saw that this was not the intention of the United States, he organized a revolt against the Americans. He continued fighting from swamp and jungle for more than three years before he was captured.

The campaign for Cuba. While Dewey was waiting in Manila Bay, another Spanish fleet was entering Santiago (san-tee-ah'-go) harbor in Cuba. It was commanded by Admiral Cervera (ser-vay'-ra). The American fleet, under Admiral William Sampson, immediately blockaded the harbor and bottled the Spanish there.

In the meantime, an army under General Shafter was preparing to aid the American fleet. The most picturesque division of this army was called the "Rough Riders." It was commanded by Colonel Leonard Wood and Lieutenant-Colonel Theodore Roosevelt and was composed largely of cowboys from the western plains, as well as ranchmen and Indians.

General Shafter and his army landed in Cuba and headed for Santiago. The march across Cuba was difficult because of swamps and jungles. Besides this, the island had been well fortified by the Spanish. On July 1 and 2, the army captured the strongholds of El Caney (el cahn-ay') and San Juan (san-hwan), which barred the way to Santiago. The next day, Admiral Cervera ordered his fleet to leave the harbor of Havana. The American fleet quickly followed him and, after a wild run up the southern shore of Cuba, completely destroyed the Spanish fleet. The Admiral and 1,200 of his men were taken prisoner and sent to New England, where they would be safe from any attempt at rescue or escape.

This was the first experience the United States ever had in caring for war prisoners of another nationality. They were treated humanely by American guards. When the prisoners were returned to Spain after the war, they cheered the Marines who had taken charge of them. Many prisoners did not want to return to their native land.

How does this prove the value of kindness and justice?

American Sisters do their part. The story of the war would be incomplete without mentioning the part played by the Sisterhoods of the United States. Even before the war began, the Sisters of the Holy Names of Jesus and Mary offered their convent and schools in Florida for hospital purposes. They asked for no reward from the government except the return of buildings in the same condition as they were before their use as hospitals. One of the first patients to be admitted was Father Chidwick, Chaplain of the *Maine*.

While the Red Cross existed at

Nurses in a Spanish-American War Hospital

Brown Brothers

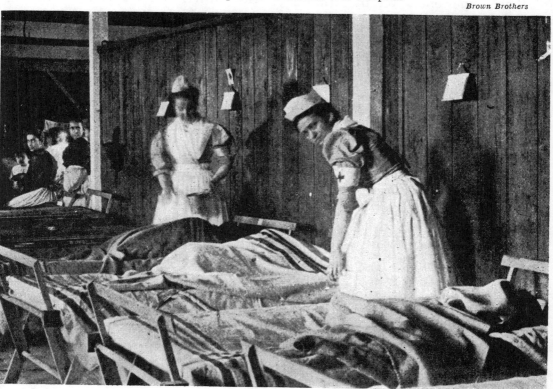

this time in the United States, it was not so well organized as it is to-day. Consequently, when the government asked for nurses, about three hundred Sisters of various Communities volunteered. Five of them gave their lives in the service of their country. The Sisters of Charity of Emmitsburg gave the most Sisters, nearly 200.

It is interesting to note that the Congregation of American Sisters sent four nurses to camps. This Congregation was composed entirely of American Indians. It was founded by Mother Catherine Sacred White Buffalo, a member of the Sioux tribe of South Dakota. They asked to be permitted to care for the wounded under fire because their experiences on the frontier had fitted them for that dangerous work. Although this request was not granted, these Sisters eventually went to Havana where they remained until after the war. This Community was disbanded around 1900.

3. Results of the Spanish-American War

The Spanish-American War lasted scarcely more than eight months. The treaty of peace which was signed in December, 1898, at Paris, brought to the United States possessions which reached halfway around the world. Even though the war was of short duration, it was a turning point in the history of the United States. From this time on, our interests had to expand beyond the boundaries of the continent of North America.

The terms of the peace treaty. Spain gave up all claims to the island of Cuba and turned it over for temporary occupation by American troops. The island of Puerto Rico in the West Indies, and the islands of Guam and Wake and the Philippines in the Pacific were ceded to the United States. For improvements which Spain had made in the Philippine Islands, the United States paid her $20,000,000.

Midway Island, which became an American possession when Hawaii was annexed, together with Guam and Wake, are under the supervision of the Navy and are important stopping-places for airplanes. They played a large part in winning World War II.

The United States develops a new world outlook. When the Spanish-American War was over, the United States had gained a colonial empire in both the Caribbean Sea and the Pacific Ocean. It now controlled about 120,000 square miles more land and some 8,500,000 more people. What was to be done with these people? Should they become American citizens?

Other nations of the world began to realize that the United States was fast becoming a very powerful member of the world family. Another way of saying this is that the United States had become a *world power.* Our policy now began to change from one of partial isolation to one of *imperialism.* Imperialism is the policy of acquiring and extending authority over territories outside a country, and over peoples with a different background. The big problem facing the United States in 1899 was the government of these newly-acquired lands.

4. The United States Manages the Philippines

Many people in the United States, as elsewhere in the world, thought that we should not take complete control of the Philippine Islands. A German statesman wrote to President McKinley that the United States should remain true to its promise that "this is a war of deliverance and not one of greedy ambition and conquest."

The President consulted Cardinal Gibbons of Baltimore in the matter. Cardinal Gibbons replied that the Catholic religion was safer under the American flag than anywhere else, but in regard to complete American control of the Philippines, the Cardinal said: "Mr. President, it would be a good thing for the Catholic Church, but . . . a bad one for the United States."

Let us briefly look into the history of the Philippines to see if we can clear the doubt which was raised in peoples' minds.

The inhabitants of the Philippines. For the most part, the people of these islands belonged to a large group of brown people known as the Malays. It was believed that the first Malayans came to the Philippines thousands of years before we became acquainted with them. The geography of the islands tended to keep the natives in separate tribes. Mountains covered with

Brown Brothers

Cardinal Gibbons

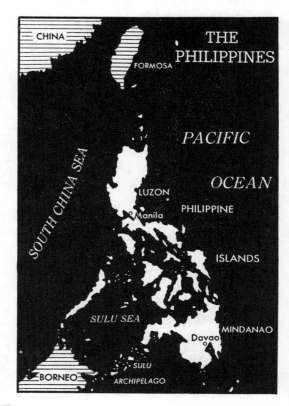

thick tropical forests made communication nearly impossible. As a result, each tribe had its own way of living and its own dialect, or way of speaking.

When the United States acquired these islands, it was surprised to learn that there were over seven thousand in the group. Four thousand of them were never named. Although the Spanish had made permanent settlements in the Philippines as far back as 1565, they had done very little towards improving the life of the people as a whole. Only a few profited by the Spanish rule. If it were not for the Spanish priests, who brought Christianity into the islands, the people would have been even less civilized than they were in 1898.

The problem of the Friars' land. One of the big problems which arose after the Spanish-American War concerned the Friars' lands. Under Spanish rule, the members of various Religious Orders had built up a great deal of power, temporal as well as spiritual. They had acquired large tracts of land and had a voice in civil affairs. They had the authority to inspect schools and prisons. They also helped recruit soldiers for the Spanish armies.

During the revolt of Aguinaldo these lands were seized, and the Friars were driven from the Philippines. When the Americans came into power the Friars were permitted to return, but they did not get back into governmental positions.

No doubt it was a good thing that the Church and state were separated. But when the Friars departed from the Philippines, the islands were left with very few priests. The Spanish missionaries had labored zealously and had made the Philippines the only Catholic and Christian nation of the Orient.

The Church had hoped that the Faith would spread from the Philippines throughout the Far East. For a long time this had seemed possible, but the days following the Spanish-American War looked dark indeed. America had taken the responsibility of the Philippines. Was it not up to her to provide priests, either native or American, to save a people that was rapidly becoming lax in its religious practices?

Education suffers also. While the Friars were active in the Philippines, Catholic education was safeguarded. With American occupation, the public school system of education was introduced. This was one of the worst features that resulted from the Filipino's revolt against Spain. So many teachers and government officials who went to the Philippines from the United States were non-Catholic, that the Filipinos began to think that Americanism meant the same as Protestantism.

Catholic education was saved by the appointment of one of the naval chaplains, Father William McKennon, as Superintendent of Catholic schools. He was responsible for the introduction of English as the only official language for education.

The beautiful Cathedral at Manila

America supplies priests. When America realized that the Filipinos were inclined to think of the United States as Protestant, American Jesuits were sent to continue the work of the Spanish Friars. Under the American Jesuits, the work of the Church flourished. They erected schools and colleges and continued the work of the Spanish Jesuits in operating the government observatory and weather bureau. From Manila, where this observatory is located, valuable weather information is provided, which greatly aids commerce.

Other benefits of American control. The material benefits with which God had blessed America were soon carried to the Philippine Islands. One of the first improvements made was the organization of a Board of Health at Manila. Through this bureau, a constant warfare against cholera, smallpox, malaria, and tuberculosis was waged.

The swamps and unsanitary conditions were causes of much disease. Consequently, the swamps were drained, and a sewage system was begun. Hospitals were opened, and trained nurses were brought in from the United States. As is often the case in hot climates, leprosy attacked many of the natives. By gathering them together on one island, the government hoped to check the spread of this disease.

Standards of living on the islands were also raised by improving transportation, building roads, constructing telephone and telegraph lines, and establishing police and

William Howard Taft

fire departments. The latest methods in agriculture were introduced to increase the production of sugar, rice, and tobacco. All of these products, plus valuable woods and dyes, are exported principally to the United States.

Early government under the United States. When military rule on the islands ceased, William H. Taft was made Civil Governor. He was aided by a Commission appointed by the President of the United States. The Governor and the Commission made up the upper house of the governing body. The lower house consisted of an assembly of eighty members elected by the Filipinos. The Americans and the Filipinos worked together to teach the Filipinos how to govern themselves.

Towards complete independence. The Filipinos had always wanted independence. It was discussed in the Congress of the United States many times. But not until 1934 did the United States feel that the Filipinos were almost ready to govern themselves. President Franklin D. Roosevelt signed the Tydings-McDuffie Act that year. This act gave the Filipinos a ten-year period of trial. During this time, they could form their own constitution. Manuel Quezon (kay-thone′) was the first President of the Commonwealth of the Philippines, as the territory was then called. Complete independence was promised the Filipinos by 1946.

For a time it seemed as though World War II would delay Philippine independence. However, the end of the war in 1945, plus the remarkable loyalty of the Filipinos to the American cause, made certain their independence. They chose July 4, 1946, as their Independence Day and celebrated it fittingly. Manuel Roxas (roe′-hass) was elected the first President of the new nation.

Human rights violated? You have learned, in both religion and history classes, that every human being or nation has rights. You know that a right is that which is justly due to anyone. Both individual and national rights come from God. An individual has such rights as those to life, property, true liberty, and to freedom of conscience. Nations have the right to conduct their own government and carry on any ac-

The Philippines became independent in 1946. Here President Roxas addresses the audience at the celebration on July 4.

tivity that is for the welfare of their people.

Since these rights come from God, no individual or public authority may interfere with them without just cause. The practice of justice protects these rights.

Did the United States violate the rights of the Filipinos by stepping in and governing their country? We have learned that the Filipinos did not really want that. They had hoped merely to be freed from Spain, which had treated them unjustly. The Filipinos did not desire

freedom from Spain only to be forced to bow to another country. Let us see what some great Catholics, who lived in 1898, thought about this.

John Lancaster Spalding, Bishop of Peoria, Illinois, said: "We have a compact territory, sufficient to support three hundred or more millions of human beings. Why should we go to the ends of the earth to take forcible possession of islands lying in remote oceans? . . . Spain deserved to be driven from her possessions. Her rule was unjust

Bishop Spalding

and cruel. We have done noble work; but having done it, we shall not be unwise or unpatriotic enough to jeopardize [that is, endanger] the fortune and future of our own country by annexing the conquered islands and becoming an imperial power."

Bishop Spalding said further that, while we had all the blessings of freedom, we should not force any people to come here to live, nor should we thrust our way of life on them.

Bishop James Ryan of the Diocese of Alton, Illinois (now the Springfield Diocese), believed that the voice of America should be heard when imperialism or *militarism* (that is, government by an army) threatens a country. "But," he said, "the path of justice is also that of honor. May the Stars and Stripes never cease to be the hope of the oppressed and the pride of all men who love liberty!"

Cardinal Gibbons felt that temporarily it would probably be safer for the Philippines to be under the direction of the United States than of any other country. He stated: "There is a great difference between independence and liberty. There are countries which have independence but no liberty or freedom, whereas the Philippine Islands, although for the present not enjoying independence, have freedom and liberty."

Although the Filipinos protested against American rule, they did not revolt, and when war swept the islands in 1944, they were loyal to the United States. This was largely because they trusted our promise to give them independence. This trust was not misplaced; we have fulfilled our pledge.

Do you understand these words?

"Pearl of the Antilles"	guerillas
West Indies	neutral
concentration camps	imperialism
sensational news	militarism
Apostolic Delegate	recruit

How well have you read?

1. Why was the United States interested in Cuba?
2. Find three general conditions on the Philippine Islands that were improved through the United States' occupation.

3. What part did American Sisters and priests play in the Spanish-American War?

4. Why was the Spanish-American War a turning point in the history of the United States?

5. Discuss the attitude of the Catholic Church towards American occupation of the Philippines.

6. Discuss this statement made in a magazine in 1899: "If an American says just government rests on the consent of the governed, he speaks wisely, but if a Filipino says the same thing, he is guilty of rebellion."

7. Is isolationism a good policy for America to follow in the modern world?

8. Discuss the question of imperialism and indicate its effects on the United States.

9. Discuss the opinions of Bishop Spalding and Bishop Ryan on the question of annexing conquered lands.

10. How have we fulfilled our pledge to the Filipinos?

To see what you remember

I. Arrange the following events in the order in which they occurred:

Sinking of the *Maine*

The Defeat of Admiral Cervera's Fleet

Election of President McKinley

Passage of the Tydings-McDuffie Act

The Battle of Manila Bay

II. On a separate piece of paper, write the numbers 1 to 13. After each number write the word or words that correctly fill the blanks in the following statements:

1. The most important event during President McKinley's administration was the................

2. Americans were interested in Cuba because they had invested money in.............and........... plantations.

3. The concentration camp was introduced before the Spanish-American War by..............

4. Most of the fighting during the war took place on.................

5. America became a world power at the end of the............century.

6. ....was the first Civil Governor of the Philippines.

7. The Filipinos under .... rebelled against the United States when they learned that they were not..............

8. Because the United States acquired land outside the continent of North America as a result of the Spanish-American War, she began a policy of.................

9. The Filipinos were granted a period of trial government by the ....Act.

10. Complete independence was given the Philippine Islands on

....

11. The peace treaty following the Spanish-American War added the following land to the United States:
a. In the Pacific Ocean ....
....

b. In the Atlantic Ocean ....
....

12. A sad state for the Catholic Church was the expulsion of the ....from the Philippines.

13. American control of the Philippines improved their...................,
...............and ....

43

CHAPTER III

WE STRUGGLE TO KEEP PEACE IN FOREIGN COUNTRIES

Points to remember. According to Christian principles, every nation is permitted to take all necessary precautions to safeguard its liberty. But it has no right to do so at the expense of the liberty of a weaker nation. Has the United States ever acted unjustly towards smaller, weaker nations?

In the first two chapters we learned that the United States acquired new territories in far-distant places. When a country acquires new land, either through annexation or purchase, a natural channel of trade is formed with it. In order to keep this trade flowing smoothly, it must be protected.

The United States purchased the Philippines and annexed Hawaii in order to have some control in the Pacific Ocean against possible Oriental invasion. The southeastern defenses of our country were strengthened by freeing Cuba from the control of a foreign nation.

In the previous chapter we learned something about how the United States handled its possessions in the Far East. In this chapter we shall see how Cuba was governed. We shall learn, too, that in order to permit an easy flow of trade from our eastern to our western possessions, the Panama Canal was built.

The points to keep in mind are: (1) Widening Our Interests, (2) Protecting Cuba and the Caribbean Lands, and (3) Securing Land for a Canal.

1. Widening Our Interests

Although the United States is rich in natural resources, you will find many items on your tables and in your home which are not produced in this country. Can you name some of them? Since America depends upon people in other parts of the world for the raw materials it does not have, it is natural that it also would send its own products to the peoples of other countries.

As we use up our oil, metals, minerals and forest products, we become increasingly dependent on foreign sources. A recent survey showed that we have just reached the point where we are using these basic resources at a faster rate than we can find new domestic sources of supply. Besides, new materials such as uranium, are becoming important. The United States depends

44

Commodore Perry opens the door to Japan. "When Japan became acquainted with Western ways and customs, it did not take her long to adopt them."

on foreign countries for most of the materials for atomic energy.

If we look into this topic, we shall find that if there were not a free flow of products to foreign countries, American farmers, businessmen, and workers would suffer. The prosperity of America, then, depends upon the rest of the world. Can you see how important it is that the United States make every effort to preserve peace in the world? Does the prosperity of the rest of the world depend on America?

Early contact with the Far East. You recall how Marco Polo visited China in the thirteenth century. You learned how China had a civilization of her own centuries before that time. For years she had been carrying on a spice and silk trade with European nations.

The United States, too, through trade, was an old acquaintance of China and Japan. There were great barriers which had to be broken down, however. The Oriental nations did not want to be disturbed by Europeans.

The credit for opening trade between Japan and Western nations is due to Commodore Matthew C. Perry of the United States Navy. In 1854, he signed a treaty with the Japanese which stated that the President of the United States would act as an umpire in any disputes which might arise between Japan and any European country. When Japan once became acquainted with Western ways and customs, it did not take her long to adopt them. It was not so with China. However, in this case, too, it was

John Hay, Secretary of State

policy too willingly. For a time, the plan reestablished peaceful relations among nations, but Japan did not fully observe the agreement.

The Boxer Rebellion. China has long been troubled with floods and famines. Some Chinese began to blame such natural disasters upon the foreigners. In 1900, a group of Chinese patriots, known as "Boxers," rose in rebellion. A reign of terror began. Foreign residents in China flocked to the missionaries for protection. They themselves, being foreigners, were not spared by the Chinese, and some of them lost their lives. The rebellion was finally stopped by armed intervention of the Great Powers, and the efforts of John Hay brought a promise from the foreign nations to stop encroaching on China.

Chinese leaders agreed to punish the organizers of the rebellion. They also agreed to pay all the damages caused. To the European nations, China paid something over a hundred million dollars. To the United States, she paid $24,000,000. However, when all claims were settled, the United States discovered that China had overpaid her. When China refused to accept a return of this money, the United States placed it in a fund for the education of Chinese students who might be sent to American colleges.

The following questions may be asked about the violation of the rights of a nation. Did European nations have the right to enter China and simply claim portions of that country for themselves? Did

the United States which aided in breaking down barriers.

The open door policy in China. At the close of the nineteenth century, Germany, France, Great Britain, Russia, and Japan decided that they wanted certain sections of land in China. It seemed as though China was going to be chopped to pieces. Fearing that the scramble by European nations for "pieces" of China would ruin American trade, the United States decided it had a right to interfere.

In 1899, John Hay, American Secretary of State, suggested the *open door policy* to the leading nations of the world. By this policy, all foreign powers would have equal trading rights in China. European powers, with the exception of Great Britain, did not accept the new

Bettmann Archive

American Marines take the wall of Peking during the Boxer Rebellion.

the fact that China was economically backward and the other nations more advanced give these nations a right? Of course not. So the United States was correct in taking steps to prevent further violation of Chinese rights, even though her main reason was not so much the protection of China as the protection of her own interests.

American Missionaries in China. The Boxer Rebellion caused a great deal of damage to the Catholic missions in China.

Perhaps you will be surprised to know that America itself was considered a mission country until the twentieth century. It was through Cardinal Gibbons, whose name you will so often meet in these pages, that the first American Foreign Mission Seminary, now known as Maryknoll, was established in 1911. Cardinal Gibbons was urged to send missionaries to foreign lands, regardless of how badly we needed priests in America, because our own faith would be endangered unless we shared it with others.

Between 1918 and 1943, missionaries increased from a mere handful to nearly three thousand. Of this number, China received the most.

There were several reasons why China should be more fortunate than other mission countries. Probably one reason was that English was studied in Chinese schools more than in other foreign schools. This enabled the English-speaking missionary to have advantages that others would not have.

Present mission field in China. Of the 4000,000,000 people in China, about 4,000,000 are Catholic. Today, most American priests have been driven from China. Many American Sisterhoods have worked in China.

The last twenty-five years in China have been the most eventful. The priests and Sisters have had to cope with civil war, bandits, Reds, famine, and flood. Every mission was affected, but this offered occasions for more charity. While missionary work was appreciated by

the Chinese, it was hindered on all sides by hostile forces. The worst effect was felt when World War II broke out in 1941. Nearly half of the American missionaries were removed and placed in concentration camps at that time. In these last twenty-five years, over fifty-three priests, Brothers, and Sisters have died in China, but the remaining ones have gone on cheerfully doing their duty. The greatest tragedy of all came with the Communist conquest of China. Under Red control, the missions are being systematically destroyed, but Chinese Catholics have remained firm and many have been put to death.

Theodore Roosevelt's part in world peace. The United States' growing interest in world affairs, which followed the Spanish-American War, enabled us to have a share in striving for world peace. In 1899, through the influence of President Roosevelt, a Court of International Arbitration was set up at the Hague in Holland. Our country had recourse to this court on several occisions.

The treaty at Portsmouth. You have already read that in 1854 the United States had signed a treaty with Japan, stating that the President of the United States could assume leadership in trying to settle disputes between Japan and any European nation. When Russia and Japan went to war over Manchuria, President Roosevelt tried to bring about peace. He offered to receive representatives from these two countries at Portsmouth, New

Russians and Japanese at Portsmouth

Brown Brothers

Hampshire, to help them settle their differences. They accepted his offer and a peace treaty was signed in 1905.

The conference at Portsmouth greatly increased the influence of the United States in world affairs, and added to the popularity of President Theodore Roosevelt. The Treaty of Portsmouth was considered the most notable achievement of Roosevelt's career and won for him the Nobel Peace Prize in 1906.

You will learn more about the relations of the United States with the Far East when you study Unit Five.

Unfortunate Maximilian of Austria. We have seen how the United States handled affairs for its own protection in the Far East. Now we shall consider some of the incidents which threatened our liberty in places to the south of the United States.

While the Civil War was being waged, there occurred the last attempt of any foreign power to try to control the nations in the New World. Mexico was the scene of this attempt, and Napoleon Bonaparte III, the nephew of Napoleon Bonaparte of France, was the man who planned it.

The Emperor Maximilian says farewell to his confessor and a servant before he is executed by the Mexicans.

European nations were often accustomed to seize the ports of a country that owed them debts. These ports could be held, and any trade duties taken until the debts were paid. Now, Mexico owed France, Spain, and England some money. Soldiers of these three nations landed on the coast of Mexico, in 1861, to collect this money. The governments of Spain and England then withdrew their soldiers.

This left France free to carry out Napoleon III's desire to spread French influence in foreign lands.

Napoleon did not think the United States would interfere, since it was busy with its own war. The French soldiers overthrew the Indian President, Benito Juarez (hwa'-reth), and made Maximilian, a younger brother of the Emperor of Austria, ruler of Mexico. Maximilian was entirely unaware of the unjust incidents that had happened in Mexico.

When our Civil War ended, the United States was free to look into the Mexican situation. General Sherman was sent to the border with American troops. The Americans informed the French that they considered "the occupation of Mexico a violation of the Monroe Doctrine." Napoleon III was requested to withdraw the French troops from Mexico. He complied. As soon as the French troops had left, Juarez captured Maximilian and had him shot, in spite of the fact that the United States pleaded that his life be spared.

No European nation ever again attempted to establish an empire in any independent American republic.

The Venezuelan boundary dispute. The next test of the effectiveness of the Monroe Doctrine was made in 1895, during President Cleveland's administration. Along the northern coast of South America is located the Republic of Venezuela. Directly to the east of this country is the British-owned portion of Guiana. The boundary line between these countries was never exactly determined.

When gold was discovered in this region, England declared it was within her boundary. Venezuela became alarmed and immediately appealed to the United States, using the Monroe Doctrine as her reason. **President Cleveland defends a weaker nation.** President Cleveland felt that Great Britain was taking advantage of a weaker nation in this matter. At first England refused to accept the offer of our Secretary of State, Richard Olney, to help settle the dispute. The President then took the matter up with Congress. A commission was sent to South America to determine, if possible, the exact boundary between these two countries. The entire affair created a tense feeling in the United States. War could have broken out. But England did not want war and finally agreed that a settlement be made by arbitration. The commission decided that England had the better claim to the territory.

When the Monroe Doctrine was

put forth in 1823, it merely stated that no foreign power could colonize in America. In the Venezuelan case, a new interpretation, or meaning, was given to this doctrine. It now came to mean that the United States was ready to come to the defense of any American nation that was unjustly treated by a foreign nation.

A boundary dispute in the north. The discovery of gold was the occasion for another boundary dispute in the North. It, too, was settled by arbitration. Here is that story.

If you look at the map, you will see that a portion of Alaska borders Canada and extends about five hundred miles southward along the Pacific coast. A dispute arose over this boundary for two reasons. *First,* northern Canada was cut off from the possibility of good ocean trade. *Second,* Canada was deprived of easy access to the gold which was discovered in Alaska in 1896.

When Russia owned Alaska, she had signed a treaty with Great Britain setting the Canadian boundary thirty miles east of the Pacific Ocean. When the United States purchased Alaska, England wanted to push Canada's boundary to the ocean in order to give her the advantage of fine harbors afforded by many deep bays in this region. The United States felt that the boundary should be left in accordance with the old treaty Great Britain had made with Russia. For many years this dispute went on.

In 1903, Theodore Roosevelt submitted the dispute to an arbitration commission of Americans, British, and Canadians. The boundary line was finally settled in accordance with American claims; in other words, as the treaty between Russia and England had originally fixed it.

2. Protecting Cuba and the Caribbean Lands

The Stars and Stripes flies over Cuba. When the United States helped Cuba to gain its freedom in 1898, our government promised it would recognize Cuban independence. After the war, the island lay in ruins. Many of the people realized that they were in no condition to carry on an efficient form of government. So the United States established a protectorate over Cuba, with the promise that as soon as it was able to govern itself it would gain complete independence.

An American Military Governor. When the Rough Riders returned to the United States after the Spanish-American War, General Leonard Wood remained in Cuba as Military Governor. He had a gigantic task before him but did not turn back.

There were two particularly difficult obstacles to overcome on the island. The first was a high percentage of illiteracy, that is, inability to read and write. The second was the conquering of epidemics of yellow fever, malaria, smallpox, and typhoid fever. Because of tropical diseases, thousands of Americans lost their lives during the first year of our occupation.

The fight against yellow fever.

Bettmann Archive

The Conquest of yellow fever

General Wood believed that the most important thing for him to undertake was the improvement of sanitary conditions on the island. He had to find a man who would work efficiently and self-sacrificingly. Dr. William C. Gorgas met these qualifications and was appointed Health Commissioner. Gorgas and Wood bravely began their struggle against disease in Havana. They ordered the streets and cisterns to be cleaned, had a sewage system installed, and soon sanitary conditions were much improved. Just when everything seemed in their favor, yellow fever reappeared. It looked as though unsanitary conditions were not the immediate cause of the scourge.

The American health commission. A Cuban physician, Dr. Carlos Fin- lay, believed firmly that yellow fever was carried by the silver-striped mosquito. The United States sent a commission headed by Walter Reed, an army physician, to investigate Dr. Finlay's claim. Two American doctors, James Carroll and Jesse Lazear, were members of the board. They exposed themselves to the bite of this mosquito, and both became seriously ill. Dr. Lazear died, a martyr to the cause of humanity.

After much more experimentation, Dr. Reed was satisfied that it was the silver-striped mosquito which carried yellow fever. The next step in this struggle was to rid the island of the mosquitoes. Dr. Gorgas found that their breeding-places were pools of water. Soon he discovered that if the water was covered with a thin film of oil, the mosquitoes could not breed. Within a very short time the island was freed of the scourge of yellow fever.

A grateful but restless people. The Cubans appreciated the conquering of disease, together with the establishment of schools, the building of roads, and the organization of local governments. However, they had been promised their independence, and that was what they wanted. General Wood became aware of this feeling, and determined that he would help the Cubans accomplish their aim.

A convention of Cubans was called in 1900. They framed a constitution and sent it to Washington for approval. The United States, however, felt that Cuba was not yet able to stand alone. So the Platt Amendment provided that:

1. Cuba should never sign a treaty with any foreign nation which would endanger her independence.
2. She should never go into debt beyond her power to pay.
3. She should permit the intervention of the United States in order to preserve her independence.
4. She should allow the United States to buy or lease coaling or or naval stations on the island.

The United States at once acted to fulfill its agreement with Cuba. In May, 1902, Cuba became a republic.

A new treaty was made with Cuba in 1934 by which the right of intervention by the United States was given up.

A Rough Rider becomes a President. While General Wood was working diligently in Cuba, his friend, Theodore Roosevelt, was elected Vice President of the United States in 1900. William McKinley, the defender of American imperialism, was reelected President at that time. His second term, however, was destined to be very short. Six months after his reelection, President McKinley was shot by an anarchist, and Theodore Roosevelt, the hero of San Juan Hill, became President. His two terms of office were notable for their many reforms, about which we shall read later.

The Monroe Doctrine develops into a "big stick" policy. In 1823, the Monroe Doctrine meant protection against colonization by a foreign power. President Cleveland extended its meaning to include the protection of a weaker American country from the injustice of a foreign nation. President Roosevelt, in 1904, announced to Congress that he would interpret this doctrine in another way. He declared that if a Latin American republic could not carry out its obligations peacefully, or was unable to keep order within itself, the United States could exercise an international police power to enforce order. This policy is frequently referred to as the *big stick policy.* Can you tell why?

Our possessions in the Caribbean area. The United States owns the following territories in the Caribbean Sea area: Puerto Rico, the

President Theodore Roosevelt
Brown Brothers

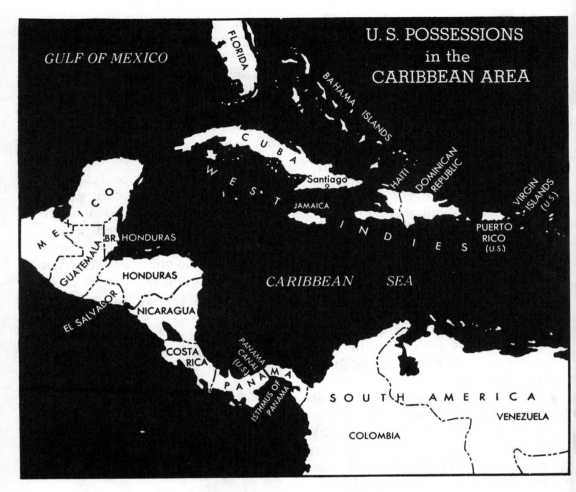

U. S. POSSESSIONS
in the
CARIBBEAN AREA

Panama Canal Zone, and the Virgin Islands. The United States has at times used the big stick policy in other territories of this region because they showed inability to protect themselves. Disturbances occurred so frequently in Santo Domingo and Haiti, for example, that the United States Marines had to be sent there to maintain order. The Marines were withdrawn from Haiti in 1934 and from Santo Domingo in 1940.

Puerto Rico. This island is economically valuable to us because of its sugar and tobacco plantations. Since it is a possession of the United States, these products come to us duty free, thereby giving the Puerto Ricans a great advantage over other Caribbean planters.

American rule has helped Puerto Rico in other ways, besides opening up trade with our country. Although many of the people cannot yet read and write, education is making progress on the island. In 1917, the people became citizens of the United States. The inhabitants themselves have elected a governor and a legislature since 1948. At that time they were also given the power to formulate laws, although any law not approved by the United States could be vetoed. The purpose of this supervision is to train the citizens in the ways of democracy.

The most important benefit gained by the Puerto Ricans is that, with their citizenship, they can enter the United States without restriction. An increasing number comes to our eastern cities each year because the country remains desperately poor. The tiny island, thirty-five by one hundred miles, has few industries; it depends mostly on its sugar crop.

Puerto Rican Independence. July 25, 1952, was a day of great rejoicing in Puerto Rico. On the fifty-fourth anniversary of the landing of American troops on the island, Puerto Ricans celebrated the adoption of their new constitution. This constitution—accepted by a referendum of the people and approved by the United States Congress— puts the island's internal affairs completely in the hands of its elected lawmakers. It abolishes the power of the United States Congress to repeal insular laws, leaves the way open for Puerto Rico to become a state of the Union later, and takes away from the United States President the power to appoint judges and officials.

The Catholic Church in Puerto Rico. Puerto Rico was discovered by Columbus in 1493. By 1513, the first bishop to set foot on American soil had arrived. He began his diocese in San Juan, which is now the capital of the island. Spanish bishops cared for the spiritual needs of the people until after the Spanish-American War.

The work of the priests and Sisters has spread. Today there are homes for the aged, schools, many types of religious communities, and hospitals. There are now two dioceses in Puerto Rico, with a total of nearly two million Catholics, over two hundred fifty priests, and about one hundred parish churches. Since there are so few priests many Puerto Ricans are not being instructed in the Catholic faith.

3. Securing Land for a Canal

Binding our possessions together. When the Spanish-American War broke out, the *Oregon*, one of the first American battleships, was needed in Cuba; but it was in San Francisco. Many long and anxious days were passed waiting and watching for its appearance in Cuba. The journey around South America was the cause of the delay. It was then that Americans determined to carry out their long-desired ambition to build a canal which would bring our possessions in the Pacific and Atlantic Oceans into closer contact.

Possible sites for a canal. The Isthmus of Panama, a narrow stretch of land between Central and South America, belonged to Colombia in South America. When the need for a canal became more acute, the United States immediately thought this would be a good location for it.

A ship in a lock of the Panama Canal. The large machines at right and left control the filling of the locks.

Nicaragua was another possible site for a canal, but England was in strong control there. The United States realized that if England decided to build a canal in this region, she could be a dangerous neighbor. Some understanding had to be reached with England.

The Clayton-Bulwer Treaty. In 1850, England and the United States made a treaty, known as the Clayton-Bulwer Treaty. The terms of the treaty satisfied both countries for a time. According to this treaty, neither country would have ex-

clusive control of any canal which might be built. Neither country could fortify the land around the canal, nor could it establish a colony in Central America. Merely discussing the possibility of a canal was all that was done at this time.

A bad beginning. In 1878, when Colombia granted a French engineering company the right to construct a canal through Panama, American interest was revived.

The great French engineer, Ferdinand de Lesseps (les-seps') had just completed cutting the Suez

56

Canal between the Red Sea and the Mediterranean. His work was so successful that Colombia placed great confidence in him. Little did De Lesseps and the French realize that they would have to work under vastly different conditions in Panama. They did not foresee that the tropical diseases of yellow fever and malaria would hamper work. Hundreds of the French died, and those who were left had not the courage to fight disease, together with tropical rains which caused landslides. They gave up in despair.

The Hay-Pauncefote Treaty. By 1901, with Theodore Roosevelt as President, the United States had decided that it should undertake the building of the canal. In accordance with that decision, the Hay-Pauncefote Treaty was drawn up. This treaty freed us from the obligation to consult England about the construction of the canal, and gave the United States the right to carry out plans as it pleased.

There were two limitations placed on the United States by the agreement with England. One was that the canal was to be open to ships of all nations, and the other was that equal toll rates would be charged to all.

Revolution without bloodshed. The next step was to secure the necessary land. The United States decided in favor of Panama. First, the purchase of the French claims to the Panama route was necessary. When that was settled, the United States offered Colombia $10,000,000 for the land in Panama, but Colom-bia had hoped to get more and rejected the proposition. This angered the people of Panama, who revolted.

President Roosevelt immediately recognized Panama as an independent country and sent the United States Marines to protect it. The entire revolution was over in a day, and Roosevelt purchased from Panama a strip of land ten miles wide for the canal.

The nations of South America were angry at the United States for taking this stand against Colombia. They accused our government of treating a weak nation unfairly. In 1921, the United States tried to make up for its action by paying Colombia $25,000,000. Friendship between the countries was again sealed, and the Canal Zone, as we now know it, belonged to the United States.

At last a canal begins. President Roosevelt profited by all of the difficulties which the French had encountered. He was determined to make this project one of the most outstanding engineering accomplishments ever undertaken. He appointed Colonel George Goethals (go' thalz), a graduate of West Point, as engineer, and chose Dr. Gorgas of Cuban fame to help combat disease. Under the guidance of these two men, a region which at one time was uninhabitable became a place where people could live comfortably. The canal was completed in 1914, just at the outbreak of the First World War.

Importance of the canal. The Panama Canal is one of the most important trade routes of the world. For the United States in particular, it is an important point in our system of global defense. Our ships can move from one ocean to the other easily and, therefore, can be on hand quickly to guard our island possessions. Trade between East and West has been greatly increased because of the canal, and cities in the southern part of the United States have developed more rapidly.

Protecting the canal. At either end of the canal, forts have been erected for its protection. Detachments of the Army and the Air Corps are always on duty. Military protection makes clear to European nations that the United States will tolerate no attempt by any foreign country to gain a foothold in this region.

In 1917, the United States purchased the Virgin Islands from Denmark. Their location near Puerto Rico makes them a valuable guardian of the entrance to the Panama Canal region.

Words to remember

open door policy   dispute
encroaching   "big stick" policy
interpretation   anarchist

To make you think

1. How did the United States protect her possessions in the Far East? In the Caribbean region?
2. Find evidences in this chapter of weaker nations being unjustly treated by stronger ones.
3. What part did Theodore Roosevelt play in striving for world peace?

4. Discuss the Maximilian Affair in Mexico. Try to find more information about it.
5. What were the three interpretations of the Monroe Doctrine mentioned in this chapter?
6. How did Cuba benefit by the guidance of the United States?

To see what you remember

Number your paper from 1 to 15. Find the word or phrase in Column II that is connected with a word in Column I. Write the letter of that phrase opposite the correct number on your paper.

Column I
1. China
2. Boxer Rebellion
3. The Hague
4. Mexico
5. Manchuria
6. Theodore Roosevelt
7. William Goethals
8. Dr. Gorgas
9. Cuba
10. Dr. Lazear
11. Puerto Rico
12. Virgin Islands
13. Nicaragua
14. Hay-Pauncefote Treaty
15. Cardinal Gibbons

Column II
a. International Arbitration Court
b. Maximilian Affair
c. foreigners in China
d. "big stick" policy
e. open door policy
f. Treaty of Portsmouth
g. complete control of canal by U. S.
h. Yellow fever
i. Panama Canal
j. guardian of Canal Zone
k. Platt Amendment
l. a martyr for humanity
m. first diocese in New World
n. joint control of Panama Canal
o. possible site for a canal
p. first American Foreign Mission Seminary

58

CHAPTER IV

AN ALL-AMERICAN TEAM IS FORMED

A bird's-eye-view of this chapter. The United States had attained its full growth as a world power. The countries which would feel the effects of this power naturally would be those closest to the United States. These countries are located in Central and South America. Together with Mexico and the West Indies, they are often spoken of as Latin America. This name is given to them because their inhabitants speak Spanish or Portuguese, languages which are derived from Latin. Since these people are our neighbors, it is for our common interest that we keep on friendly terms.

The country which caused the greatest disturbance of our peaceful relations early in the twentieth century was Mexico. In 1914, a rebellion broke out in that country after a period of political unrest. Serious injury was done to the Catholic Church, and it looked very much as if the revolution was in reality a revolt against religion. The principle that all men have the right to worship God according to their conscience was attacked in that country. Many people endured great suffering, and were even put to death for the Faith.

Our relations with Latin American countries were strengthened by the "Good Neighbor Policy" of President Franklin D. Roosevelt. Conferences, known as Pan-American Conferences, were frequently held with a view to binding all of the Americas closer together. Whether or not this policy will always ease any strained relations which might arise in the Western Hemisphere is still to be seen. It has, however, tended to make a more solid line of defense in this section of the world.

The main points of this chapter are: (1) Our Relations with Mexico, and (2) Pan-Americanism—A Union of the Americas.

1. Our Relations with Mexico

For over fifty years after the unfortunate Maximilian affair, the relations of the United States with Mexico were peaceful. Mexico is rich in natural resources, particularly oil and silver. Many Americans invested their money in developing these resources. When unrest spread throughout Mexico, American interests were at stake.

President Diaz of Mexico

We had a right to protect them, provided we exercised justice in doing so.

Early Mexican history. You have already learned that Mexico was discovered by Hernando Cortes and claimed for Spain. Cortes had found a flourishing civilization in Mexico, but it was completely pagan. The Spaniards brought Christianity to the Mexican Indians. They tried to raise their standards of living. Soon Catholic schools, colleges and universities, and hospitals were erected for both whites and Indians.

But Spain failed to keep pace with the Mexican desire for independence and was forced to withdraw.

A land of revolution. Between the years 1877 and 1911, Mexico was ruled by Porfirio Diaz (pore-fee'-ree-o de'-as). He exercised his presidential power with the iron hand of a dictator, that is, with unlimited authority. During his early administration, he constantly persecuted the Catholic Church. However, religious freedom was restored towards the close of his period of control.

Diaz was responsible for improving some conditions in Mexico. He developed the natural resources of the country, built factories and railroads, and fostered education. But he always favored foreigners who had invested money in Mexico. When he could no longer satisfy their desires, he was forced out of office in 1910 by Francisco Madero (ma-day'-roe). Although Madero meant well, he was too weak to control the revolutionary spirit which he had aroused.

Recognition of Huerta. In 1913, Victoriano Huerta (ware'-ta), another revolutionary general, had Madero arrested and proclaimed himself President of Mexico. Madero was assassinated on the way to prison. At this point President Taft became alarmed but would not permit any arms to be sent to either the Mexican rebels or to the government. Troops hurried to the border, however, to keep the disorder south of the Rio Grande River.

A few days after the murder of Madero, Woodrow Wilson became President of the United States. With his administration began a sorry relationship between our country and Mexico. Although a score of foreign governments, plus most of the Mexican provinces, recognized Huerta as President of Mexico, the United States hesitated.

"Watchful waiting." President Wilson adopted the policy of waiting to see if Mexico could straighten out her own affairs without our help. Formerly, we had recognized governments which were formed through revolution, but now Wilson declared that he would not "extend the hand of welcome to anyone who obtains power in a sister republic by treachery and violence." He sent a message to Mexico to cease hostilities and hold an election, in which Huerta would not be a candidate. When Huerta refused these terms, the United States ignored Mexico, hoping by this method to embarrass it in the eyes of the rest of the world.

In a message to Congress, in December, 1913, Wilson stated that he would not change his policy of "watchful waiting." Wilson was really waiting for some incident which would furnish an excuse for our participation in Mexican affairs. At last this incident occurred.

The Tampico Bay incident. Early in 1914, a boatload of United States Marines landed at Tampico, a city on the eastern coast of Mexico, to purchase gasoline. Orders had been given by President Huerta to close the roads in this section, and because our Marines had trespassed they were arrested. Although Huerta ordered their speedy release, the United States demanded a salute to the American flag as an apology. Huerta refused. He rea-

Brown Brothers

U. S. Marines at Vera Cruz

soned that since the United States would not recognize him as the Mexican President, he had no obligation to fire a salute to our flag. President Wilson directed that armed force be used to secure "proper recognition of the dignity of the United States."

Battleships landed at Vera Cruz (vay'-ra Croos) a little to the south of Tampico, and the customhouse there was seized. Some American and Mexican lives were lost, and Huerta resigned his office. War was prevented, however, by the intervention of Argentina, Brazil, and Chile, three South American countries, often called the A. B. C. countries.

A series of presidents. The next Mexican President was General Carranza (kar-ran'-sa), one of the

61

many revolutionary leaders of the army. When the United States recognized him, another revolution broke out in protest. Francisco Villa (vee'-ya), angered at this action of the United States, raided the town of Columbus, New Mexico, in 1916. Again, United States troops, under General John J. Pershing, were sent to Mexico. He was ordered to capture the bandit Villa, but after a six-month search our soldiers were recalled. The First World War was claiming the attention of the world. Trouble in Mexico, however, did not cease.

Mexico gets a constitution. In 1917, Mexico finally drew up a constitution. The United States would not recognize it because it affected our investments in Mexico. One of the articles declared that all land, water, and minerals belonged to the

Father Pro, S. J.

state, and that "only Mexicans by birth or naturalization" had the right to acquire land or develop any of the country's resources. Immediately, protests arose on the part of American investors. This led Mexico to agree not to apply this law to property acquired before 1917. The United States was satisfied and, for a brief period, peaceful relations were restored.

Blood-drenched Mexico. While the rest of the world was busy fighting the First World War, Mexico was going through days of political and spiritual wretchedness. Carranza and Villa were both driven out of public life. The country was being governed by politicians and army chiefs who were both tyrannical and incapable of public office. In 1923, Plutarco Calles (kah'-yase) became President of Mexico. During his administration, persecution of the Church flared up anew.

The constitution—a menace to the Church. The new constitution threatened religious liberty, and Calles put this part of the constitution into forceful effect. All religious services were discontinued. It was up to the government to decide how many priests were needed. No religious habits were permitted to be worn. Many priests and Sisters were driven into exile without a trial. Religious, as well as the Catholic laity, were executed on charges of disloyalty to the government.

You will get a good picture of this persecution if you read a life of Father Miguel Pro, a Jesuit, who for a long time resisted capture by the Mexicans. The story of how he upheld the right of the Mexican people to religious freedom is most interesting. Father Pro finally was put to death by the Mexican government in 1927. His Cause is now in Rome, and some day the Church may declare him a saint.

That same year, at the unofficial intervention of Dwight W. Morrow, our Ambassador to Mexico, the Mexican government pledged itself to end its interference with the Church's affairs and allow freedom in the practice of religion. The Church promised to give up its claim to any land which the Mexican government had already seized from it. The Government brutally broke its word, but the Church, as always, was faithful to its promise. The Mexican constitution proclaimed liberty of thought and conscience but in practice it contradicted these freedoms. There are some governments today doing much the same things.

2. Pan-Americanism

In the preceding chapters, we have seen that the United States tried various means to keep good order in those countries which were near our shores. Latin American countries declared the United States was interested only in "big business" developments in their territories. You will learn about big business in the next Unit. Our neighbors also resented our big stick interference in their affairs.

The United States insisted it was for the good of the weaker nation

By Burton Holmes, from Ewing Galloway
The "Christ of the Andes"

that she interfered. We shall see how the United States tried to defend her point of view and became the leader in forming a strong union for the preservation of peace in the Western Hemisphere.

Christ—the foundation of friendly relations. Latin Americans quickly learned to settle some of their differences by arbitration. They learned that wars do not solve difficulties; they only lead to other wars. Christian principles are the best guides for building good feeling between nations.

A good example of settling a dispute in a Christian manner occurred in South America. Argentina and Chile argued over the possession of some land at their boundaries. Bishops in both countries urged the people to resort to the principles of Christ, and so avoid war. They finally agreed to arbitrate, and thus settled the question peaceably.

The joy and thanksgiving of the people were expressed by the erection of a large, bronze statue of Christ, high in the Andes Mountains in 1904. This statue, on the Argentina-Chile border, is often called the "Christ of the Andes." This statue testifies that the people believed in the words of Christ, Who said, "Without Me, you can do nothing."

The Pan-American movement. The desire for good Latin American relations dates back to the days of Simon Bolivar, who is called the George Washington of South America. In 1826, he tried to form a union which would bind Latin American countries together, but this movement was not successful. Several later attempts also met with failure.

When James G. Blaine was Secretary of State in 1889, the United States made an effort to form a union for better relations. The first meeting was held in Washington, D. C., on April 14, 1890. This date has been considered "Pan-American Day" ever since.

The achievements of this meeting were not outstanding. The South American republics were dis-

The Headquarters of the union of twenty-one American republics—the Pan-American Union Building, Washington, D. C.
By Ewing Galloway, N. Y.

trustful of the United States, and the United States did not seem interested in their problems. Then, too, South America was bound by economic ties to various European countries. These countries had lent money to Latin American republics and, frequently, took over their financial affairs until any debt was paid. What instance of this has been previously mentioned?

The inter-American conference of 1890 paved the way for later ones. Today, there are twenty-one republics in this union. Its permanent headquarters is the Pan-American Union Building, one of the most beautiful buildings in Washington, D. C. Altogether, there have been nine conferences held in a different American capital every five years. They are held, not for treaty purposes only, but to promote friendship, cooperation, better understanding, and appreciation of the cultures of the various American countries.

President Hoover pleases Latin American countries. For many years, one point in particular was brought up at the inter-American meetings. This point was the fact that Latin American countries resented interference in their affairs by the United States. Herbert Hoover, elected President of the United States in 1928, determined he would make every effort to improve relations. Consequently, during the months between his election and inauguration, he made a tour of about a dozen Latin American countries. Wherever he traveled, he spoke of mutual understanding and friendship.

When he returned to the United States, he had the State Department prepare a statement of the Monroe Doctrine, which omitted the addition which President Theodore Roosevelt had inserted fifteen years previously. That addition was the offensive clause stating that the United States had the right and duty to intervene in the affairs of weaker nations if necessary. Latin American countries rejoiced, and another step was made towards strengthening good feeling between them and the United States.

We become a good neighbor. When Franklin D. Roosevelt was inaugurated in 1933, he announced the "Good Neighbor Policy." This policy played an important part in gaining the confidence of Latin America. President Roosevelt, like Hoover, said the United States was opposed to armed intervention in the affairs of smaller countries.

He gave several reasons why our past imperialistic policy should be replaced by a good neighbor policy. First, Latin American countries seemed to be able to take care of themselves. Second, Roosevelt believed stronger ties would be formed if better trade relations existed between the Americas. And third, there was definite need for closer union in order to overcome the influence of powerful European nations, such as Germany, which were trying to spread false ideas in Latin America.

President Roosevelt put the good

The wealth and culture of our South American neighbors is reflected in Rio de Janeiro, Brazil.

neighbor policy into effect by recalling the Marines from Haiti and by withdrawing from the internal affairs of Cuba and Panama.

Misunderstanding to be overcome. While the good neighbor policy has considerably improved our relations with our neighboring republics, there is still much to be accomplished. A great deal depends upon mutual knowledge. There are several sources of misunderstandings. Some people in the United States have been accustomed to think of Latin Americans as being backward. We must learn that many of these people are highly cultured. Another source of mis-

understanding is the refusal to grasp the fact that Latin America is Catholic.

Latin Americans, too, often misinterpret American customs because they know us only through our motion pictures, which are often bad. They remember, too, that once we took Cuba, the Philippines, New Mexico, and California from Spain. They sometimes look upon our good neighbor policy as a cloak to hide our "Yankee imperialism." In other words, they doubt our sincerity.

A common enemy — a common bond of union. The period between the First and Second World

Wars saw the rise of Nazism and the growth of Communism. The threat which they both raised, and the continuing menace of Communism, have brought all the Americas closer in the realization that they must protect each other.

All of the American nations have a common bond which will help to conquer this enemy, and that is the Christian religion. While we should never use religion as a political tool, it can be used as a bond of friendship and a help to a common understanding among nations.

A pledge of assistance. In 1947, at Rio de Janeiro, Brazil's beautiful capital, the American nations made a treaty which was intended to preserve the peace and independence of the 290,000,000 people of the Western Hemisphere.

In substance, this is what it said: "If any American country is attacked by any other nation from outside or inside the Western Hemisphere, we shall consider it an attack against all, and shall all help to meet it."

Canada does not belong to the inter-American union but to the British Commonwealth of Nations. However, she has an agreement with the United States to help defend North America in case of attack.

Spreading the good neighbor policy. Since the development of the good neighbor policy depends upon mutual understanding, there must be some means of spreading a knowledge of the culture of the nations that strive for friendship.

The United States Government Printing Office in Washington publishes a monthly bulletin called *Americas.* This formerly was known as the *Pan-American Bulletin.* Much valuable information can be learned from this bulletin.

The N. C. W. C. News Service of the National Catholic Welfare Conference in Washington also publishes *Noticias Catolicas,* regular news stories about Latin American countries. The library of The Catholic University of America in Washington has more material on Latin America than any library outside those countries.

The value of the good neighbor policy. During the Second World War the United States passed a Neutrality Act, which declared we would not carry war equipment under our own flag to any warring nation. We succeeded in getting shipments through to help England and France, however, because through inter-American agreement, any American nation might fly the flag of any other American nation. The ships of the United States flew the flag of Panama, and the necessary war materials reached their destination. Whether this was right or wrong, it did show the value of a close union between the Americas.

The organization of American states. In 1948, the meeting of the American republics was held at Bogota (boe-goe-tah') in Colombia. At this meeting, the structure of the union of the American countries was changed, and it is now called the Organization of American States. The reason for this change was to make certain that no impression would be given that one nation was superior to the others and the leader in the union. The Pan-American Union still exists, but it is now merely one of the six divisions of the larger Organization of American States.

A new charter was also drawn up at this time, which stated that the Organization of American States would operate within the United Nations, which is an organization of leading nations in the world. It was made clear, however, that all the American nations would attempt to settle within their own organization disputes arising among them before they would appeal to the United Nations.

Sharing resources to foster peace. The main reason for starting the inter-American conferences was to work out the problems of trade relations between Latin America and the United States. If nations can find a way of sharing the goods they produce, this is a big step towards forming friendly relations. Our Holy Father, Pope Pius XII, has stated that nations have the right and obligation to share resources with others.

Recognizing the value of trade relations, not only among the Americas but throughout the world, the United States made a number of suggestions for expanding world trade. One was the formation of an International Trade Organization. This agency seeks to lower trade barriers among nations and keep open the channels of international commerce. The dropping of trade barriers is a very important factor in promoting peace.

Why we must be friendly neighbors. There are three main reasons why there should be a spirit of cooperation between the United States and Latin America.

First, We must be friendly in order to protect each other. If any unfriendly country succeeded in making an entrance in a Latin American country, our own peace would be endangered.

Second, we must be friendly in order to keep democracy alive. Our neighbors must be democracies too, because the more democratic governments there are, the stronger will we be to oppose some of the tyrannical governments in the world.

Third, we must be friendly in order to keep our trade from collapsing. War has disturbed our trade with Europe. Thus, our trade with Latin America is important, for it has abundant resources that we need, a growing population, and an expanding economy.

All the points mentioned in the second section of this chapter have the same goal—peace and lasting friendship among the Americas. With Christ, this can be achieved; without Him, our cause will fail.

Terms to remember
dictator
"watchful waiting"
revolutionary spirit
a sister republic

unofficial intervention
Pan-Americanism
Latin America
Inter-American Conference
Good Neighbor Policy
Organization of American States
International Trade Organizations

How many can you answer?

1. Why did President Wilson refuse to recognize Huerta as President of Mexico?
2. Why was the religious persecution in Mexico a violation of the rights of the Mexican people?
3. Why are we more interested now in the Caribbean region than we were in the nineteenth century?
4. What caused Wilson to change his policy of "watchful waiting"?
5. Explain the purpose of the Pan-American Conferences.
6. How can you help to build more friendly relations between people of the United States and Latin America?
7. What did Presidents Hoover and Roosevelt do to build friendlier relations between the countries of the Americas?
8. How can the United States keep cordial relations with the other American republics?

Answer *yes* or *no*

1. Mexico persecuted the Church when the Spaniards were in control there.
2. The attitude of the United States towards Mexico in the early twentieth century is one of which we can be justly proud.
3. Latin American countries are those whose languages are derived from Latin.
4. The "Christ of the Andes" is a token of peace between Argentina and Brazil.
5. The permanent headquarters for the Organization of American States is in the Pan-American Building in Washington, D. C.
6. The "watchful waiting" policy towards Mexico was followed by President Taft.
7. The Mexican Constitution of 1917 aroused American anger because we were fearful that we might lose our investments in Mexico.
8. The revolutionary movement in Mexico never was carried across the boundary into the United States.
9. Dwight W. Morrow, United States Ambassador to Mexico, tried to bring peace between Mexico and the Church, even though he was not officially told to do so by the United States.
10. A common bond of friendship between the United States and Latin America is the Catholic religion.
11. Porfirio Diaz is known as the George Washington of South America.
12. The first Pan-American Conference was held in Washington in 1890.
13. The Organization of American States operates within the United Nations.
14. President Roosevelt was responsible for omitting the clause of the Monroe Doctrine which stated that the United States could intervene in the affairs of Latin America.
15. If the American countries are to build good neighbor relations with each other, they must overcome sources of misunderstanding.
16. Canada is a member of the Organization of American States.

17. President Roosevelt in his Good Neighbor Policy expressed the desire that the Americas should be friendly.
18. It is necessary that American republics be united if democracy is to be preserved.
19. The International Trade Organization was formed in 1945 to aid in the easy flow of world commerce.
20. The best way to build good feeling between nations is through Christian living.

Highlights of the unit

1. Isolationism was:
   the policy which our founding fathers believed in.
   opposed to entangling alliances which might involve the United States in world affairs.
   stated in the Monroe Doctrine in 1823.
2. Climb these *steps* to see how the interpretation of the Monroe Doctrine changed:
   Step 5: being a "good neighbor"
   Step 4: interference when a smaller American country was unable to keep order within itself ("big stick" policy)
   Step 3: interference to protect a weaker American nation from an aggressor
   Step 2: interference when our possessions were endangered by others
   Step 1: isolation: attending to our own affairs; non-interference
3. Our policy of isolation had to change because:
   American investments and trade spread throughout the world.
   no country should sit idly by while a stronger one oppresses a weak one.
   modern inventions have brought countries closer together.
4. Draw a chart showing dates when territories were annexed.
5. WHO'S WHO in this Unit
   WILLIAM SEWARD —
   Secretary of State in 1867
   Arranged for purchase of Alaska
   CAPTAIN VITUS BERING —
   Discoverer of Alaska
   JOSEPH CRIMONT —
   Jesuit missionary
   First Bishop of Alaska
   FATHER BERNARD HUBBARD —
   explorer, lecturer, and photographer
   studied glaciers in Alaska
   studied plant life in Alaska
   furnished valuable information to U. S. Army
   WILLIAM McKINLEY —
   President during Spanish-American War
   annexed Hawaii to U. S.
   shot by anarchist
   defender of American imperialism
   FATHER DAMIEN —
   Belgian missionary to Hawaii
   Chaplain to lepers at Molokai
   improved housing, food, and water supply for lepers
   contracted leprosy before he died
   COMMODORE GEORGE DEWEY —
   hero at battle of Manila Bay
   in command of American fleet in Pacific
   EMILIO AGUINALDO —
   Filipino guerilla who led revolt against Americans

ADMIRAL CERVERA —
  Commander of Spanish fleet in
  Santiago harbor
ADMIRAL SAMPSON —
  Commander of American fleet in
  battle for Cuba
GENERAL SHAFTER —
  leader of American army in
  Cuba
WILLIAM H. TAFT —
  first Civil Governor of the Philippines under American rule
FRANKLIN D. ROOSEVELT —
  signed Tydings-McDuffie Act in
  1935
  strengthened the good neighbor
  policy
JOHN HAY —
  American Secretary of State
  suggested the open door policy
  in China
  helped stop the Boxer Rebellion
CARDINAL GIBBONS —
  advised President McKinley in
  regard to U. S. control of
  Philippines
  urged the U. S. to send missionaries to foreign lands
  sanctioned the beginnings of
  Maryknoll
THEODORE ROOSEVELT —
  hero of San Juan Hill
  a leader of the Rough Riders
  a leader in striving for world
  peace
  set up the Court of International
  Arbitration in Holland
  arranged for the Treaty
  of Portsmouth
  author of the "big stick" policy
MAXIMILIAN OF AUSTRIA —
  sent to Mexico by Napoleon III
  to establish a French colony
  lost his life at the hands of Mexican patriots
PRESIDENT CLEVELAND —
  tried to settle affairs between

Queen Lil and American
  planters in Hawaii
changed the interpretation of the
  Monroe Doctrine to intervention in case of foreign attack
  on a weaker nation
settled Venezuelan boundary
  dispute by arbitration
COLONEL LEONARD WOOD —
  first military governor of Cuba
  leader of Rough Riders
DR. WILLIAM GORGAS —
  health commissioner of Cuba
  conquered yellow fever in Cuba
  fought malaria in building of
  Panama Canal
COLONEL GEORGE GOETHALS —
  engineer in building of Panama
  Canal
PORFIRIO DIAZ —
  dictator of Mexico
  persecutor of Catholic Church
  modernized Mexico
PRESIDENT WILSON —
  policy of "watchful waiting" regarding Mexico
  sent John J. Pershing to capture
  the rebel, Villa
FATHER MICHAEL PRO —
  Mexican Jesuit put to death for
  the Faith
DWIGHT W. MORROW —
  American Ambassador to Mexico who asked Mexico to ease
  relations between Church and
  state
PRESIDENT HOOVER —
  improved relations between
  U. S. and Latin American
  countries by withdrawing the
  intervention clause from the
  Monroe Doctrine

More points to remember

1. People of all nations have obligations of justice and charity towards one another.

2. It is better to settle disputes peacefully through arbitration than by war.
3. A stronger nation has a right to help a weaker nation to learn to govern itself, provided it does not force its way of living upon the weak nation.
4. A nation has an obligation of justice to help a weaker nation when unjustly attacked by a stronger one.
5. A nation which has agricultural or industrial interests in another country has a right to protect those interests against unjust attack.
6. Nations have the right to conduct their own government and carry on any activity which is for the welfare of their people, without interference from other nations.
7. Catholics, as good citizens, have an obligation to defend their country when it is unjustly attacked.
8. Agreements made in good faith are sacred obligations and must be kept.
9. No nation has a right to interfere in the affairs of another nation simply in order to secure its own selfish ends.
10. Nations should share with each other the material goods which God has given them because He created these goods for all men.
11. Mutual understanding and knowledge are of great benefit in improving relations between countries.
12. The Bering Sea dispute led to an international agreement for the protection of seal-fishing in Alaska.
13. Points about Hawaii:
is called the Crossroads of the Pacific; the Paradise of the Pacific
has improved educationally, industrially, and socially because of American influence
since 1900 all its citizens are American citizens
the naval station, Pearl Harbor, on one island
Molokai, a leper colony, on one island
14. Spanish-American War:
occurred in 1898
began with the sinking of the battleship *Maine*
was fought mainly on the water in both Pacific and Atlantic Oceans
made the United States a world power
15. The Philippine Islands:
were purchased from Spain at the end of the Spanish-American War
gained complete independence in 1946
taught the world that the United States was not all Protestant
are a source of sugar, rice, tobacco, and valuable woods and dyes
16. The Boxer Rebellion was a protest by Chinese patriots against the presence of foreigners in China.
17. The Panama Canal:
was first attempted by the French engineer De Lesseps
was completed in 1914
made protection of our possessions easier
facilitated trade
helped to build up the southern part of the United States
is protected by the Virgin Islands and American military detachments
18. The Mexican Constitution of 1917

was a menace to the Catholic religion because it provided that the state make decisions regarding religious matters.

19. Pan-Americanism unites all of the Americas in a common bond for protection from aggressor nations.
20. The Pan-American Movement dates back to 1890.
21. The headquarters for the Pan-American Union is in Washington, D. C.
22. The new name for Pan-American Union is the Organization of the American States.

Clinching the highlights through activity

1. Make a series of slides depicting life in our possessions. These might include industries, recreation, customs, etc.
2. Find in the Official Catholic Directory the name of a Catholic school located in one of the places mentioned in this Unit. Write a letter to the seventh- or eighth-grade class there. You might include in your letter the following points: your kind of education, description of your city, its industries and customs. Ask them to send your class an exchange letter. Perhaps you would like to make this a letter-booklet which would include pictures.
3. Make a pictorial date-line of the acquisitions which made the United States a world power.
4. Draw a cartoon of some idea that has impressed you as you studied this unit.
5. Have a round-table discussion on whether or not the United States has been imperialistic.

A final check-up

I. Copy the following list of names. After each name, there are three other words or phrases. Choose the one with which the person named was connected, and write it after his name on your paper.

William Seward
Alaska, Hawaii, the Philippines
Father Bernard Hubbard
Samoa, Molokai, Alaska
Father Damien
Japan, Venezuela, leper colony
William McKinley
Purchase of Alaska, Panama Canal, Spanish-American War.
Aguinaldo
Boxer Rebellion, Philippine Revolt, Tampico Bay Affair
Admiral Dewey
Battle of Manila, Sinking of the *Maine*, Mexican Revolt
Franklin D. Roosevelt
Independence of Philippines, Panama Canal, Boxer Rebellion
Cardinal Gibbons
Maryknoll Seminary, Mexican persecution, Good Neighbor Policy
Theodore Roosevelt
Open Door Policy, "Big Stick" Policy, Pan-American Union
President Wilson
"Watchful Waiting," yellow fever, seal fishing

II. Choose the word or phrase from the following list which correctly fills the blank in each of the sentences below:

seal-fishing
sinking of the *Maine*
isolationism
good neighbor

Theodore Roosevelt
Hawaii
1867
Cuba

73

Mexican Constitution of 1917
Boxer Rebellion
Cervera
Virgin Islands
Organization of American States
imperialism
nineteenth
Court of International Arbitration

Pacific
Russia
mineral resources
Maryknoll
arbitration
sugar plantations
furs
Mexico
Jesuits
1946
twentieth
open door
Dr. Gorgas
Spain

1. The founding fathers of our country adopted a policy of .... in connection with foreign nations.
2. The United States purchased Alaska from .... in the year ....
3. Alaska has been valuable to the United States because of its .... and ....
4. The peaceful settling of a dispute is known as ....
5. The Bering Sea dispute was concerned with ....
6. The first successful missionary activities in Alaska were carried on by the ....
7. The expression "Crossroads of the Pacific" refers to ....
8. The United States was interested in Hawaii because Americans had invested money in its ....
9. The "Pearl of the Antilles" was a name given to .... because of its beauty.
10. The event which finally brought about the Spanish-American War was the ....
11. Commodore George Dewey commanded the American fleet in the .... area during the Spanish-American War.

12. The Spanish Admiral, whose fleet was pursued along the shores of Cuba, was ....
13. After the Spanish-American War, the United States began to change its foreign policy from isolationism to ....
14. The Philippine Islands became completely independent in the year ....
15. The United States became a world power at the end of the .... century.
16. The United States purchased the .... in 1917 to guard the entrance to the Panama Canal Region.
17. The Monroe Doctrine developed into a "big stick" policy during the presidency of ....
18. At the end of the Spanish-American War .... withdrew forever from the Western Hemisphere.
19. The .... was a protest by Chinese patriots against the presence of foreigners in China.
20. The Church considered the United States a mission country until the .... century.
21. President Theodore Roosevelt was influential in setting up the .... at The Hague.
22. The last instance of any foreign nation attempting to set up an empire in North America was that of the French in ....
23. The .... was a violation of the right to worship God according to the dictates of one's conscience.
24. United States' relations with South America were greatly strengthened by the .... policy of Franklin D. Roosevelt.
25. The policy which gave all nations of the world equal trading rights in China was the .... policy.

74

26. The leader in the struggle against disease in Panama during the building of the Panama Canal was ....

27. The first American foreign mission seminary was founded at ...., New York, in 1911.

III. Write X for any of the following statements which are true, and — for those which are false. Write a correct statement for each incorrect one. It will earn you an extra point.

1. Father Hubbard's work in Alaska was that of a missionary only.
2. The port of Pagopago in the Samoan Islands is an important coaling station for the United States.
3. The people of Alaska show their hospitality to visitors by decorating them with leis.
4. People born in Hawaii are citizens of the United States.
5. Pearl Harbor is an important naval station for the United States because it lies about midway between the United States and Asia.
6. The Filipinos, led by Aguinaldo, revolted against the United States because they desired to be a free people.
7. Our founding fathers' policy of isolation should never have been changed.
8. The Spanish-American War began and ended in the year 1898.
9. The Spanish-American War interrupted the spread of the Catholic religion in the Far East.
10. The Friars' lands were located in Cuba.
11. The United States still controls all of the territory she acquired at the end of the Spanish-American War.
12. One important reason why the United States desired control of Cuba and the Philippine Islands was to protect American trade.
13. The Spanish-American War led the United States to take the lead in striving for world peace.
14. The United States secured the land for the Panama Canal, with very little resistance from South America.
15. One purpose of the Panama Canal was to make it easier to protect our possessions in the Atlantic and Pacific Oceans.
16. American relations with Mexico during the early twentieth century were a blot on United States history.
17. The United States and Mexico went to war over the Tampico Bay incident.
18. The Mexican Constitution of 1917 eased the strained relations between the Catholic Church and the Mexican Government.
19. "Christ of the Andes" is a symbol of friendly relations between two South American republics.
20. The Pan-American Movement was begun by President Franklin D. Roosevelt.
21. Canada is a member of the Organization of American States.
22. President Hoover gained the confidence of Latin American countries because he canceled the claim of the United States to a right to interfere in the affairs of a weaker nation.
23. The good neighbor policy was the policy of the United States towards Latin America.
24. Misunderstandings are often the cause of conflicts between nations.
25. The common threat of Communism has bound all American countries closer together.

Mary's Assumption

HISTORY. The Assumption of Our Lady was the occasion when her body and soul, after her earthly life, were taken up into heaven. There she received a crown of glory from her Son. The feast-day of the Assumption is August 15. Although defined in 1950, Catholics have always believed this dogma.

BELIEF. Catholics believe that "The Immaculate Mother of God, Mary ever Virgin, having completed the course of earthly life, was assumed body and soul into heavenly glory."

This privilege was granted to Mary because God did not wish her body to remain in the grave, since she was the Immaculate Mother of the Son of God.

Prayer

GRANT, we beseech Thee, O Lord God, unto us Thy servants, that we may rejoice in continual health of mind and body; and, by the glorious intercession of blessed Mary ever Virgin, may be delivered from present sadness, and enter into the joy of Thine eternal gladness. Through Christ Our Lord. Amen.

An indulgence of 3 years. A plenary indulgence once a month under the usual conditions for the daily repetition of this prayer (See "The Raccolta," the official book of indulgenced prayers, page 255).

DOGMA. The Assumption is a dogma (a truth solemnly declared by the Church to be an article of Catholic faith), and was defined by Pope Pius XII, on November 1, 1950. It is one of the five great truths pertaining to Mary. The other four are: Her Immaculate Conception, her Divine Motherhood, her Perpetual Virginity, her Plenitude of Grace.

Courtesy of Rev. J. B. Carol, O. F. M.

UNIT TWO

THE AMERICAN BUSINESS WORLD—OWNERS, MANAGERS AND WORKERS

PART ONE—THE OWNERS AND MANAGERS

CHAPTER I—CONDITIONS RESPONSIBLE FOR THE RISE OF BIG BUSINESS

Development of Natural Resources
Inventions and Science
Immigration
Rise of Industrial Leaders

CHAPTER II—BIG BUSINESS AFFECTS STANDARDS OF LIVING

The Importance of the Business Man in Modern Life
Advantages and Disadvantages of Big Business
Dangers of Complete Control by the Few
Effects upon Owners of Small Businesses

CHAPTER III—THE GOVERNMENT PROTECTS AND REGULATES INDUSTRY

Tariff Regulations and Politics
Regulation of Money
Federal Reserve System
Government Regulation of Big Business

PART TWO—AMERICAN WORKERS

CHAPTER IV—IMPORTANCE OF THE WORKER IN AMERICAN SOCIETY

Kinds of American Workers
Conditions Affecting Labor before the Days of Big Business

CHAPTER V—SOCIAL JUSTICE—AN IDEAL GOAL

Christian Ideals in Industrial Relations
Encyclicals on Labor
Organization of Labor
Weapons of Industry

CHAPTER VI—MODERN LABOR PROBLEMS

Effect of World War I on Industry
The Depression of 1929
Attempts to Relieve the Suffering Caused by Depression

UNIT TWO

THE AMERICAN BUSINESS WORLD — OWNERS, MANAGERS AND WORKERS

IN THE first Unit, we learned how the United States acquired more territory and began to take an important place in world affairs. Do you think that this was accomplished simply because the United States enlarged its possessions? No, a nation achieves importance when it becomes influential.

One of the factors which made our country influential was its manner of carrying on business dealings. We know that today a country does not develop rapidly without trade. No nation, including the United States, is self-sufficient, that is, completely independent of all other nations. The United States, however, through her ability to utilize the resources with which God has blessed her, has developed enormous business projects within her own boundaries.

We shall see in this Unit how various factors, such as an abundance of raw materials, inventions, mass production, and an increasing population tended to make business grow rapidly. In fact, it grew so rapidly that the small businessman was often swept away in the fast-moving stream of modern industrial activities.

Some of the men who controlled big business enterprises frequently misused their power. They forgot that unless an employer lives up to Christian ideals and respects his employees, there will be social unrest and disturbances. This also happens when the laborer forgets his obligations.

By the end of the nineteenth century many men became convinced that the government should regulate big business, lest it become harmful to society, as well as dangerous to democracy. In this Unit, we shall see how the government attempted to solve some of the problems by passing a number of bills or acts. We shall learn, too, that the Church played an important role in suggesting remedies.

CHAPTER I

CONDITIONS RESPONSIBLE FOR THE RISE OF BIG BUSINESS

Short story of the chapter. Although the Civil War was a calamity, it brought a period of great prosperity to the North. The need for supplies and equipment for the government to carry on the war caused industry to put forth its best effort. After the war was over, enterprising business leaders combined to build truly great industries.

The Civil War developed industry, but there were other factors that played a greater part. Perhaps the most important of all was that of the rich natural resources found in the United States. These were utilized by men who saw their value in developing huge industries, such as steel and oil. A large supply of labor was needed to carry on these mammoth projects and it was furnished by a great wave of immigration from Europe. With good transportation facilities and a world that was waiting for the products, big business grew by leaps and bounds.

In this chapter, therefore, we shall study some of the factors underlying the growth in industry.

These are: (1) The Development of Natural Resources and the Progress of Science; and (2) the Rise of Industrial Leaders.

1. The Development of Natural Resources

Discovery of natural resources. There have always been treasure seekers who have been attracted by something that glitters. Do you recall the years when the forty-niners, lured by the prospects of gold in California, left homes in the East to make their fortunes in the West? When the western frontier disappeared, people in various regions gradually discovered other natural resources in the nation.

Up to the middle of the nineteenth century, gold was about the only mineral that affected deeply the lives of the people. Before the century was over, however, the American people began to realize that within their boundaries lay greater wealth than they had ever imagined. They began to understand that such metals as iron and copper could create more wealth

80

Mining iron ore. An open pit mine at Hibbing, Minnesota. Huge steam shovels strip off the soil, then dig the ore.

for them than the precious metals of gold and silver. Can you see why this is possible?

Use of natural resources. After the Civil War, business grew until it was large enough to be called "big business." It became more powerful all the time. Great industries, such as steel, oil, and rubber, came into existence during this period.

The application of power to machinery on a large scale began with the use of coal which produced steam. With sufficient power supplied, industry could furnish more of the products needed in American life. As extensive deposits of iron ore were discovered in the country, the United States became the industrial leader of the world.

With these two minerals, coal and iron ore, we can make the most important metal used in modern times — steel. It replaces wood in any number of ways. It is the framework of our big buildings. It is used to make most of our farm implements, without which we could not secure enough food. It is the basic metal used in most types of modern transportation.

The United States is fortunate in having easy transportation facilities between its coal and iron deposits. Trace the route it travels on the map. This enables it to produce steel at less expense than many other nations. Andrew Carnegie,

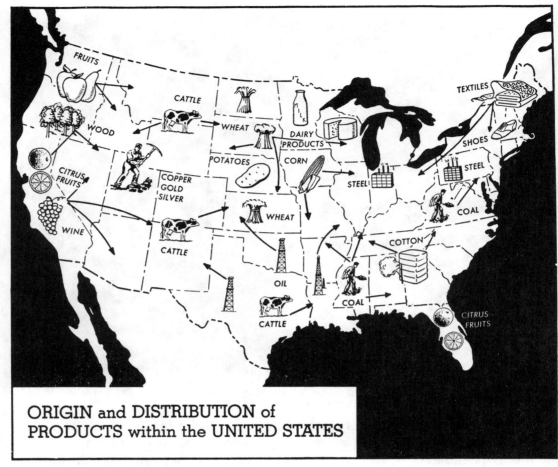

ORIGIN and DISTRIBUTION of PRODUCTS within the UNITED STATES

who was probably the greatest steel manufacturer in the country, once said: "The nation that makes the cheapest steel has the other nations at its feet." Was he right?

Second in importance to steel in this rapidly developing country of ours is oil. At first, it was used only for lighting purposes but gradually it revolutionized the industry of the whole world. Oil is indispensable wherever machinery is employed. It is a source of power and lubrication for steamships, railroads, airplanes, and almost every other form of transportation.

Communication developed just as rapidly as transportation. The telegraph, telephone, cables and radio, are necessary for the efficient transaction of business. All of these inventions, about which you studied last year, have brought the various people of the United States and the world closer together. Rapid contact between dealers in raw materials and factory owners aids in the development of business. **Influence of science.** Nearly all great industries in the United States have developed large scientific laboratories. Without these laboratories, industry would probably not be so successful as it is. The steel industry has been aided by the chemist, who combines iron with carbon and other metals to produce different types of steel. An amazing number of products have been developed from coal, petroleum, and wood. Which ones can you name?

The automobile industry, which grew in leaps and bounds, would have been halted during World War II had it not been for chemists who learned how to make synthetic rubber for tires. Rubber companies employ many expert chemists. In the laboratories of such great industries, scientists are constantly searching for improved methods in manufacturing.

Father Julius Nieuwland. One of our great scientists lived at the University of Notre Dame. His name was Father Julius Nieuwland (new'-land), and it is to him that we owe the discovery of synthetic rubber.

Some years before his discovery, Thomas Edison remarked that one of our weaknesses was our "lack of certain essential raw materials in case of war. The most important of these," he added, "is rubber." Americans did not fully realize the importance of these words of Thomas Edison, but the Japanese did. When they struck Pearl Harbor in 1941, they deliberately cut off our rubber supply from the Malay Peninsula.

The Japanese did not know that synthetic rubber had already been

Father Julius Nieuwland, C.S.C.

discovered by Father Nieuwland. Although he had discovered it in 1906, his discovery was not fully developed until 1931, when the first synthetic rubber was made commercially on a limited scale.

It was not until after Father Nieuwland's death in 1935 that synthetic rubber became widely used. It replaced the natural rubber which the Japanese tried to withhold from us, and helped carry us through the Second World War.

You can see from the previous paragraphs how science has aided the growth of business. You may find many more ways.

2. The Rise of Industrial Leaders

You may remember that the immigrants from European lands played an important part in populating the United States. Most of these people came because they

83

Andrew Carnegie.

Henry Ford.

wanted democracy or freedom of religion, which they were denied in their own land. They thought there was more freedom and opportunity in a new land. They hoped to find more comfortable homes for themselves and their families. The large factories that had developed in the latter nineteenth century needed workers and hired great numbers of these immigrants. The increase in population furnished a ready market so that industry had little trouble in selling its products.

Besides contributing strength and numbers to America, immigrants furnished leaders in many fields. Alexander Bell and Andrew Carnegie came from Scotland. J. J. Hill, the railroad builder, was born in Canada. These men, and many others who were native Americans, like Henry Ford of Detroit, had the vision and ability to see the possibilities of the great natural resources in our country. Practically all of them began as poor men but eventually they came to be known as *captains of industry*.

Do you like this definition of a captain of industry—"one who is responsible for the growth of business from small beginnings to a great industry"?

The "Steel King." Without doubt, Andrew Carnegie and his partner, Henry Clay Frick, did more to organize the steel industry than any other men in the country. Carnegie, the son of a wool-weaver, was born in Scotland. In 1848, his father decided to seek his fortune in

America because the Industrial Revolution had forced him out of his trade. The Carnegies settled in Pittsburgh, Pennsylvania. Here, too, Andrew's father found he was unsucccessful because the machine age had begun. He was obliged to give up his trade and take a position in a cotton factory.

As Andrew grew older, his father obtained a job for him as a bobbin boy in the cotton factory. He worked for $1.20 a week. Yet, in his autobiography, he tells us that he was more proud of that first week's salary than he was of his later millions. Can you think why?

An ambitious youth. Soon Andrew became a messenger for a telegraph company. One day he came to the notice of a high official of the Pennsylvania Railroad because of his coolheaded behavior at the time of a tragic accident. This man helped him to get a job in the railroad company. While working there, Carnegie noticed that steel for rails was coming from England. He was sure that steel could be made just as well in the United States, at less expense to the railroad. He bought a small furnace and began. His determination led to success.

Two heads better than one. Carnegie's success did not come until after he had become a partner of Henry Frick, a bookkeeper in a neighboring village. From his office window, Frick often watched some small ovens which were used for making coke. Like many other small factories, these failed during

Open hearth furnace.

the depression of 1873. Frick saw his opportunity, bought some of the ovens, and in a few years became the greatest coke producer in the United States.

Andrew Carnegie knew coal had been used for making steel and could not see why coke would not produce just as good a type of steel. He invited Frick to enter a partnership with him, and they set up a steel factory near Pittsburgh.

By the end of the nineteenth century, Carnegie had the most complete steel organization in the world. He owned iron ore mines in Wisconsin and Minnesota. Along Lake Erie he had docks, where his own ships could unload the ore. Between Lake Erie and Pittsburgh, he had built his own railroad line; and in that city he built his own blast furnaces. His coal mines completed the picture. This shows how different industries, thousands of miles apart, could work together to contribute to the success of one industry.

By the end of the nineteenth century, Carnegie, one of the richest men in the world, retired from the steel business. Although he may not always have used fair methods to acquire his wealth, he, like some other industrialists, contributed large sums to education and social service. He established the Carnegie Foundation for the Advancement of Teaching, the Carnegie Institution at Washington, and various other organizations to promote education.

When he retired, he sold his mills to the United States Steel Corporation. This was the largest corporation in the world. The next few paragraphs will explain the word *corporation*.

A modern type of business organization. Carnegie could never have developed the steel industry as he did without the form of business known as the corporation. In the eighteenth century, most Americans went into business alone and relied on their own money and efforts. In the early nineteenth century, men often took a partner, as Andrew Carnegie did, thus creating a *partnership*. Do you know any types of partnerships that are in existence today?

As time went on, business men saw that the single ownership and partnership forms of business could not accumulate enough money for vast undertakings. About 1865, corporations began to be formed. A corporation is a legal association of men who supply *capital*, or money, for a business.

A corporation operates under a board of directors and obtains a charter from the state. It acquires its capital by selling shares of stock. If it is determined that each share is to be valued at $100, a man who invests $1,000 owns ten shares. Those who buy such shares are called *shareholders*.

In the eyes of the law, a corporation is regarded as a person. That is why it can own wealth and be responsible for its debts; why it can buy and sell; why it can hire and borrow. Its profits are shared by the shareholders. One advantage of this type of business is that individual members are not liable in case of bankruptcy. They may lose the money they invested, but their other property cannot be touched to pay the debts of a corporation which fails. Do you think there are other advantages in this type of business? Do you think there are any dangers in it? Perhaps, after you read the next chapter, you will be able to make a decision.

A great oil company. One of the best examples of the growth of industry to large proportions is the production and refining of oil. John D. Rockefeller is the man responsible for its growth. Born in the State of New York, he came to Cleveland, Ohio, at an early age,

A forest of oil wells at Beaumont, Texas. Can you tell why oil is sometimes called "black gold"?

and worked for three years at a job on the docks.

Rockefeller watched the oil business expanding and determined he would take part in it. He had acquired amazing business ability and, by 1863, he decided that he would gain control of the entire oil industry. It was a seemingly unattainable goal, but in ten years he had accomplished his aim. He established the Standard Oil Company of Ohio, with capital of $1,000,000. Today the Standard Oil Company operates in many states.

This company manufactured its own barrels, built its own railroad cars, and laid its own pipe lines from the oil fields to the refineries.

It often forced railroads to carry its oil at a cheap rate, under the threat that it would build its own roads. Do you think action like that conforms to Christian ideals? Why, or why not?

An oil trust. The Standard Oil Company, which soon expanded beyond the State of Ohio, became the first *trust* in the United States. A trust is made up of several corporations. Rockefeller's trust consisted of thirty-nine corporations and controlled about ninety percent of the refining business of the country.

Other types of trusts. By 1880, people began to refer to all great combinations of industry, railroads,

A gasoline tank farm.

today only by larger ones. Nevertheless, he states that it is better for society in general if any given job is done by the smallest organization that can handle it efficiently. This insures more liberty and affords less chance of tyranny.

The automobile industry. Although Henry Ford of Detroit, Michigan, did not invent the first automobile, he made it available to the common people of the country. At first, only the wealthy could afford to own and run an automobile. By mass production and the assembly line he was able to produce cars at a low price.

Ford's venture proved to be such a financial success that another big trust soon developed in the United States. Before long, Ford had acquired iron and coal mines, mills,

or banks, as trusts. There were combinations in the sugar industry, the meat industry, the tobacco industry, as well as various other industries. One combination controlled over half of the iron ore mined in the country.

In recent years, we find that a few large companies control the making of automobiles. The motion picture industry, too, comes under the influence of two or three companies. Even such public utilities as the telephone, telegraph, and electricity are controlled by a small group of great corporations.

In 1931, Pope Pius XI, whose teachings you will study later in this Unit, stated that history clearly proves that business cannot be carried on today as in the past. Much that was formerly done by smaller associations can be accomplished

The first Ford car.

factories, and even forests, so that every part of his machine could be manufactured at the least expense. Today, the Ford Motor Company also controls rubber plantations in South America for the manufacture of tires.

Besides being a business genius, Ford had some concern for the interests of his workmen. He established an eight-hour day, set a minimum wage at five dollars a day, and provided excellent sanitation and even hospitalization service for his employees. But his system of mass production through division of labor tended to reduce man almost to the level of a human *robot*. You have probably seen pictures of a robot and know that it is a "mechanical man." Reduced to this state, man had less opportunity to use the talents which God had given him. Any business which affects man in this way may become harmful to him. However, in the minds of his workers, the increased wages and the social and medical services provided by Henry Ford counteracted the disadvantages of the ever-moving assembly line.

Whether we like it or not, the assembly line in industrial plants is here to stay. In order to produce enough to satisfy the purchasers and to produce it as fast as they desire it, mass production must be accepted. There can be bad features about it, such as reducing man almost to the level of a machine. However, an employer who has at heart the interests of his employees will provide means which will counter-

From Ewing Galloway
An automobile assembly line.

act the tensions or strains caused in his plant.

Money — a necessity in industry. One hundred years ago, banks were small local establishments. Each banker knew all his customers, just as the owner of a small shop did. But, gradually, small banks were absorbed by larger and stronger ones. They, too, became corporations.

For business and industry to be carried on in a big way, money had to be kept in circulation. The large banking houses of today developed from this need. In the second half of the nineteenth century, bankers loaned large sums of money to corporations that were building railroads, or engaged in manufacturing and mining. As a result, Americans did not have enough capital to develop the natural resources of the country. People in Europe, particularly in England, had long been watching the development of business in the United States. Hoping to make money for themselves, they were glad to invest their capital in American enterprises.

The man who took the lead in bringing this money from Europe was J. Pierpont Morgan. He was born in Connecticut and came from a family of financiers. A financier is sometimes referred to as a *master of capital*, that is, one who controls the money of thousands of other people.

At the beginning of the twentieth century, two great masters of capital, J. Pierpont Morgan and John D. Rockefeller, controlled practically all of the mines, railroads, and factories of the United States. These men and their associates are often called the Morgan group and the Rockefeller group. Although every mine, railroad, and factory in the country did not actually belong to these men, they were so powerful that they had a voice in deciding how these industries should be managed.

Early in the twentieth century, the United States had become the leading manufacturing country of the world, and the northeastern quarter of the nation became the greatest industrial center in the country.

Word study

captains of industry	trust
competition	partnership
corporation	capital
robot	shareholder

Think before you answer

1. State two main factors which hastened the development of big business. Can you find any others in this chapter?
2. What types of work would the rubber industry have to control to make it a trust?
3. Discuss some points brought out in this chapter which would be contrary to Christian ideals.

A Matching Game

Place on a paper the numbers from 1 to 10. Match Column II with Column I by placing the correct letter after the number on your paper.

Column I	Column II
1. captain of industry	a. business rivalry
2. scientific laboratories	b. United States—industrial leader
3. trust	c. advance of big business
4. mass production	d. European investments
5. corporation	e. a person responsible for the growth of big business
6. competition	f. a number of corporations
7. J. Pierpont Morgan	g. Andrew Carnegie
8. Standard Oil Company	h. first trust in the United States
9. synthetic rubber	i. Father Julius Nieuwland
10. development of rich natural resources	j. Henry Ford

CHAPTER II

BIG BUSINESS AFFECTS STANDARDS OF LIVING

Looking ahead. In Chapter I of this Unit, we discussed some of the most important factors underlying the growth of business in the United States. We know that God blessed our country with a wealth of raw materials which contributed to the growth of industry. This growth was aided by immigration and the clever, if not always just, handling of money. The age of big business was bound to have its effect upon living. In this chapter, therefore, we shall study: (1) the Importance of Business in Modern Life, and (2) The Advantages and Disadvantages of Big Business.

1. The Importance of Business in Modern Life

If a man attempts to carry on a business, whether small or large, a department store or a factory, he does it on his own responsibility. He goes into business not only to make money but, if his sense of justice is correct, to be of service to the community in which he lives. No one has a right to engage in any business which is directly harmful to his fellowmen. You remember from your study of history that God has given all of us certain inalienable rights. However, each right with which He has blessed us has its corresponding obligations.

Virtue in business. With the rapid growth of industry, there crept into the country a cold-hearted, selfish spirit. Conflicts often arose among people who wanted to improve their financial position on any terms. Some of these people were quite willing to ignore the laws of God to gain material wealth. They took advantage of others in every possible way. Some industrialists tried to save expenses by paying their workers an unfair wage. At times, workers have gone on strike to secure benefits to which they are not entitled. The Church condemns the unjust treatment of workers. She teaches that honesty, justice, and fairness, rather than the gaining of riches, must be the goal of both employer and worker.

Necessary elements in running a business. From the beginnings of civilization to the present time, there have always been people who hire others to work for them. These people are called *employers*. Sometimes the employers are the owners of businesses, but when these firms

A large manufacturing plant. Raw materials such as iron ore are delivered to the plant by boat and train, and the entire product is made at one plant.

become too large, the owners hire *managers*, who carry on the business for them. The people who accomplish the work in the factories are known as *employees*.

Employees are sometimes referred to as *labor*, while those who supervise and direct work are called *management*. When labor and management, together with capital, work out their difficulties according to the principles of justice, then we have good working conditions.

2. Advantages and Disadvantages of Big Business

Last year you learned how the United States changed rapidly into a nation of city-dwellers.

People left their farms because they thought they would be happier and could accumulate more money by working in cities. Machine production made low-cost luxuries possible, and, even though hard times have occurred frequently within the past fifty years, most people have been able to keep a rather high standard of living. In fact, there is no other country in the world where the ordinary working man has been able to afford so many conveniences as in the United States.

Some good points about big business. Big business would not have developed if men had not seen its advantages. Experience had taught them that a large factory could be run more cheaply than two small ones. Men learned, too, that raw materials could be bought more cheaply in large quantities than in small.

Large concerns usually make more profits. Therefore, they can afford to hire experts who can experiment to improve their products. Then, too, a big business can supply better social benefits for its workers because it has more capital. All of these advantages result in cheaper products for people with average incomes.

Some bad points about big business. In the nineteenth century, as today, big business was not all a matter of conveniences and advantages. As it became larger and larger, thoughtful men began to fear that it was becoming harmful to society and dangerous to democracy. Justice-loving Americans began to weigh questions like the following: Is it right for the natural resources of a country to be controlled by a few men? Could any man be trusted enough, or was he wise enough, to have control over the railroads of ten or fifteen states? Is it not possible for a banking house that controls the money of dozens of industries to injure as well as benefit the country? What is to become of the small businessman, such as the grocer or the butcher around the corner? Does not a man's energy and ability mean anything in industry? Is it right that he be treated as a machine?

A new view of business. Modern science has changed the world so greatly that some things which were considered advantageous fifty years ago are not so now. Formerly, it was thought more profitable to *centralize*, or gather together, one big business in a certain section of the country. For example, the automobile industry is centered in Detroit, Michigan. Today, there is a movement towards *decentralization*. This means that the operations of a particular industry are distributed in various parts of the nation.

There are several reasons why this practice is being adopted. First of all, it is safer. In case of attack during war, an entire industry, if centralized, would be crippled. Secondly, decentralization provides work for more people. And lastly, *economy*, or the management of

A small factory.

Brown Brothers

Pope Leo XIII.

Brown Brothers

Pope Pius XI.

money matters, in the country is better balanced. In other words, one section of the country does not have many financial advantages, while another has very few.

Two rays of hope in the business world. While it is true that big business raised the standards of living in the United States, much more good would have come from it if industry had adopted principles of social justice. The phrase, *principles of social justice,* needs to be explained. In this case, a *principle* is a standard by which people ought to act. *Justice* is the virtue by which a person gives to everyone what is due to him. The word *social* has to do with groups of people. Therefore, a principle of social justice is a standard, or a rule, according to which members of society perform actions for

the common good of that society.

The Catholic Church has always been interested in the welfare of the common man. Within the last seventy-five years especially, the Church, through her Popes, has issued letters or *encyclicals* to the world. These are sent by the Pope to the bishops throughout the world for the guidance of the faithful.

Two encyclicals in particular have to do with the human side of business. One was written by Pope Leo XIII, who is often spoken of as "the Pope of the working man." It is called *On the Condition of the Working Classes* and was written in 1891. The other, which was written forty years later, by Pope Pius XI, is called *On the Reconstruction of the Social Order.* During the course of this Unit you will learn that many principles, which should guide the conduct of business, are found in these two encyclicals.

The right to own property. Both Pope Leo XIII and Pope Pius XI condemned any act by which man is deprived of his right to own property. God has so made man that he has a right to acquire and possess property. God created the material things of the world in order that man might own them and use them to attain the purpose for which he was created.

Pope Pius XI declares that, while a person has a full and strict right to what he owns, he may not always use it as he pleases. His use of it is limited by obligations to his fellowmen and to the common good.

If a businessman were to donate large sums of money to erect hospitals, orphanages, or schools, but neglected those whom he employed, would he be fulfilling his first obligations? He might appear charitable to the world but, in reality, he would not be.

The Church teaches that private ownership of property is necessary for the liberty of the individual and for the progress of society. If any type of business or government violates this right, that business or government is unjust. One of the main purposes of the Constitution is to protect the individual.

Increasing your "industrial" vocabulary

employer
employee
management

managers
decentralize
encyclical

On the Condition of the Working
  Classes
principle of social justice

Can you answer these questions?
1. What should be the main motive of any man who opens a business establishment?
2. When are good working conditions present in industry?
3. In this chapter we learned what is meant by a principle of social justice. Can you give an example of one?
4. Name the authors of the two encyclicals regarding the working man which are mentioned in this chapter. Name the two encyclicals.
5. Explain the following statement made by Pope Pius XI: "While a man has a full right to what he owns, he may not use it as he pleases."

Fill the blanks
1. The goal of employers and workers, who have correct Christian principles, is................, ..., and................ .
2. Every right which God has given us demands a corresponding............
3. When labor and management obey the laws of God, a man labors under ....
4. Several reasons why decentralization in industry is being practiced are:
   a. ....
   b. ....
   c. ....
5. In 1891, Pope Leo XIII wrote an encyclical called ....
6. Man's right to own property comes from............ .

95

CHAPTER III

THE GOVERNMENT PROTECTS AND REGULATES INDUSTRY

What is in this chapter. The first two chapters of this Unit have explained how business developed and grew. We learned that while there were a number of advantages to business on a large scale, there were some disadvantages also. People realized that something had to be done to keep business from getting beyond control.

When industries were young, the government passed laws which would protect business. Later, when business was able to stand on its own feet and went so far as to influence politics, the government of the United States saw that it was necessary to regulate business activities.

You learned in the last chapter that, in order to carry on business, a certain amount of money is necessary. You also know that we have to pay taxes on various items, even on income. Both of these things, money and taxes, play a large part in business enterprises. Consequently, if business needs to be controlled, so do money and taxes.

This chapter discusses in detail the following topics: (1) Tariff Regulations and Politics, (2) Regulation of Money, and (3) Government Regulation of Big Business.

1. Tariff Regulations and Politics

A backward glance at the tariff question. From the time the United States set up a government of its own, down to the present day, the tariff question has been a leading political issue. Do you remember that a tariff is a tax levied on goods coming in from a foreign country? Under the Articles of Confederation, each state passed its own tariff laws, which caused great confusion in trade. Consequently, in 1789, Congress was given the power to regulate tariff.

Kinds of tariff. There are several reasons why a tariff may be levied. Sometimes it is to procure money which is needed by the government. At other times, it is to protect home industries from competition with foreign countries. Do you remember what the word "competition" means? A tariff that would be levied for *revenue*, that is, for government income, is apt to be placed on something that is not produced in the country. Modern governments no longer depend to any extent on this type of revenue.

The purpose of a *protective tariff* is to limit the importation of goods from other countries, so there will be a better market for those produced in the United States. In the early nineteenth century, when American factory owners found it difficult to sell their goods because English goods were cheaper, they asked the government to protect them by putting a tax on imported goods.

Protective tariff controversy. Even before the Civil War, the North and the South disagreed about the protective tariff. The South, being an agricultural section, wanted a low protective tariff, while the North desired a high tariff to protect its manufacturing. This controversy about the tariff has lasted over a century.

Those who argued in favor of a high protective tariff gave the following reasons:

1. It helped to develop and unify our country.
2. It made our standard of living higher by keeping wages up.
3. It provided a home market for our products and protected our industries from foreign competition.

On the other hand, the opponents of the protective tariff declared:

1. It raised prices, thus helping the producer and not the majority of the people.
2. It interfered with the natural movement of trade.
3. It caused political corruption because the tariff cannot be regulated except by Congress.

The tariff and political parties. The Republican Party has generally favored a high tariff, while the Democrats have steadily demanded a low one. We know that the Republicans came into power during the Civil War and, immediately, they raised the tariff. It remained high long after the war.

In 1884, Grover Cleveland, a Democrat, made the tariff question a leading issue in his campaign. He believed that a high tariff not only robbed the working people, but that it led to an unhealthy alliance between manufacturers and politicians. Too frequently it happened that agents of large corporations worked for the kinds of laws the corporation wanted. These "lobbyists" would go to Washington and try to influence Congress to pass a tariff that would benefit their industry. Does this violate justice?

Twentieth-century tariffs. As the tariff battle continued, the country found itself at one time with a high tariff and, at another, a low one. Few tariffs in the nineteenth century had a sound foundation. President Taft was aware of this, so when the *Payne-Aldrich Tariff* was passed in 1909, it provided for the establishment of a commission to study the tariff question. Although the tariff was high, the creation of this commission was the first step towards regulating import duties. In the future, the commission was to have the power to regulate tariff regardless of what political party was in office.

A number of tariffs were passed

during the first part of the twentieth century but none of these is enforced now. As the years passed, the Presidents were given the power to either lower or raise any tariff rate as much as fifty percent, if they thought it necessary to meet foreign competition.

In 1930 Congress passed, and Hoover signed, the *Smoot-Hawley Tariff Bill*. This tariff carried some of the highest rates ever levied by the United States. Hoover's intention was protection of our industries, but the results he desired did not follow. What actually happened was that other nations of the world raised their tariff on American goods. What was the result? American exports suffered a sharp decline.

The Trade Agreements Act. In an effort to revive our foreign trade, Congress passed the *Trade Agreements Act* in 1934. This gave the President the power to make *reciprocal trade* agreements with other nations without the approval of the Senate.

A "reciprocal trade agreement" means that the United States admits products without duty, or with a certain specified percent of duty, from countries that will do the same for our products. This new tariff policy improved American trade relations to a great extent. By the close of 1938, reciprocal trade agreements had been made with nineteen nations, the two leading ones being Canada and Great Britain.

2. Regulation of Money

Because business cannot be conducted without the use of money, something had to be done about controlling it, so there would be a sufficient amount throughout the country. Before beginning our new topic, however, just a few words about the growth of the banks in the United States should refresh your memory.

Early American banks. The First Bank of the United States was founded in 1791 by Alexander Hamilton, who was Secretary of the Treasury under George Washington. After its charter had expired, it was replaced in 1816 by the Second Bank. During Andrew Jackson's administration in the early nineteenth century, private banks began to spring up.

National Bank Act of 1863. During the War between the North and the South, a new kind of bank was created in the United States to replace these private banks. It was known as the National Bank. The law which created it stated that any group of five men could establish a national bank if they purchased a certain number of government bonds and deposited them with the Treasury at Washington. These banks were efficient but they were disliked by the farmers and the small tradesmen because they favored big businessmen. The people, in general, wanted a banking system that would be controlled by the government for the benefit of the common man.

The panic of 1893. During the

latter half of the nineteenth century, as you learned last year, there was great discussion about the basis of United States money. The Sherman Silver Bill, in 1890, had provided that silver could be exchanged at the United States Treasury for paper dollars. These, in turn, could be redeemed for gold, which was more valuable than silver. As a result, the Treasury was being drained of its gold, which the government needed to pay for its imports. Everything bought from foreign countries had to be paid for in gold. President Cleveland hoped to save the country from another panic by repealing the Sherman Silver Bill but he was just a little too late. Do you remember what a "panic" is?

There were several reasons for the panic of 1893, which crept upon the nation rather slowly. There was an overproduction of silver in the country. People turned this in for paper dollars and then exchanged them for gold, which they began to hoard. Foreigners had ceased to invest their money in American industries. Soon factories, mills, and business houses had to close their doors. Industry came to a standstill, and thousands of people found themselves out of work. More than six hundred banks failed, and railroad building almost ceased. The people demanded that the government do something to help the situation.

A dollar saved but a reputation lost. Throughout the autumn and winter of the year 1893, charitable organizations did their part in supplying food and clothing to relieve the distress of the unemployed. At first, the government did nothing. President Cleveland knew that the only thing that could save the country from bankruptcy was to put the dollar on a firm basis. Twice he asked the people to buy United States interest-bearing bonds. As fast as they withdrew gold from the banks to purchase the bonds, just so fast did the banks demand more gold from the Treasury in Washington.

Cleveland was forced to turn to J. P. Morgan, the great master of capital, about whom you learned in Chapter I of this Unit. Morgan secured the necessary amount of gold for the Treasury at a great cost to the government. The cost to President Cleveland, however, was nothing less than his popularity because he was accused of allying himself with the bankers.

The Federal Reserve System. During the next twenty years, brief periods of panic occurred in the country. Finally, a group of men was appointed to study the problem of organizing the banks so as to avoid future panics.

When President Wilson came into office in 1913, he made a careful study of the reports made by this group. After serious consideration, in this same year, Congress passed the Federal Reserve Act. This act created a new type of bank known as the Federal Reserve Bank. According to this act, the country was divided into twelve districts, each

Interior of the Federal Reserve Bank, New York. How does a Federal Reserve Bank differ from a National bank?

of which contained one of these reserve banks.

Federal Reserve Banks operate somewhat differently than ordinary banks. Most banks deal with individuals, but these deal with other banks. Perhaps you are wondering how a reserve bank receives its money. Every national bank within a district is obliged to belong to the Federal Reserve Bank and deposit some of its funds therein. The United States Treasury, too, can put some of its *reserves,* or surplus money, into the federal banks. The entire system is placed under the control of a Federal Reserve Board of six members, which has the power to transfer money from one member bank to another. The formation of this system, one of the outstanding achievements of Wilson's administration, was a great step towards preventing future bank failures and panics.

3. Regulation of Big Business

Before the 1880's the United States government did not regulate industry. It kept a "hands-off" policy towards big business, which means that it did not interfere too much with it. It felt that keen competition between business enterprises would benefit industry and make the country prosperous. Not only did the government permit business to go its own way but, as we learned in the first part of this chapter, enacted protective tariffs in order to assist the progress of industry.

Evils and abuses. Some of the earliest abuses which crept into our industrial life were those concerning railroads. *Industrial magnates,* another expression for captains of industry, often succeeded in gaining control of several railroads. They induced the railroads to charge low rates where competition was high, but unusually high rates where there was no competition. Sometimes the railroad companies would give better service at cheaper rates to gain certain business. In other cases they charged higher rates for a shipment over a short distance than over a long distance. Some favored shippers got *rebates,* or a portion of the charges given back, for long-distance shipments. How do all of these evils violate social justice?

Beginning of railroad regulation. The farmers, in particular, had long been trying to fight these abuses. Very little success had been achieved because each state had tried to enact its own laws without considering how they would affect the country at large. Do you recall the Granger Laws which were passed by some of the western states? In 1886, the Supreme Court decided that the Granger laws applied only to territory within a single state. In other words, the Court held that these laws regulated *intrastate commerce,* or commerce within a state.

A different type of legislation had to be enforced to regulate *interstate commerce,* or commerce between states. Congress alone had this authority. As a result, the Interstate Commerce Act was passed in 1887. This was the first step made by Congress in the regulation of any type of business.

The Interstate Commerce Act forbade rebates and unreasonable transportation rates, and attempted to secure equal rates for all. No longer was there to be one rate for the captains of industry and another for the small farmer. Most important of all, the new act created an Interstate Commerce Commission, which was to investigate any violations of transportation laws. While this act did not entirely solve the problems of railroad rates, it paved the way for better legislation in the future.

The Northern Securities Case. As railroad lines began to form themselves into great networks across the country, two great railroad lines developed in the West. One was the Great Northern Railway, controlled by James J. Hill, and the other was the Union Pacific, which had been developed by Edward H. Harriman. Eventually, these two companies merged, and the entire transportation of the West was controlled by Harriman and Hill.

Transportation in the East was almost entirely in the hands of J. P. Morgan. In order to secure complete control of railroads in the country, Morgan formed the Northern Securities Company by joining his line with that of Harriman and Hill. The farmers became alarmed because they felt they would be at the mercy of these railroad magnates. They protested to President Theodore Roosevelt, who ordered this railroad trust dissolved immediately. When the case was brought before the Supreme Court in 1904, the Court upheld the President's order and the Northern Securities Company was condemned as interfering with trade. This proved that the law of the nation was supreme over any corporation.

The Hepburn Act. The second law, passed in 1906, for the regulation of the railroads, was the Hepburn Act. It enlarged the Interstate Commerce Commission from five to seven members. Its authority was widened by being extended over oil pipe lines, express companies, and Pullman-car companies. It had the power to fix freight rates, to inspect records, and to demand that those records be kept in a uniform manner on all railroads.

A number of other railroad laws were passed at this time but, since they are more concerned with labor, we shall learn about them when we study the workingman and his problems.

A government's right. During World War I, the government took control of the railroads for military purposes, but in 1920 they were returned to private control. By this time, the railroads had lost so much money that they needed protection rather than regulation. By operating as individual lines, they could not give efficient service, so Congress passed a law which *consolidated* them, or banded them together into larger systems. This was a different consolidation than that attempted by Northern Securities Company. The purpose of the new law was not to make money for a privileged few, but to give better service to the people in the United States.

During the panic of 1929, about which you will read later, many railroad systems went into bankruptcy. But Congress enacted some emergency legislation during the presidency of Franklin D. Roosevelt, which helped to check wasteful practices, thereby enabling railroads to continue their valuable service.

The Sherman Anti-Trust Act. Government regulation of railroads was only part of the regulation of big business. Separate states had tried to regulate trusts, but after unsuccessful attempts they began to realize that the trust problem, too, was one that could be handled best by the federal government.

The first big attack on the trusts was the Sherman Anti-Trust Act of 1890. This law declared that all business combinations which interfered with interstate commerce were illegal. It also condemned any trust which grew so large that it could control the price of any particular commodity, thereby leading to *monopoly*. It was not, however, strictly enforced, and so it did not stop the growth of trusts.

The Trust-Buster. When President

Theodore Roosevelt came into office, he began such a steady warfare against trusts, that he was called the "trust-buster." This nickname was not given to him because he was opposed to all trusts. He approved of big business that was beneficial to the public welfare. In his estimation, men who had the courage and perseverance to build up big business enterprises had done an immense good for the people. Roosevelt felt that regulation was necessary only when evil practices crept into these industries.

In a move to check unfair business practices, Roosevelt invoked the Sherman Anti-Trust Law, and brought suit against the American Sugar Refining Company, which had defrauded the government of customs duties on raw sugar. The company was convicted and compelled to pay several million dollars in fines.

Roosevelt considered it the right of the government to know the real facts concerning business activities, and, consequently, he created a new Federal Department of Commerce and Labor. Its Secretary became a member of the President's Cabinet. The new department had the power to check all the records of big business deals.

President Taft wages war against Trusts. Although Roosevelt has name of the "trust-buster," his successor, President Taft, also carried on his policies of checking trusts. The public, which was paying high prices for the necessities of life, demanded the enforcement of the

FOLLOW THE LEADER

The "Trust-Buster."

Sherman Anti-Trust Law. President Taft in 1911 secured two notable decisions, among many others. One concerned the Standard Oil Company and the other the American Tobacco Company. Both of these companies were ordered by the Supreme Court to dissolve into smaller companies. They obeyed the order, but the former affiliates remained friendly to the original company.

Chief Justice White. At the time these decisions were made, Edward Douglas White, a Catholic, was a Justice of the Supreme Court. He was made Chief Justice during Taft's administration. As Chief Justice, White endeavored to insure the civil rights of all people. He fought for them against illegal trusts. His motto was that in law

Chief Justice White.

suits against trusts, the Court should be guided by the "rule of reason." In other words, no decision should be made against a trust until, after thorough investigation, it could be proved harmful and unjust.

President Wilson's attitude towards trusts. The fact that the Sherman Act was unable to curb the monopolistic power of the trusts had been shown over and over again. Justice Harlan of the Supreme Court went so far as to say that "the nation had been rid of human slavery . . . but was in real danger from another kind of slavery . . . namely, the slavery that would result from . . . capital in the hands of a few, . . . controlling for their own advantage the entire business of the country." How would a condition such as this vio-

late the principles of social justice?

President Wilson, recognizing the weaknesses of the Sherman Act, with the assistance of Congress, passed another act called the *Clayton Anti-Trust Law* in 1914. This act was intended to prohibit such unfair practices as price cutting, bribing, and forcing customers to use certain brands of products. Up to this time, directors of one corporation had been serving also on the boards of other corporations engaged in the same industry. The Clayton Anti-Trust Law forbade this practice.

The Federal Trade Commission. The provisions included in the Clayton Anti-Trust Law were to be enforced by the establishment of a committee of five members called the Federal Trade Commission. Its general purpose was to regulate trusts or corporations. In this respect, it was similar to the Interstate Commerce Commission, which supervised and examined railroads.

The great A & P muddle. The Great Atlantic and Pacific Tea Company is perhaps the greatest system of chain stores in the United States. This corporation has its own units for processing foods; that is, canning, baking, and packing foods. It also has large selling units, such as the stores and markets which you know. Because of this wide control, it can undersell other food merchants.

In 1944, the A & P was accused by the Department of Justice of having violated the Sherman Anti-Trust Law. The case dragged on even after the company paid a fine of $175,000. It was brought up again in 1949. The Department of Justice asked the court to break up the A & P into seven sections, corresponding to its seven regional divisions.

The trust question in the middle of the twentieth century. In spite of all the attempted regulation of trusts, there are still some with incomes of unheard-of figures. The report of the Economics Committee of 1949 showed that the profits of large corporations were 90% higher than in 1948. The control of business and the national wealth today, then, tends as much as ever to be concentrated in the hands of a few.

New and review words

tariff	over-production
revenue	"hands-off policy"
controversy	interstate commerce
rebates	intrastate commerce
commission	consolidated
panic	monopoly
reserves	reciprocal trade

More questions about industry

1. How are tariff regulations and politics related?
2. Explain how tariff laws affect trade.
3. How is the Federal Reserve System organized? How did it remedy the weakness of the banking system of the United States?
4. How did railroads violate principles of social justice before the creation of the Interstate Commerce Commission?
5. Find as many instances as you can in this chapter to prove that the government was trying to regulate trusts.

Answer *yes* or *no*

1. The main reason for levying a protective tariff is to raise revenue for the government.
2. The tariff question is a comparatively new one.
3. The Smoot-Hawley Tariff carried the highest tariff rates in the history of the United States.
4. The Trade Agreements Act of 1934 greatly improved American trade relations.
5. President Cleveland was responsible for the formation of the Federal Reserve System.
6. States retain the right to regulate commerce which passes from one state to another.
7. Violations of transportation laws are investigated by the Interstate Commerce Commission.
8. The Hepburn Act gave more power to the Interstate Commerce Commission.
9. A monopoly is the ability to control an entire business or industry.
10. President Theodore Roosevelt was given the name "the trust-buster" because he did not favor any kind of trust.
11. Chief Justice White, a Catholic, favored the "rule of reason" when dealing with trusts.
12. The Sherman Anti-Trust Law was seldom used after it was written in 1890.
13. The Clayton Anti-Trust Law declared that strikes and boycotts were legal.
14. The only type of trusts which have never been guilty of unfair practices are railroads.
15. At the present time the trust problem is completely under control.

PART TWO—AMERICAN WORKERS

CHAPTER IV

THE IMPORTANCE OF THE WORKER IN AMERICAN SOCIETY

Introducing the chapter. In the first part of this Unit we read something about the growth of large industries, but we have not looked into the story of the American workingman. All of the huge industrial projects that have been started in the United States, as well as anywhere else, would never have been accomplished without workers. Each of these very valuable people has his own place to fill in order that a finished product will be as perfect as possible.

Of course, you realize that all people must work to earn a living. There are many kinds of work besides employment in factories. What other types of employment can you name? Are you thinking of the man who carries your mail, or the one who brings your milk each morning, or the man who helps keep your city sanitary by collecting garbage? All these and many others are workers, and play an important role in gaining the respect of other nations.

This chapter will tell about:

(1) the kinds of workingmen you will find in the United States and (2) some of the conditions which have affected the laboring classes in the past.

1. Kinds of American Workers

Our Divine Lord taught us that work is not beneath our dignity. He worked as a carpenter, He supported our Blessed Mother after St. Joseph died and, like all other workers in Nazareth, He knew the hardships of labor. His experience prompted Him to choose as His closest friends men who toiled in order to make a living. Christ's example of respect for labor has been continued by His Church.

Need for workers. From the beginning of its history, America has needed workers to carry out its plans for development. The rich natural resources of metal and coal in our country would have remained untouched had it not been for workers such as miners. This is just one example of the necessity for workers. All true Americans

The model of Christian workers. The Boy Jesus taught us that work is not beneath our dignity.

want to use the natural resources of the nation so as to secure its welfare, even though there might be differences of opinion as to how this can best be accomplished.

Skilled and unskilled labor. Before the factory system, manufactured articles were made in the home. If a man was a carpenter, he worked at making a table until the whole was completed. He was a *skilled laborer* because he had to know exactly how to fit all the parts together to make a complete product.

Since the coming of machines, each step in making an article is divided. There is a machine for each part of the work, and a man is put in charge of each machine. He does not need to know exactly how to complete the whole article. He merely needs to know how to run his own machine. This aspect of modern manufacture is called *division of labor* because the work is divided among many people.

While the machines increase the amount of goods which can be made, they may also, at times, increase the number of unemployed

By Ewing Galloway, N. Y.

A skilled worker.

A white-collar worker.

By Ewing Galloway, N. Y.

in a community. Those who have suffered especially are the *unskilled laborers*. These are men who are not trained in any special type of work. Modern machinery is generally run by *semi-skilled* workers, with some skilled workers to supervise or repair it.

White-collar workers. During the early history of the United States, most labor was farm labor. When people began to move to the cities, new types of workers came into existence, the factory worker, about whom you have just read, and the white-collar workers. These latter are salespeople, clerks, typists, and government employees. Today, white-collar workers comprise as large a group as factory workers.

Unrecognized workers. There is another group of workers who are often forgotten but who must be considered because they are necessary for our community welfare. These are the people who provide various services. What would happen to our cities if, suddenly, no one would collect rubbish? What would happen to our trade if those who drive trucks would refuse to do this type of work? Perhaps you have experienced the effects of a bus strike. Can you name any other type of public service carried on in the nation? These workers should, in justice, receive as much consideration as the factory and white-collar workers.

2. Conditions Which Have Affected Labor in America

Labor in the United States has developed differently than in most countries of Europe because there are different factors influencing it here.

An abundance of land. The United States was settled first along the coast. Beyond the Appalachian Mountains were vast stretches of cheap, unoccupied land. After immigrants from Europe arrived in this country, it was fairly easy for them to leave the industrial centers in the East, if they were dissatisfied with conditions in the factories, and go to the West to become farmers. This caused competition to arise between industry and agriculture. The result was that, if industry wanted to keep good labor, it had to pay good wages.

Newcomers to the United States. A second factor influencing labor was the continued immigration from Europe. Between 1820 and 1920 about thirty-five million immigrants entered our country. Many of these were content to work for low wages in our factories because they were willing to get any kind of work in order to make a living. This had a bad effect on labor because it tended to lower the standard of living and made the organization of labor difficult.

The Blessing of Democracy. Perhaps one of the greatest factors influencing American labor was democracy itself. As you have learned, many immigrants were able, through their own ambition and perseverance, to rise from a low position to a very high one in business, government, or in a profession. Can you name some of these

Brown Brothers

A humble but important job.

An abundance of land.
By Ewing Galloway, N. Y.

Newcomers to our land. These immigrants are ready to start life in a new land. Many such new arrivals started in lowly jobs and rose to positions of wealth and prominence in our country.

people? A laboring man realized that he need not remain in that position all his life. He knew, too, that his children did not have to follow in his footsteps but that they could choose their own work and become better off than he. Also, it was fairly easy for the immigrant to gain citizenship, and once he had the vote, he could voice his needs.

As time went on, however, and work became more complicated in the United States, frequent conflicts arose between workers and employers.

Just a few more new words

skilled laborer   white-collar workers
division of labor   unskilled laborer

Now answer these questions

1. Prove that labor should not be beneath our dignity.
2. How would you group workers?
3. How did an abundance of land, immigration, and our democratic way of living influence labor in the early history of the United States?

Complete the following sentences

1. Our Divine Lord showed us the dignity of labor by..............................
2. A country needs workers to............
3. Several types of workers mentioned in this chapter are....................
4. Division of labor has the following effects on production:.........................
5. Three important factors which have influenced the development of labor in the United States are:

....

CHAPTER V

SOCIAL JUSTICE—AN IDEAL GOAL

Overview. We have seen how the workingman was gradually getting less and less consideration from those who controlled business. It seemed that his skill or strength was not sufficient to warrant justice from his employer. He had nothing to say about his wages or the length of time he worked; that was the privilege of the employer.

We have mentioned the fact that Our Holy Mother the Church always has at heart the welfare of her children. We have also learned that encyclicals were written to advise the leaders of industry what principles they were to follow in dealing with the workingman. Now we are ready to learn some of the points contained in these encyclicals.

Labor often became desperate and tried to solve its problems in its own way. But eventually it realized that if a difficulty was to be solved, it would have to be through a cooperative effort. So, in the hope of improving working conditions, workers combined into organizations or unions.

In order to get a clear picture of various viewpoints on labor, we shall study in this chapter the following topics: (1) Christian Ideals in Industrial Relations, and (2) the Organization of Labor.

1. Christian Ideals in Industrial Relations

In modern times the best teachers of Christian social principles have been the Popes. They wrote encyclicals to improve working conditions, not only in one country but in the entire world. In the United States, archbishops and bishops applied the principles contained in these encyclicals to American conditions. In the following paragraphs we shall learn what some of these principles are.

Rerum Novarum. The title of this paragraph is the Latin name of Pope Leo's encyclical on labor. The words mean "of new developments," namely, those brought about by the growth of business.

It will be sufficient at this time to learn the major points which Pope Leo stressed. He said that workers should receive enough pay to support themselves and their families in comfort, with some money over and above this to provide for sickness and old age. This kind of wage is called a *just wage*. He recommended that working hours should not be too long and that employers should avoid in their business any practices injurious to health or safety. Special care should be taken that women and children, who are obliged to work, would not have too strenuous jobs. He suggested that workers be permitted to share in the wealth and profits they help to produce. He recommended that money be available to workers who were injured, ill, or suffering from some other misfortune.

In order to secure these benefits, the Holy Father advocated that workers organize into unions. He believed that both workers and employers should be able to come to agreements through talking over industrial problems. He warned that these unions should have for their officers capable men who are devoted to the common good, not men who would be influenced by greed or a desire for power. We will learn more about the organization of labor in the next section of this chapter.

The Bishops' Program. It was partly through the efforts of the bishops of the United States that American industry has adopted some of the principles which Pope Leo suggested. In 1919, the bishops outlined the following eleven-point program of social reconstruction, based on Pope Leo's encyclical. Even though you need not memorize all of these points, it is good for you know them in a general way.

1. Every worker is entitled to a just wage.
2. There should be insurance against unemployment, sickness, and old age.
3. Children, under sixteen years of age, should not be permitted to work in full-time jobs.
4. There should be legal enforcement of the right of labor to organize.
5. The National War Labor Board should be continued. (You will read about this later in this Unit)
6. There should be national employment service.
7. There should be public housing for the working classes.
8. War-time wages (this refers to the First World War) should not be decreased considerably. Keeping high wages would bring about general prosperity.
9. There should be a regulation of the amount of profits permitted to owners of public utilities.
10. There should be greater participation of labor in management, and a wider distribution of ownership among the workers.
11. There should be control of monopolies, even by government competition if that should be necessary.

All of these recommendations have been carried out to some degree in industry. The tenth point has not been heeded to any great extent; but later in this Unit you will see that profit-sharing has at least had a beginning.

This eleven-point program has made history in the American Catholic Church. Non-Catholics, too, regard it as one of the outstanding Catholic contributions of the twentieth century.

Monsignor John A. Ryan. A great part of the work of organizing this Bishops' Program was done by Right Reverend Monsignor John A. Ryan. He was the director of the Social Action Department of the National Catholic Welfare Conference and a professor at The Catholic University of America in Washington, D. C. Many years of his life were devoted to studying and applying the principles of social justice to working conditions. His influence has been great in America, and we need many more leaders as fearless and self-sacrificing as he.

Labor grows up. When the Bishops' Program was set forth in 1919, two problems were not mentioned. One was the very serious problem of unemployment. In the early twentieth century, there seemed to be plenty of employment for all, so this point was omitted from the program.

No one could foresee the second problem, namely, the great scientific improvements which would still further substitute machines for men.

Accordingly, when these two problems arose, Pope Pius XI wrote his encyclical in 1931. It was called *Quadragesimo Anno,* which means "in the fortieth year," that is, after *Rerum Novarum.* Pope Pius endeavored to explain how the principles stated by Pope Leo should be applied to the new problems of the twentieth century.

Monsignor John A. Ryan

In 1940, the American bishops again met and summarized Pope Pius XI's encyclical. Five important points, to which the bishops called attention for our times, are:

1. Men have the right to own private property, but it must be used for the common good.
2. Employers should not abuse their workers, and workers should not allow themselves to be misled by men of evil principles.
3. Laborers should receive just wages.
4. Workers should be made secure against unemployment, sickness, accident, and old age.
5. Groups of management and labor should be formed to work together for the common good. The government should aid but not control the workings of these groups.

If these Christian principles should be followed in the industrial world, they would lead us to a better social order, based on justice and charity. Our chief hope is found in this statement made by the bishops in 1940: "We must bring God back into government; we must bring God back into economic life; we must bring God back, indeed, into all life, private and public, individual and social."

2. The Organization of Labor

During the nineteenth century, not only men, but women and children, worked long hours in surroundings that often bred illness and discontent. In order to improve these conditions, workers began to form unions.

The strength of union. In most of the early factories, the length of

An early union meeting

working day, the wages, and the conditions under which employees worked gradually came less and less under their control. They had to accept whatever the employer decided upon. If he was guided by principles of justice, then conditions were not too bad. But if he was without principle, the following practices could be found in his establishment: low wages, long hours, unhealthful working conditions, and child labor.

The protests of individual workers against these injustices were of little avail. But when a large number of workers agreed to act together, they found they could force employers to listen to their demands. These groups of workers came to be known as *trade unions*.

The Christian basis of unionism. Pope Leo urged workers to organize and form strong unions by which they could secure their rights. He explained that the need for unions springs from man's social nature. God made men dependent upon each other. The Pope quoted the Old Testament: "It is better that two should be together than one, for they have the advantage of their society. If one fall, he shall be supported by the other. Woe to him that is alone, for when he falleth, he hath none to lift him up." Both Pope Leo XIII and Pope Pius XI insisted that the right to organize unions is "a natural right of man, and the government is obligated to protect natural rights, not to destroy them."

A Catholic's obligation. While the

Pope has urged Catholics to join labor unions, he specifically states that they may join only those which will in no way interfere with their religious obligations. If the temper of a country is such that Catholic unions are not advisable, then our Holy Father recommends that a Catholic should also make every effort to join some Catholic study club which will supply the religious background needed in industrial relations.

Association of Catholic Trade Unionists. One such organization has already been formed in various parishes throughout the United States. The *Association of Catholic Trade Unionists,* often spoken of as the *ACTU,* is doing excellent work in training Catholics to be leaders in the workers' search for justice. Of course, there must be justice on both sides, labor as well as capital. It is not a one-sided affair. If labor wants a fair wage, then it has to give honest, faithful service.

After a study of the labor encyclicals, the ACTU drew up the following set of workers' rights and duties.

The worker has a right to:
1. have a steady job
2. get a just wage
3. talk his problems over with employers
4. share in the profits of industry
5. strike and picket peacefully for a just cause
6. be charged only a fair price for purchases
7. have working conditions suitable to human dignity.

The worker has a duty to:
1. join a trade union
2. strike only after all other means have failed
3. refrain from violence
4. respect the property of others
5. live up to all agreements freely made
6. enforce strict honesty in his union for all, regardless of race, color, or creed.

You will learn more about some of these topics later in this Unit. But you can see from this list that the "rights of a worker" are points which the employer must respect, thereby making mutual obligations. Do you know what the word "mutual" means? Pope Leo XIII defined its meaning when he stated that capital and labor are necessary to each other. If there were no labor, what could capital do towards completing the projects it had thought out? On the other hand, how much could labor accomplish if it had no capital with which to build large projects? These Christian principles must become part of our American heritage if justice is to be obtained.

The Knights of Labor. Labor organization began in the United States early in the 1800's. Most of these early unions, however, were local and not national. In 1869, the garment cutters of Philadelphia organized a union which they called the Knights of Labor. This was the first union to become truly national. In fact, it even spread into Canada.

You will remember that in 1873 there occurred a panic in the United States. During the years which followed, violent strikes swept the country. So much unrest was caused by some union members that Church leaders, especially in Canada, became fearful of all unions. In the hope of avoiding disturbances, the Holy Father was asked to condemn the branches of the Knights of Labor in Canada.

Archbishop Gibbons and his zeal for the workers. The Knights of Labor had a true friend in the person of Archbishop Gibbons of Baltimore. He feared that if the Holy Father condemned this organization, the Church would be looked upon as an enemy of labor. The Archbishop realized that the laborers were honestly seeking a just wage. Consequently, after a talk with Terence Powderly, president of the Knights of Labor, and President Cleveland, he invited Powderly to explain the purpose of the Knights of Labor to the bishops of the country.

The president of the Knights assured the bishops that the organization was not a secret society, nor did it uphold any principles which were contrary to Catholic teaching. It was decided at this meeting that the Holy Father should be asked for his approval of the society.

Archbishop Gibbons intended to explain the whole matter to Pope Leo. The Archbishop had the opportunity of going to Rome sooner than he had expected, for within a year he was summoned there to receive the cardinal's hat. At this time, he explained that the Church in America would suffer if she did not uphold the rights of the workingman. As a result, the Knights of Labor was saved as an organization, and Catholics were urged to join labor unions in order to receive protection from unjust employers. The visit of Archbishop Gibbons to Rome was one of many incidents which paved the way for the great encyclical letter of Pope Leo XIII, mentioned above.

The American Federation of Labor. Cardinal Gibbons' efforts saved the Knights of Labor in this country, but the organization was doomed to failure. The fact that it was composed of both skilled and unskilled laborers was probably one cause of its gradual decline. The interests of skilled and unskilled laborers were not the same. Consequently, the need seemed to be for a union organized on the basis of different crafts or skills.

In 1881, such a union was formed in Terre Haute, Indiana, by Samuel Gompers. It was known as the American Federation of Labor. Only skilled workers were admitted to membership. This new organization was composed of groups of local unions. For example, there were local carpenters' unions in various cities. These all belonged to a national carpenters' union, which in turn was one section of the A. F. of L. These various sections form the American Federation of Labor. It has become a strong labor force in the United States today.

Samuel Gompers gave untiring service to the A. F. of L. until his

Samuel Gompers, founder of the A. F. of L., addressing a meeting in the early days of the labor movement.

death in 1924. Some of the outstanding achievements of his presidency were: the abolition of child labor, the establishment of an eight-hour day, and half-holidays on Saturdays. He urged each local union to control its own affairs, and insisted that no decision be made before general discussions of the matter were held. His successor, William Green, attempted to carry out the same democratic procedures.

Kinds of unions. Not all unions are the same. The two most important types are the *craft unions* and the *industrial unions.* We have learned that the A. F. of L. is made up entirely of craft unions. All members of a particular craft union do the same kind of work. For ex-

ample, there is a union for carpenters, another for plumbers, and another for electricians. All of these workers are skilled in their own trade.

As the machine age progressed during the twentieth century, many union leaders came to believe that labor should reorganize. They saw that there was a place for both skilled and unskilled workers in practically every industry. The steel industry is one example. There are many types of workers engaged in this business, some doing highly skilled work, and others sweeping floors, or loading trucks. All, however, work for the steel industry. Why, then, should each type of worker belong to a different union?

117

Brown Brothers

Philip Murray

Could there not be one union which would include, for example, all steel workers? This problem was solved by the formation of an industrial union, to which all workers, in any industry, skilled and unskilled alike, could belong. Such a union greatly strengthens large-scale industry.

The Committee for Industrial Organization. It is unions of the type just explained that form the Committee for Industrial Organization, which was started by John L. Lewis in 1935. A glance at the labor situation at that time will show how this new organization came about.

Before World War I, the United Mine Workers belonged to the A. F. of L. When the war was over, John L. Lewis became president of this union. An earlier leader, the staunch Catholic, John Mitchell, had made the United Mine Workers into the first American industrial union which united all coal miners into a really strong organization. Lewis fought to have the A. F. of L. sponsor the industrial type of union. When he failed, he broke away from the A. F. of L. with several other groups and formed the "Committee for Industrial Organization" (1935). In 1936 it became the independent "Congress of Industrial Organizations," commonly known as the C. I. O.

As a result, there are many industrial unions within the C. I. O., such as the United Automobile Workers, the United Electrical Workers, and the United Steel Workers. Each group had its own president. Philip Murray, a Catholic, was later made president of the entire organization. The United Mine Workers belongs to neither the A. F. of L. nor the C. I. O., but is an independent union.

Of the 15,500,000 Americans who carry union cards, 7,000,000 are enrolled in the A. F. of L. and 6,000,000 belong to the C. I. O. The others belong to independent unions.

Weapons of industry. Labor comes into conflict with capital for various reasons. Some of them are: (1) to secure the rights of collective bargaining, (2) to prevent non-union members from coming into an industry, and (3) to secure favorable laws from the government to protect the welfare of the worker.

In its long struggle for social justice, labor has used a number of means to attain these objectives.

One important method is the *strike*. This means that employees cease working until the employer gives them what they ask. They demonstrate their dissatisfaction by picketing, or marching in front of the factory. The purpose of this is to inform everyone that a strike is in progress and to prevent anyone from taking their jobs.

Is a strike just? A strike may be just, but there is often a better way of securing justice. Our Holy Father has urged workers to join with employers to decide upon such points as better wages, hours of work, or other matters. This general discussion is known as *collective bargaining*. It is a democratic way of handling grievances.

Below are some points regarding strikes which Catholics must remember:

1. A strike may not be called except for a just and serious reason. If employers refuse to bargain collectively, if they refuse to give a just wage, or if working conditions are gravely harmful to health, life, or morals, there may be a just cause for a strike.
2. The strike should be the last resort after all other means of securing justice have failed.
3. Violence must be avoided during the strike.
4. There must be some hope that the strike will be successful.

Pope Leo urged Catholics not to follow men of evil principle, who may stir up dissatisfaction in labor, because these men often "raise foolish hopes which usually end in

Brown Brothers
Scene during a strike

disaster." Has not experience proved this?

Other ways of securing justice. In the previous paragraphs we have learned something about the strike, which is one method of securing justice for labor. There are a number of other weapons also. The *boycott* is one. A boycott is placed on goods when members of the union urge the public not to purchase the products of any employer who is unfair to organized labor. The strike, picketing, and the use of the boycott were all made legal when Congress passed the Clayton Anti-Trust Law in 1914.

Capital, too, has certain means with which to oppose labor. There is the *open shop,* which means that an employer hires non-union labor for his factory. If an employer closes his factory doors until his em-

Brown Brothers

The Homestead strike

ployees meet his terms, this is called a *lockout.*

Often in the past, when strikes occurred, employers sought help from a court. In such instances, the court issued an *injunction,* or order, forbidding a person or a group of persons to carry out some act, such as organizing a strike. If they refused to obey this order, they were guilty of "contempt of court." This could result in fine and imprisonment.

The Homestead Strike. The strike was not made legal until 1914, but there were a number of violent work stoppages before that year. In 1892, the Carnegie Steel Company in Homestead, Pennsylvania, lowered the wages of its workmen, in spite of its huge earnings. As a result, the men went on strike. According to law, a company is permitted to secure police protection. Instead of doing this, the Carnegie Steel Company hired private detectives and surrounded its yard with live electric wires. This angered the workers, and they resorted to acts of violence. So many people were killed and wounded that the Governor of Pennsylvania had to send troops to settle the struggle.

The Pullman Strike of 1894. The Pullman Strike was of national concern because it tied up the railroads of about twenty-seven states. President Cleveland sent federal troops to Illinois in order to open the railroads so the mail could go through. He issued an injunction forbidding the strikers to interfere with the operation of the trains. Because the union leaders refused to obey the injunction, they were arrested and imprisoned.

Perhaps you have been wondering whether or not it is permissible for the government to interfere in these labor questions. While the President does not have the power, Congress can and does give him the power to interfere when the general welfare demands it. The Church also approves of such action. Our Holy Father, Leo XIII, stated in his encyclical: "Whenever the general interest, or any particular class, suffers or is threatened with injury which can in no other way be met or prevented, it is the duty of the public authority to intervene."

Whether the public authorities were justified in the cases mentioned above, depends on their intentions and on the circumstances. **The Coal Strike of 1902.** In 1902, the Anthracite coal miners in Pennsylvania went on strike. It was the fall of the year, and since winter was not far off, President Roosevelt realized he had to step in. Working conditions had been going from bad to worse. The miners, like the factory workers, were entitled to a just wage but they were not getting it.

John Mitchell, president of the United Mine Workers of America, tried to have the dispute submitted to arbitration, but the mine owners refused. Many organizations asked the operators of the mines to settle the strike quickly, if possible. Archbishop Ireland of St. Paul, Minnesota, and Father J. J. Curran of Wilkes-Barre, Pennsylvania, did all they could to aid in a settlement.

However, the strike reached such great proportions that President Roosevelt formed a board of five men, some of whom represented the mine owners and some the miners. The miners agreed to accept this board, provided Bishop John Lancaster Spalding of Peoria, Illinois, were also appointed. Their desire signified their trust in Bishop Spalding. They relied on his wisdom and his sympathy with the workingman.

As for President Roosevelt's feeling in the matter, he tells in his autobiography how he added to the Arbitration Commission, on his own authority, a sixth member, Bishop Spalding. Roosevelt declared that the bishop was one of the best men to be found in the whole country. The story of this strike is important, since it shows how Catholic influence can be a guide to correct thinking.

The coal strike ended a few months later when the board awarded the miners a wage increase and shorter hours. Their union, however, was not recognized.

Significance of coal and steel strikes. Coal strikes can paralyze a nation. While oil is replacing coal in many instances, coal is still a very necessary item for a nation the size of the United States. Can you name any times when coal is indispensable?

John L. Lewis, head of the coal miners' union for many years, has helped his men in many ways, such as procuring better housing, safer working conditions, and the like. As a result, the miners rally round him. But sometimes he calls strikes when they are not just.

The record of labor-management relations in the steel industry has also been marked by many disputes.

Perhaps you have read somewhere that we are living in a "steel age." What is meant by that statement? Can you see why steel is very important, and why a steel strike also could cause many difficulties in the United States?

Steel dispute of 1952 and Presidential powers. As a result of a dispute over wages between employers and employees of the steel industry, President Truman, on April 8, 1952, ordered government seizure of the steel mills in order to maintain uninterrupted production for the war in Korea and national defense.

The President's action was opposed on the grounds that it violated private enterprise's right to property. A matter of greater importance thus came to the foreground. Did the President have the power to seize the mills?

On June 2, 1952, the Supreme Court announced its decision that, in seizing the industry, the President was making use of lawmaking power reserved to Congress.

Department of Labor. As far back as 1913, President Wilson realized that labor was a major concern of the federal government. Consequently, he added the Department of Labor to his Cabinet, with a Secretary of Labor at the head of it. Today, this department is very active. By investigating conditions in factories, it promotes the welfare of the wage earner, especially women and children in industry.

Enlarging your historical vocabulary

Rerum Novarum	strike
workmen's compensation	picketing
reconstruction	violence
industrial union	boycott
weapons of industry	open shop

How would you answer these questions?

1. Refer to Chapter II in the first part of this Unit for the meaning of "principles of social justice." Do the strikes mentioned in this chapter violate them?
2. How can you determine whether or not a strike is just?
3. In order to be able to defend Christian social principles which may arise at labor meetings, what does the Church urge Catholics to do?
4. Explain the different types of unions mentioned in this chapter.
5. Why do labor and capital frequently come into conflict? Is this necessary?
6. Find out how the word "boycott" originated?

Which is the incorrect word?

Here are twelve groups of three words. In each group there is one word which does not belong to the other two words. Find it.

1. Encyclical	Popes	John Mitchell
2. Rerum Novarum	Pope Leo XIII	1931
3. Pope of the Workingman	Pope Leo XIII	Pope Pius XII
4. Bishops' Program	Monsignor John Ryan	Bishop Spalding
5. Trade unions	steel industry	carpenters
6. A. F. of L.	Samuel Gompers	industrial unions
7. Knights of Labor	Theodore Roosevelt	Archbishop Gibbons
8. Bishop Spalding	Terence Powderly	coal strike of 1902
9. Strike	unjust wages	violence
10. Pullman strike	just strike	Carnegie Steel Co.
11. John L. Lewis	coal mining	socially unjust
12. Department of Labor	President Wilson	President Roosevelt

Now make a true statement about the correct words in each group.

CHAPTER VI

MODERN LABOR PROBLEMS

Preview. When wars occur they change ways of living greatly. During war time, industry usually reaches a very high peak of production. But when the war is over, periods of unemployment often follow. Do you remember what these periods are called? You are correct if you thought of the word "depression."

Perhaps the greatest depression which ever occurred in the United States started in 1929. It affected nearly everyone in the country and even the rest of the world. The President came forward with a plan which he hoped would remedy the situation. While it was partially successful, it did not go far enough. Our Holy Father, Pope Pius XI, also had a plan, and although the country did not adopt it at the time, wise men are beginning to see its value now.

The points which you will study in this chapter are: (1) The Effect of World War I on Industry, (2) The Depression of 1929, and (3) The New Deal of President Franklin D. Roosevelt.

1. World War I and Labor

Before the United States en-tered the first World War, there had been many strikes. However, during the war the demand for labor was so great, and the government had intervened so often in strikes, that they began to lessen in number. Labor organizations were contented because, for the most part, they had secured what they desired.

The Adamson Law. In 1916, a strike on the railroads threatened to tie up supplies and troops which were necessary to the war effort. The railroad unions, or brotherhoods, demanded an eight-hour day and time and a half for overtime. Attempts were made to settle the question by *arbitration,* but they failed. Do you recall what the word "arbitration" means? President Wilson appealed to the Congress of the United States. The result of his appeal was the passage of the Adamson Law, which prohibited a working day of more than eight hours on railroads. This was a victory for labor.

War speeds up industry. When the United States actually entered the war in 1917, a real boom in industry began. Factories worked day and night to speed up production for the army. High salaries were paid to those who were not inducted into the service. Everyone enjoyed an almost luxurious living.

The aftermath of war. But when the Armistice was signed in 1919, the condition of labor presented a sorry picture. Young men, returning from Europe, expected to resume the jobs they had vacated. Instead, they found themselves unemployed because their jobs had been filled by those who had remained at home. Besides, many highly-paid workers also found themselves out of employment because there was no longer any call for the particular commodity they had been manufacturing.

There was some hope for industry because, due to the damages of the war, Europe needed our products. But after a brief spurt to meet immediate needs, the reconstruction in Europe was over, trade suffered, prices fell, and many factories had to close, thus throwing more people out of work. There was great discontent. Both capital and labor used many of the weapons we have already described. Do you remember them?

At this time another type of union, the *company union*, was formed. Employers set up these unions within their own companies and required that anyone who obtained employment from them had to sign a contract that he would not join any other union. These contracts were called "yellow-dog contracts." How would such contracts violate social justice?

The company-union men and the non-union men really weakened the cause of labor in the United States. If labor and capital had been united, misunderstandings could have been solved more easily.

Everyone thought the United States was heading for another depression in the years immediately after World War I, but the strain on our economic system lasted only a few months.

2. Prosperity Followed by the Great Depression

When the fear of the depression of 1920 was over, the United States settled back to comfortable living. By 1922, the financial condition of the country was back to normal. In fact, the years between 1922 and 1929 were so prosperous as to be called "the Seven Fat Years." Everyone lived a carefree life, but over it hung a fear. The war had left wounds which did not heal too rapidly. Each nation had come to believe that it must produce as much as possible within its own boundaries, so it would not have to be dependent upon an outside nation for the necessities of life. This spirit of isolation had penetrated into the United States also. It took another great war to make us understand that no nation can be completely self-sufficient.

The Stock Market crash. Practically over night, the prosperous condition of the United States was changed. If you recall Chapter III of this Unit, it was at this time that one of the highest tariffs, the Smoot-Hawley tariff, was levied. It resulted in building up a high wall around our trade with other countries. When these countries could not pay the tariff, business with them ceased. When business declined, stocks declined in value. This, coupled with large-scale speculation caused a collapse to come suddenly in October of the year 1929.

The breakdown was felt in nearly every phase of life. Some schools had to close for lack of funds. Millions of men and women found themselves without money for food and clothing. Professional men, like doctors and lawyers, found it difficult to live because they could not collect their bills. Many people lost their homes and property because they could not keep up payments on them. Many banks failed.

Why the depression of 1929 was so great. Earlier depressions in the United States had not lasted too long, so the people hoped that in a short time this one would be over. They did not understand that much more was involved in this depression. In the first place, it affected the whole world. Secondly, so many people were living in cities by this time that it was more difficult for them to make a living when they were dismissed from their usual jobs. Perhaps you are wondering why they did not move into the country, start a farm, and raise their own food.

This brings up the third reason why the depression of 1929 was the worst in our history. There was no good, cheap land to be found anywhere. Previously, when depres-

Brown Brothers

The New York Stock Exchange

Unemployed men selling apples
By Ewing Galloway, N. Y.

sions had occurred, the government had been able to sell at a low price or give away land which it owned. By 1929, there was no more good land available to the government. Besides, a drought in 1930 ruined crops and brought many farm families almost to starvation.

President Hoover's Plan. A number of relief measures were passed by Congress during President Hoover's administration. The Reconstruction Finance Corporation was formed. It provided that the government lend millions of dollars to banks, business firms, and railroads that were in financial difficulties. An organization called the Home Owners' Loan Corporation loaned money to people to keep them from losing their property.

In spite of these and other efforts on President Hoover's part, the unemployed increased in three years from two million to twelve million.

The presidential election in 1932 showed that the people blamed the depression upon the Republican party, which was in power. The Republicans nominated Hoover for reelection, while the Democrats nominated Franklin D. Roosevelt, who was elected in a sweeping victory.

3. A New President Promises a New Deal

During his campaign, Roosevelt used the term "New Deal" to ex-

The Inauguration of Franklin D. Roosevelt for his first term as President. Here he told the people: "We have nothing to fear but fear itself."

press his belief that the welfare of the people required that government aid directly those who could not earn enough to support themselves. He declared that since a country was blessed with such great resources as ours, this wealth should be more widely distributed among all the people.

The Bank Holiday. One of the first things which the President did to relieve the strained financial situation was to close the banks of the country for four days. During this time the government examined the banks to see which were sound. The sound banks were permitted to reopen at the end of about two weeks. This action gave the people confidence in President Roosevelt.

The President forbade the banks to pay out gold as they had been doing in President Hoover's time. The gold which the people had been withdrawing was being hoarded in their homes or in safe-deposit boxes. Roosevelt recalled all of this gold, and people had to turn it in.

Emergency powers of the President. In the presence of this emergency the President took upon himself powers which were never used before. After the banking problem had been fairly well settled, it became evident that other relief measures had to be adopted. President Roosevelt's central plan was to raise the prices of goods produced by the farmer and to increase the wages of the laborer. He felt that in this way they could both purchase the manufacturer's products, thereby allowing him to make a profit.

The President planned to accomplish this by creating two new organizations. To increase the amount of money received by the farmers, he set up the Agricultural Adjustment Administration. We shall learn about this plan in the next Unit. To improve the labor situation, the President established the National Recovery Administration, commonly referred to as the NRA. This gave Congress control of all types of industry.

The NRA. The NRA was organized under the National Industrial Recovery Act. Under the NRA each industry drew up a code of fair practices and methods of work. The code established shorter hours and minimum wages. Unfair competition was forbidden. The worker was guaranteed the right to collective bargaining.

The Blue Eagle emblem

By Ewing Galloway, N. Y.

By Ewing Galloway, N. Y.

The CCC built roads and worked on other public projects. This organization did much to relieve unemployment.

Altogether, a great deal of good had been accomplished through this act. In spite of this, however, the Supreme Court declared in May, 1935, that the National Industrial Recovery Act was unconstitutional because it permitted the government to interfere too much in business.

The C.C.C. Camps. In order to relieve the unemployment situation, President Roosevelt organized the Civilian Conservation Corps, which was referred to as the CCC. Young men went to camps which were under military supervision. All of the camps had chaplains which cared for the spiritual needs of these young men. They built roads, planted trees, and worked on flood projects. While in camp, they also had the opportunity to continue their education. The bill which created the CCC was one of the most successful measures which President Roosevelt carried out.

Public Works Administration. Another department of the National Industrial Recovery Act was the Public Works Administration. It, too, was created to provide work for the millions of Americans who were unemployed. Many public works, such as the construction of dams, bridges, and highways, were started throughout the country. Unskilled laborers were given work they could do.

The Works Progress Administration, commonly known as the WPA, gave work to unemployed artists, writers, actors, and musicians.

The Wagner Labor Relations Act. After the Supreme Court declared the NRA unconstitutional, Congress replaced it with a new law known as the Wagner Labor Relations Act. This act was proposed in 1935 by Senator Wagner of New York, a convert to Catholicism. It was intended to prevent unfair practices on the part of employers.

The Wagner Act also created a board which was to conduct elections among the workers so they could select the group that would represent them for bargaining purposes. This board was called the National Labor Relations Board, or the NLRB.

By the year 1939, the labor situation was fairly good. When the United States entered the Second World War, industrial production was at another peak in its history.

Coal miners work for Uncle Sam. In order to keep war materials in constant motion, serious strikes were avoided during the Second World War. However, discontent arose among the miners in the spring of 1946. The government finally had to take over the mines. A contract between the government and the miners made them government employees.

John L. Lewis, President of the United Mine Workers, charged that the government had failed to keep certain provisions of this con-tract. He informed the miners that the contract no longer existed, and they immediately began to leave the pits. President Harry S. Truman was in office at this time. At his direction, the government obtained a court order requiring Mr. Lewis to withdraw his charges. He ignored the order, and for seventeen days the mines were again closed.

For disobeying this injunction, Mr. Lewis and the United Mine Workers were tried by the Supreme Court and found guilty of contempt of court. Both were fined. Lewis' action had seriously threatened the constitutional government and the welfare of the nation. The miners were government employees so long as the government had control of the mines. Therefore, the court could issue an order in the emergency.

The Taft-Hartley Act. Labor leaders and the American workers were very well satisfied with the Wagner Act. Between 1935 and 1947, the unions had expanded greatly and had became powerful. The situation became "big unions" against "big business." To control the "bigness" of the unions, the Taft-Hartley Act was proposed. Workers generally were opposed because they realized they were well off under the Wagner Act.

The coal strike of 1946 was the event which moved Congress to pass the Taft-Hartley Act. This act was an attempt to ward off strikes which could paralyze the nation by tying up railroads and industrial production. It was passed in June

Senator Robert A. Taft

1947, over President Truman's veto.
Provisions of the Taft-Hartley Act.
This act radically amended the
Wagner Act. Like the latter, it indicated the list of unfair practices forbidden to employers. It also specified a number of practices which
unions themselves are forbidden
to engage in. It required that officers of unions had to state that they
were not in any way connected with
the Communist Party.

Under both of these acts, workers had the right to strike, picket,
and boycott. However, the Taft-Hartley Act guaranteed workers
the right to refrain from striking,
picketing, and boycotting, if they
so desired. All unions have democratic constitutions, and strikes
must have member support. But it
was felt that pressure was sometimes put on members to strike, and

the Taft-Hartley Law tried to prevent this. The real problem, as in all
democratic politics, is the failure of
union members to attend meetings
and vote.

Workers must be aware that
there are certain times when they
are required to take part in labor
activities. These times are:

1. When the common good requires their participation.
2. When the activity is morally good or, at least, not evil.
3. When the activity is dictated by legitimate authority, such as an election, convention, executive board, etc.

The Taft-Hartley Act also outlawed the *closed shop*. A closed
shop is one which hires only men
who belong to a union. The closed
shop may have some advantages in
skilled trades, but it also offers
labor leaders an opportunity to take
unfair advantage over their members.

The NLRB, which had been
formed under the Wagner Act, was
enlarged under the Taft-Hartley
Act to five members instead of
three. This board acts as a judge in
labor difficulties.

President Truman applied this
law for the first time during the
coal strike of 1950.

The Profit-Sharing Plan. President
Franklin D. Roosevelt's ideas for
restoring our nation to a sounder
financial condition during the depression accomplished much good.
But they did not go far enough.
Men who devote their time and
energy to the development of great

industrial projects have a right to share in the profits which result from these industries, over and above the salaries which they earn.

Pope Pius XI favored the formation of organizations, comprised of representatives of both capital and labor, to provide a sharing in the ownership and management of industries. While some legislation by the government is directed towards this goal, there has not been sufficient actual participation by labor.

There is, however, a very young but lively organization in the United States called the Council of Profit Sharing Industries. Here is the story of its beginning. On July 11, 1947, representatives of twenty firms met with employees in Cleveland, Ohio, to discuss and exchange ideas. The most important outcome of the meeting was that all who attended agreed that the profit-sharing idea would go far towards eliminating rivalry and conflict in industrial relations.

Two years later, at a conference in New York, the membership in this council had grown to 153 firms, with a total of about 225,000 employees. At the New York conference, the following principles were brought out: (1) that profit-sharing was not to be a substitute for wages, (2) that it was not to be a way of avoiding union membership, and (3) that it implies genuine employer-employee cooperation and partnership.

Profit-sharing is a great step towards curing many of the ills of labor-management relations. It contributes to the common interest, which is essential for industrial peace and progress. It is a good beginning of the application of Pope Pius XI's suggestions towards securing justice in industry.

Your part in labor's future. In this Unit you have learned that the government of the United States has attempted to carry out the policies which it hoped were for the welfare of the people. You have learned that Christian principles should be the guiding lights in industrial relations. The United States has rallied to these principles in many instances. But there is still a long road to be traveled in the right direction.

You must be aware that you have a definite obligation to spread Christian principles of justice. You must understand and be ready to safeguard the kind of industrial relations which both Pope Leo XIII and Pope Pius XI recommended.

Words used in this chapter

emergency powers	depression
financial situation	speculation
minimum wage	aftermath
economic system	profit-sharing
unconstitutional	company union
code of fair practices	"New Deal"
contempt of court	closed shop
"yellow-dog contracts"	

How well have you read?
1. What were some causes of unemployment in the United States after 1919?
2. Give some reasons why the depression of 1929 was the worst in the history of the United States.

3. What legislation did President Roosevelt recommend to relieve the labor situation?

4. Discuss the profit-sharing plan of Pope Pius XI and the N.R.A. of President Roosevelt. Why do you think the former would go further towards relieving financial distress?

5. What obligation as a Catholic will you have when you step into the business world?

Fill the blanks in the sentences with the correct words from this list:

the Adamson Law   company union
stock-market crash   "New Deal"
President Hoover   profit-sharing
President Roosevelt Taft-Hartley Act
emergency powers   closed shop
National Labor Relations Board
Civilian Conservation Corps
Public Works Administration
National Industrial Recovery Act

1. The................gives workers the right to refrain from striking if they so desire.

2. One of the most successful measures to relieve unemployment carried out by President Roosevelt was the................

3. The Wagner Act created the................
....

4. The Supreme Court declared the ....to be unconstitutional in 1935.

5. The term................refers to the plan of government control which President Roosevelt believed necessary to bring the country back to prosperity.

6. The Reconstruction Finance Corporation was one of the agencies of President .... for relieving the depression.

7. The depression of 1929 began with the................

8. A working day of eight hours was granted to railroad men by the
....

9. The term "yellow-dog contracts" is associated with ....

10. The .... relieved unemployment during the depression by beginning a number of large projects, such as the building of dams, bridges, and highways.

11. Pope Pius XI believed that better relations in industry could be brought about by means of................
....

12. The Taft-Hartley Act outlaws the
....

Highlights of the Unit

I. Catholic Principles to Remember

1. A Christian principle is a Christian standard of conduct.

2. Our Lord dignified and sanctified labor by His example on earth.

3. All men have the God-given right to acquire property, and industry may not deny this right.

4. Private ownership of property is necessary for the liberty of the individual and the progress of society.

5. The use which a man makes of his property is limited by his obligations to his neighbor.

6. An employer has an obligation in justice to pay each employee a just wage.

7. Employees are obliged to be honest, faithful, and punctual in their work.

8. Catholics may participate in just strikes.

9. Labor has the right to strike only when its rights are violated, and even then no violence may occur.

10. All just contracts between the employer and his employees should be kept.

11. Catholics have an obligation to learn the attitude of the Church in regard to relations between employer and employee.

12. A business which does not give a man the opportunity to use his God-given abilities is to be looked upon with suspicion.

II. WHO'S WHO in Unit Two

Captains of Industry:

Andrew Carnegie: the steel magnate

J. J. Hill: the railroad magnate

John D. Rockefeller: the oil magnate

Henry Ford: the automobile magnate: introduced the assembly line

J. Pierpont Morgan: a master of capital.

Father Julius Nieuwland—
discovered synthetic rubber

Henry Clay Frick—
partner of Andrew Carnegie

Pope Leo XIII—
the "Workingman's Pope"; *Rerum Novarum* in 1891

Theodore Roosevelt—
often called the "trust-buster"

Chief Justice White—
made decisions about trusts

Pope Pius XI—
wrote *Quadragesimo Anno* in 1931; endorsed the profit-sharing plan in industry

Monsignor John A. Ryan—
helped organize the Bishops' Program in 1919

Terence Powderly—
organized the Knights of Labor

Archbishop Gibbons—
friend of the workingman in the United States

Samuel Gompers—
organized the A. F. of L. in 1881

John L. Lewis—
organized the C.I.O. in 1935; president of the United Mine Workers for many years

Bishop John Lancaster Spalding—
member of the Coal Commission of 1902

President Wilson—
added the Department of Labor to his cabinet in 1913; organized the Federal Reserve System in 1913

Franklin D. Roosevelt—
the "New Deal" President

III. Important Acts or Laws Mentioned in this Unit

Tariffs—
taxes on imports

Smoot-Hawley Tariff—
passed in 1930; highest tariff ever levied in this country

Trade Agreements Act—
passed in 1934; provided for reciprocal trade agreements

Sherman Silver Bill—
passed in 1890; made silver the basis of the American dollar; caused the panic of 1893

Federal Reserve Act—
passed in 1913; divided the country into twelve districts, each having a Federal Reserve Bank; purpose — to keep money distributed evenly throughout the country, thereby preventing future panics

Interstate Commerce Act—
passed in 1887; regulated commerce between states; was the

first step made by Congress to regulate any type of business

Hepburn Act—
passed in 1906; extended Interstate Commerce regulations

Sherman Anti-Trust Act—
passed in 1890; was the first attack on trusts

Clayton Anti-Trust Act—
passed in 1914; strengthened the Sherman Anti-Trust Act; provided for a Federal Trade Commission to regulate trusts; legalized the strike and the boycott

National Industrial Recovery Act—
passed by Franklin D. Roosevelt to ease the national bankruptcy caused by the depression of 1929; declared unconstitutional by Supreme Court in 1935

Wagner Labor Relations Act—
replaced the N.R.A.; purpose — to check unfair labor practices; established the first National Labor Relations Board (NLRB)

Taft-Hartley Act—
passed in 1947; demanded that labor leaders declare whether they were Communists; outlawed the closed shop; attempted to control the "bigness" of the unions; attempted to control strikes that would paralyze a national industry

IV. Industrial Terms to Remember
corporation—
a legal association of men who supply capital for a business venture

capital—
money or property invested in a business venture; another name for the owners of a business

competition—
business rivalry

shareholder—
one who holds a share in a business

trust—
a group of corporations

labor—
a group name for employees

economy—
management of money matters

protective tariff—
a tax on imported goods with a view to protecting our own industries

industrial magnate—
a captain of industry

rebate—
a portion of money refunded

social justice—
a virtue which prompts society to perform whatever actions are necessary for the common good

interstate commerce—
commerce between states

intrastate commerce—
commerce within a state

monopoly—
complete control of a particular industry

skilled laborer—
one trained in a trade

division of labor—
the dividing of work among many people, no one person completing a job; another name for assembly-line production

just wage—
sufficient to care for one's needs

craft union—
a group of workers who do the same kind of work

industrial union—
a group of workers who partici-

pate in all the types of work which make up a particular industry

strike—
the stoppage of work to secure a desired end

collective bargaining—
general discussion between capital and labor to come to an agreement

open shop—
a shop in which non-union labor is admitted

closed shop—
a shop which hires only union members

lockout—
closing of a factory by an employer until his employees meet his terms

injunction—
a court order forbidding a person or a group to continue an activity

profit-sharing—
a plan of sharing profits between labor and management

V. New Deal Terms

the "New Deal"—
the plan which President Franklin D. Roosevelt hoped would bring back prosperity after the Depression of 1929

stock-market crash—
the failure of the stock markets in the United States, thereby causing the 1929 depression

the Bank Holiday—
the closing of the banks for four days by President Roosevelt to relieve the financial difficulties

emergency powers—
powers which President Franklin D. Roosevelt took upon himself in order to try to bring the country out of the depression

N.R.A.—
President Roosevelt's plan to help industry

Agricultural Adjustment Act—
(A.A.A.) Roosevelt's plan to help agriculture

C.C.C. Camps—
organized to give unemployed youth work

Public Works Administration—
department which constructed many public works in order to give jobs to people

VI. Catholic Contributions to Labor Problems

Labor encyclicals or letters—
Rerum Novarum; Quadragesimo Anno

Christian Social Principles found in the above Encyclicals:

The Bishops' Program of Social Reconstruction — organized in 1919, considered the greatest contribution of the Catholic Church to America in the twentieth century

Association of Catholic Trade Unionists (A.C.T.U.), an organization which trains leaders in securing justice for the workingman

The work of Bishop John Lancaster Spalding and Archbishop Gibbons

The Council of Profit-Sharing Industries organized in Cleveland, Ohio, in 1947

VII. A Few More Points for Study

1. The United States is the greatest industrial nation of the world because it possesses and has developed its wealth of natural resources.

2. Decentralization of business means the scattering of large industries in order to lessen the possibility of being destroyed by attack.

3. Unless mass production is wisely managed, it may deprive man of his dignity as a human being.

4. Big business is beneficial if it serves more people and at less expense to them.

5. The government may interfere in labor problems if the welfare of the nation is in danger.

6. The depression of 1929 was the worst in history because the entire world was involved in it.

7. The Standard Oil Company was the first trust to be formed in the United States.

8. During the panic of 1893, President Cleveland was compelled to seek financial aid from J. P. Morgan in order to keep American business from collapsing.

Clinching the highlights through activity

1. Draw a large map of the United States. Indicate the location of the Federal Reserve Banks. The *World Almanac* will give location of these banks.

2. Have a living time-line. Pick out the important dates mentioned in this Unit. Write the date and the statement about each date on separate papers and distribute them about the class. Hold a conversation similar to this:

    First Speaker: The date is 1887.
    Second Speaker: The Interstate Commerce Act was passed.

3. Make a chart on big business. Cut pictures from magazines illustrating various big industries. At the bottom of the chart list the dates and laws which attempted to control big business.

4. Draw a cartoon to show the growth of business from the private ownership to the trust.

5. Write a letter to a friend telling him about your position on the assembly line of a large industry. Be sure to include the important points mentioned in this Unit.

6. Have a round-table discussion on various viewpoints in solving labor questions. Include in your discussion such present-day methods as: the strike, collective bargaining, picketing, boycott, social justice, open and closed shops, the lockout, the profit-sharing plan, and the mutual obligations of employer and employee.

A final check-up

A REASONS TEST. Copy the number before each statement. To the right of it write the letter of the group of words which best completes the statement.

1. The United States has developed into the greatest industrial nation of the world because

    a. its scientists are wealthier than those of any other nation

    b. more nations depend upon us for industrial progress

    c. it has a greater population than most countries

    d. it possesses and has developed great natural resources

2. Many immigrants came to the United States in the latter nineteenth century because

    a. they liked the climate in the United States

    b. the English language and customs of America appealed to them

    c. they had heard about our great natural resources

d. they wanted democracy and freedom of religion

3. Mass production must be wisely managed because

a. it frequently deprives man of his dignity by reducing him to the level of a machine.

b. it accumulates wealth only for the employer

c. employees easily become tired

d. otherwise employees will develop habits of laziness

4. After World War II big business began gradually to decentralize its plants because

a. this was considered the most honest thing to do

b. more profits can be realized by the owner

c. it is safer in case of attack

d. people do not like huge industries near private homes

5. Big business is beneficial because

a. improved products result from it

b. more profits are made

c. the consumer can thereby have less difficulty in shopping

d. cheaper goods are produced for more people

6. President Theodore Roosevelt has been nicknamed the "trust-buster" because

a. he imprisoned all managers of trusts

b. he stopped the growth of trusts

c. he attacked trusts when evil practices crept into them

d. he was opposed to all trusts

7. The government may interfere in labor questions whenever

a. it wants to gain control of an industry

b. certain industries would fail due to lack of capital

c. the welfare of the nation requires it

d. labor problems occur

8. It is better to settle labor disputes by arbitration because

a. this method is generally successful

b. it takes less time than a strike

c. violence can be avoided

d. this method is more in keeping with the dignity of human beings

9. In the eyes of the Church, workingmen are required to participate in the labor organizations if

a. the common good requires their participation

b. the majority of men want better salaries

c. the labor leader suggests it

d. their families depend upon them for support

10. The depression of 1929 was the worst in history because

a. more Americans were out of work than ever before

b. many banks in the country failed

c. the government was left penniless and helpless

d. the entire world was involved in it

II. TRUE or FALSE? Below are 35 statements. On your paper write X for those which are true, and — for those which are false.

1. The development of chemical laboratories as departments of industrial plants has encouraged the growth of business.

2. Business has grown so large today that the partnership type of firm has gone out of existence.

3. Corporations developed in order to avoid the failure that would

have come about in some instances due to competition.

4. The United States Steel Corporation was the first trust in the United States.

5. Henry Ford invented the first automobile.

6. The welfare of the people and not merely the acquiring of wealth should be the goal of all honest business men.

7. The assembly-line type of industry was introduced by Andrew Carnegie.

8. Captains of industry were not always masters of capital.

9. Big business enterprises are carried on today much as they were in the past.

10. Pope Pius XI was the first Pope to write an encyclical on labor.

11. The use which a man makes of his property is limited by his obligations to his neighbor.

12. A protective tariff is placed on something manufactured in our own country to protect it in transportation.

13. It is a good thing for the United States to keep the tariff rates high.

14. A reciprocal trade agreement means that the United States will admit products without duty or with a certain specified per cent of duty from countries that will do the same for us.

15. One cause of the panic of 1893 was the over-production of silver in the United States.

16. Wilson was the President who, as a last resort to relieve the financial distress of the country in

1893, was compelled to turn to J. P. Morgan, the master of capital, for help.

17. The formation of the Federal Reserve System in 1913 was considered one of the outstanding achievements of President Wilson's administration.

18. Among the earliest abuses which crept into the industrial life in the United States and led to the regulation of industry were those connected with the railroads.

19. President Theodore Roosevelt was the only President who really fought against illegal trusts.

20. The strike and boycott were recognized as legal weapons of labor by the passage of the Clayton Anti-Trust Law.

21. By 1950, the trust question was favorably solved.

22. All labor in the United States today is skilled labor.

23. The hierarchy of the United States set forth Pope Leo's principles for this country in the Bishops' Program of Social Reconstruction.

24. It is a Catholic's obligation to learn the religious principles which are necessary in business relations.

25. The Church does not approve of unions.

26. Industry developed into big business in the second half of the nineteenth century.

27. The American Federation of Labor and the Committee for Industrial Organization are the only two labor unions in the United States.

28. An industrial union covers many kinds of employment in the same industry.

29. The United Automobile Workers is a union within the CIO.

30. The calling of a strike is the method most highly recommended by the Church for labor to obtain justice.

31. Company unions often violate just principles because they force men to sign contracts preventing them from joining another union.

32. Andrew Carnegie had at heart the interest of the common man in his business dealings.

33. The federal government is never justified in taking over a complete industry.

34. Pope Leo XIII is often spoken of as the "Pope of the Workingman."

35. When employees and employers reach the point of sharing the just profits of an industry, then peaceful business relations can be established.

III. Can YOU get 100% for these? Match Column I with Column II by writing the letter of a phrase from Column II opposite the correct number in Column I.

Column I

1. Samuel Gompers
2. competition
3. labor
4. Rerum Novarum
5. principle of social justice
6. revenue
7. highest tariff in history
8. Interstate Commerce Commission
9. Sherman Anti-Trust Act
10. Chief Justice White
11. Cardinal Gibbons
12. encyclical
13. C.I.O.
14. collective bargaining
15. Coal Strike of 1902
16. Adamson Law
17. company union
18. N.R.A.
19. New Deal
20. Taft-Hartley Act

Column II

a. letter issued by a Pope to the world
b. just wage
c. government income
d. Knights of Labor
e. eight-hour day on railroads
f. A. F. of L.
g. business rivalry
h. attempt to stop nation-wide strikes
i. employees
j. depression of 1929
k. Pope Leo XIII
l. first government regulation of large industry
m. Underwood Tariff
n. industrial unions
o. Smoot-Hawley Tariff
p. yellow-dog contracts
q. Bishop John Lancaster Spalding
r. President Wilson
s. railroad regulation
t. Franklin D. Roosevelt
u. trust decisions
v. discussions of labor and management

Mary's Divine Motherhood

HISTORY. Since Jesus is God, and Mary is His Mother, she is therefore the Mother of God. The Church has always taught this, and those who refused to accept this were condemned at the Council of Ephesus in 431 A.D. The several feasts commemorating this dogma are: The Annunciation, March 25, the Motherhood of the Blessed Virgin Mary, October 11, and the Nativity, December 25.

BELIEF. Catholics believe that Jesus Christ became man through the motherhood of the Virgin Mary, under the power of the Holy Ghost. Because of this special privilege, we pay Mary special honor, for her excellence far surpasses that of all the saints and Angels.

Prayer

REMEMBER, O most gracious Virgin Mary, that never was it known that any one who fled to thy protection, implored thy help or sought thy intercession, was left unaided. Inspired with this confidence, I fly unto thee, O Virgin of virgins and Mother; to thee do I come, before thee I stand, sinful and sorrowful; O Mother of the Word Incarnate, despise not my petitions, but in thy mercy hear and answer me. Amen.

An indulgence of 3 years. A plenary indulgence once a month on the usual conditions for the daily recitation of this prayer (See "The Raccolta," the official book of indulgenced prayers, page 247).

DOGMA. The Divine Motherhood of Mary is a dogma (a truth solemnly declared by the Church to be an article of Catholic faith), and was defined at the Council of Ephesus in 431. It is one of the five great truths pertaining to Mary. The other four are: Her Immaculate Conception, her Assumption, her Perpetual Virginity, and her Plenitude of Grace.

Courtesy of Rev. J. B. Carol, O. F. M.

UNIT THREE

THE FARMER—AN INDISPENSABLE MEMBER OF THE AMERICAN NATION

UNIT THREE

THE FARMER—AN INDISPENSABLE MEMBER OF THE AMERICAN NATION

FARMING has played a big part in the development of our nation. In fact, without the farmer the wheels of industry would not revolve. Can you think of some reasons why?

During the time that businessmen were developing huge industrial projects, the farmers were not sitting idle. The invention of improved farm machinery changed the methods and the lives of the farmers as much as big business changed the lives of factory workers. The industrial age, about which we have just learned, aided the farmer tremendously.

Inventions such as the reaper enabled a farmer to work much more rapidly. As a result, not so many farmers were needed, and many moved into the cities. This was not too happy a trend in the eyes of the Church. She knows that the countryside is a good environment for happy, Christian living. She has accomplished much towards organizing the Catholic farm population and doing educational work among this group of people.

The government, too, has made great progress in giving aid to the farmers. The struggle between capital and labor involved the farmer because high tariff, transportation rates, and the problem of money were his concern as well. When he appealed to the government for aid and was refused, he allied himself with the miners of the West in their demand for unlimited coinage of silver. Together they secured the passage of the Sherman Silver Act. From that time on, farmers began to organize into many societies.

A Department of Agriculture had been added to the President's Cabinet in 1889, and since then great strides have been made towards improving the lot of the farmer. The twentieth century, especially, has seen some important developments in agriculture.

THE FARMER SEEKS SECURITY

We look into the chapter. The Industrial Revolution helped to change the life of the American farmer. The increasing number of farm machines helped produce larger crops without more labor on the part of the farmer. Better transportation facilities made it easy to send the increased produce to the cities.

A new social life was introduced into the agricultural sections of the United States. The Catholic Church realizes that if the conditions of *rural life,* that is, life in the country, are good, society in general will benefit.

When farmers saw the favorable results of labor's efforts to organize, they took similar steps. They learned that it is a good thing to work together in such groups as the Grange, 4-H Clubs, and cooperatives. If these are conducted according to Christian principles, the justice and charity desired by the Church will be insured. Farmers can make a great contribution to America's progress by carrying out these principles.

In order to learn more about these matters, you will need to study the following topics: (1) American Rural Life and Its Problems, (2) The Farmers Organize to Secure Justice, and (3) The Work of the National Catholic Rural Life Conference.

1. American Rural Life and Its Problems

It has been said that if you wish to know how prosperous a nation is you should look at its farm life. At first it may seem that farming is so different from industry that the two have little in common so far as the prosperity of a nation is concerned. However, as you shall see, the one depends on the other.

Machinery affects farming. The invention of machinery, on the one hand, enabled the farmer to produce more food; on the other, it led to an increased demand for farm products. Various industries, like textile-making, the canning industry, and the packing industry depended to a great extent on agriculture. In fact, they are either prosperous or slack, depending upon whether farm methods are efficient or inefficient.

The spread of factories led to the growth of cities. City people had to to be fed, and since they were too busy in industrial or white-collar

144

No more horses. Tractors and improved machinery have speeded up the work on modern farms.

jobs to raise their own food, the farmer had to do it for them. This necessitated the building of better roads so that foodstuffs could be more easily transported from the country.

When iron and steel made possible such machines as reapers and threshing machines, the farmer found himself able to cultivate more land. When tractors were invented, and gasoline or diesel motors were applied to farm machines, the farmers' work was not only less laborious and tiring, but he had more leisure time.

Social improvements because of inventions. Many years ago, the farmer was almost isolated from his fellow human beings. Beginning with the latter part of the nineteenth century, however, farmers and city folk have been brought closer together. The automobile, the telephone, and good roads and bus lines have broken down the isolation of earlier years.

Surely, you have seen many modern school buildings on your trips through the country. These well-equipped schools have been made possible because several small farming communities group together and build a school. In this way, a better school can be constructed. It will have more pupils

A consolidated rural school

Farm children learn by doing

and, therefore, will warrant a more complete school faculty, that is, teaching staff.

Other educational opportunities are given to farmers through the radio and television, which bring to farm homes the finest music, scientific lectures, and news of the world.

Farm life, an aid to family spirit. In the earlier days of our country, most people were farmers. They owned large tracts of land they themselves cultivated. They were very proud of their farms, even though, at that time, they did not know all the modern ways of improving them.

All the members of the family, men, women, and children, shared the work of the farm. This made it a family enterprise. It kept the family together for meals, work, and recreation. Together they talked over their problems and made plans for improvements. This gave them a common interest which is lacking in so many homes today. Can you see how farm life would strengthen a good Christian family spirit?

Classes of farmers. There are still some large farms in the country from which the owners acquire comfortable incomes. Before the First World War, more than sixty-five percent of the farms were owned by the farmers who worked them. But during the depression of 1929, many of these farms were taken over by the banks or landlords who did not live on the farm. Today, half of the farms in the United States are operated by tenant farmers. A tenant farmer is one who works land for its owner. Usually tenant farmers receive a share of the crops in payment for their services. In some parts of the country, such farmers are called sharecroppers.

The evils of tenant farming. The tenant farmer, because he does not own the land he is working, often is not too interested in it. He often does his work carelessly or neglects the farm property. The result is that sometimes tenant farmers become poverty-stricken, and wander to another farm, hoping to better their condition. Because tenant farmers frequently lack contact with religion and good education and fail to support community social enterprises, their children often suffer.

Pope Leo XIII has rightly said that men and women always work harder on land which is their own. The earth belongs to man, and when he uses his strength and talent to make it productive, it is only just that he should be given an opportunity to own it. In the eyes of the Church, one solution to the farm problem is ownership of the land.

Farm tenancy report of 1937. In 1937, President Franklin D. Roosevelt appointed a committee to make a survey of conditions on American farms. The report stated that if the slavery of the Civil War days was undemocratic, it is just as undemocratic for a country's farms to be run by careless, landless tenants who are the victims of unjust landlords. This report further stated: "Where there is a strong trend toward a nation of tenant farmers, there is a developing a condition

Brown Brothers

The upper picture shows a sharecropper's home; the lower, the same family's home after they joined a cooperative.

Brown Brothers

147

which will endanger the welfare of the masses of the farmers." Tenant farming is really one of the greatest misfortunes in the history of agriculture in the United States.

Problems facing farmers. In spite of the improvements modern machinery has made possible on our farms, many problems still confront the farmer. His family income is usually uncertain. There are a number of reasons for this condition.

First of all, a farmer depends upon his crops for his salary. You have probably read in newspapers or magazines that in certain farming regions of the country a biting frost, a drought, or a plague of insects has destroyed crops. When these misfortunes occur, a farmer's crops are reduced and, therefore, his income will likewise be small.

Secondly, high transportation rates cut down a farmer's income. Do you recall from Unit II how the railroads violated principles of social justice where the farmer was concerned? The Granger Laws, which some western states passed, and about which you studied last year, attempted to regulate railroad rates.

Thirdly, a problem is created for the farmer when his harvest is too large. It is necessary for him to store some of his crops. If his storage space is limited, a portion of his produce will be spoiled. This will affect his income, and he may not get as much for his products.

2. The Farmers Organize to Secure Justice

Consolidation of railroads and their frequent unjust cooperation with big businessmen against the farmer, made the farmer look with suspicion upon capitalists. He realized that big business had its hand on all that concerned him. It furnished the machines he used, it controlled transportation facilities, and, in many instances, held a mortgage over his head. The only salvation for him was to organize just as labor did.

Early forms of union among farmers. Probably the first society organized by the farmers was the Grange, founded by Oliver H. Kelly. Do you recall from last year's history what a Grange is? Its purpose, in the beginning, was not political but, rather, it was hoped that farmers and their families would benefit socially and educationally from the Grange meetings.

By 1873, however, its influence began to be felt in politics. One of the biggest achievements of the Grangers was that they succeeded in interesting the government in their railroad problems. It was largely through them that the Interstate Commerce Act was passed in 1887. If you do not remember what this act was, refer to Unit II.

As the movement for securing justice for the farmer continued to sweep over the country, farmers' societies were formed in different regions. One was the Farmers' Alliance, known by various names in the North, the West, and the South. These groups finally joined with organized labor and became known as the Populist Party.

Influence of the Populist Party.
The Populist Party was also known as the People's Party. At its national convention in Omaha, Nebraska, in 1892, James B. Weaver was nominated the candidate for the presidency. The Populists urged that the government either break up or strictly regulate trusts. They demanded that all railroads, telegraph lines, and telephones be controlled by the United States government. The farmers felt certain that government regulation of these public services would assure them a more just treatment. They also asked for postal savings banks in place of the national banks, for the convenience of farmers with small earnings.

Although the Populist Party was defeated in the election of 1892, it polled over a million votes.

The election of 1896. At the next election year in 1896, the Populists united with the Democrats in support of William Jennings Bryan of Nebraska. In spite of the fact that Bryan spent months preceding the election seeking votes in the West and South, William McKinley, the Republican candidate, was elected.

The Populist party gradually disappeared after that time, and the farmers never again tried to organize their own party. They have, however, great influence over the Congressmen, especially from the South and the West. The tendency of the farmer is to vote for any candidate who will pledge support to agricultural interests.

4-H Clubs for young farmers. Have

By Ewing Galloway, N. Y.
Williams Jennings Bryan

you ever read in a newspaper or magazine about a young boy who won recognition because of a fine type of cattle which he had raised? This boy probably belongs to a 4-H Club. There are many such clubs in the United States. Over a million and a half boys and girls, between the ages of ten and twenty, belong to them. The purpose of the clubs is to give rural youth the experience and instruction which will enable them to learn productive methods of farming. The four H's stand for head, heart, health, and hands. What part would each of these play in good farming?

The 4-H Clubs began with farmers who volunteered their services and rural school teachers who instructed youth in farming and home-making. As the movement grew larger and great benefit was

4-H Clubs train rural youth

A farmers' "Co-op"

derived from it, the Department of Agriculture in Washington gave it permanent recognition in 1914.

Farmers' cooperatives. We mentioned that farmers learned through experience that, when they worked together, better results were achieved. Many farmers have lost their land through carelessness or lack of knowledge. In order to eliminate these losses, farmers established *cooperatives*. These are organizations in which the farmers work together and share profits and losses. They put money in a central fund to purchase farm equipment which is shared by the group. In this way, no one farmer has to spend a great deal of money, and yet he has the chance to use modern machinery which will help him grow better and larger crops.

If cooperatives are conducted ac-cording to Christian social principles, much good can result. The common use of farm machinery will teach farmers to be responsible. They will learn to be helpful and charitable by working together towards a common goal. This common goal is to achieve a higher standard of living and better social conditions.

3. The Work of the National Catholic Rural Life Conference

The National Catholic Rural Life Conference devotes itself to the task of improving conditions in rural areas.

Bishop Edwin V. O'Hara. In 1923, Father O'Hara, who was later to become Bishop of Kansas City, Missouri, gathered together a group of people interested in rural problems. This group consisted of bishops, priests, and lay persons who

150

were anxious to improve the economic, social, and spiritual life of American farmers. The result of a three-day session showed that some permanent organization should be formed to study rural problems and to spread Catholic rural principles. Accordingly, those present at this meeting organized the National Catholic Rural Life Conference.

Aims of the National Catholic Rural Life Conference. The purpose of this organization is to develop in youth an appreciation of the blessings to be derived from living in rural areas. It strives to accomplish this in four ways:

1. By caring for the underprivileged Catholics living on the land.
2. By encouraging Catholics who are now on the farm lands to remain there.
3. By urging more Catholics to settle on the land.
4. By converting the non-Catholics now on the land.

What the Church is doing for rural districts. Unfortunately, many rural Catholics are suffering from disadvantages. The Catholic Church is interested in improving their condition, spiritually as well as materially. The Rural Life Conference cooperates with the Confraternity of Christian Doctrine, which conducts religious vacation schools. These schools are taught by Sisters, some of whom are in full-time teaching positions in city schools during the year. A library service distributes free pamphlets to rural churches which have no schools. It

(Blackstone Studios)
Bishop Edwin V. O'Hara

fosters devotion to St. Isidore, the patron of farmers, and urges that annual retreats be given the farmers.

Priests who will labor in agricultural areas are given special training. One college which gives intensive training in working in rural areas is St. John's University, Collegeville, Minnesota.

What do these words mean?

rural life	unreliable
efficient	cooperatives
family enterprise	Populist Party
tenant farming	4-H Clubs

How would a farmer answer these questions?

1. Discuss the effect of machinery on farm life.
2. Why is tenant farming a serious problem for any country?
3. What conditions cause the income of a farmer to be uncertain?

151

4. What principles of social justice are frequently violated in relation to the farmer?
5. Discuss past and present types of organization found among farmers.
6. Does the Catholic Church approve of cooperatives? Find out whether there are cooperatives in other occupations besides farming.
7. How has the Catholic Church aided the farmers?

Choosing the best answer

Number lines on a paper from 1 to 8. Choose the best answer to each of the following statements. Place the letter of that answer after the number of the statement.

1. Modern farm machinery has changed the lives of the farmers because
    a. less men are needed on farms than ever before
    b. farmers have to work harder
    c. it makes the farmers wealthier
    d. it gives them more leisure time for education

2. The Catholic Church believes that rural life is the most complete life because
    a. it strengthens family spirit
    b. it makes children healthier
    c. it does away with tenant farming
    d. it is easier to lead a good life on a farm

3. The greatest evil of tenant farming is that
    a. farmers lose money
    b. tenant farmers often do not get enough to eat
    c. children suffer because of lack of education and social contact
    d. farmers cannot own their own land

4. According to Pope Leo XIII, the best solution to farm problems is that
    a. farmers should receive proper training on cultivating the land
    b. more people should become farmers
    c. more crops should be stored for future use
    d. those who till the fields should be given an opportunity to own them

5. It is largely because of the farmers that
    a. industry expanded in the twentieth century
    b. more silver was mined
    c. the Sherman Silver Act was a failure
    d. the Interstate Commerce Act was passed

6. The purpose of 4-H Clubs is to
    a. see which boy or girl can raise the best cattle
    b. enable young farmers to have a good time
    c. help people in foreign countries
    d. enable farm children to learn the best methods of farming

7. The Church approves of cooperatives among farmers because
    a. they give farmers the chance to use modern machinery
    b. the movement enables the farmers to become better educated.
    c. larger and better crops can be raised
    d. common use of farm machinery often teaches Christian social living

8. The main purpose of the National Catholic Rural Life Conference is
    a. to draw more converts to the Catholic Church in rural areas
    b. to develop scientific methods of farming
    c. to bring all Catholic farmers together
    d. to develop in youth an appreciation of the blessings of rural life

CHAPTER II

THE GOVERNMENT AIDS THE FARMER

By way of introduction. We have seen how the farmers in the United States formed organizations to secure just treatment from the railroads and big business. The United States government realized how valuable the work of the farmer is to the country. In order to give him guidance, it established the Department of Agriculture. This department has undertaken, among other things, immense projects of conservation and irrigation.

The First World War had a decided effect upon agriculture, just as it did on industry. During the war, there was a period of prosperity. But when the war ended, the depression left its mark on farming. The New Deal of Franklin D. Roosevelt attempted to lighten distress in the farming areas, much as it did in the field of industry.

The story of how the government has helped the farmer is divided into the following parts: (1) Laws Which Helped the Farmer, (2) Saving and Protecting the Land, (3) The Effect of World War I on Agriculture, and (4) What the New Deal Did for the Farmer.

1. Laws Which Helped the Farmer

Last year, you learned that the Homestead Act of 1862 was responsible for populating the West because many people were attracted by the land offered by the government. While this act spread the population, it did not aid the farmer. So many new farms sprang up that there was an over-production of crops. This means that crops were too large, and not enough buyers could be found for them. Farm prices fell. It was at this time that the farmers began to organize.

The beginning of agricultural education. In 1862, Congress passed the first law which was to benefit farmers. It was known as the Morrill Law and was the first of many which encouraged agricultural education. This law provided that each state was to be given 30,000 acres of land for each member it had in Congress. In other words, if a state had two Senators and three Representatives, it would receive 150,000 acres of land. The money which would be derived from the sale of this land was to be used for the erection and support of agricultural colleges.

As the nineteenth century progressed, the government aided these colleges in developing scientific experiments for the improvement of agriculture. There are now forty-

By Ewing Galloway, N. Y.

A teacher and students conduct a test in dairy farming at an agricultural college. Such colleges have greatly improved farming methods.

eight such colleges in the United States. Not only has agricultural education resulted in more efficient methods of farming, but it has developed an interest in the opportunities of farm life.

Agriculture in elementary and high schools. Agriculture is taught in some elementary schools in farming districts. It is required by law in about twenty states. In the earlier grades of these schools, it takes the form of science or nature study.

About thirty years after the establishment of the first agricultural college, a successful agricultural high school was formed in connection with the University of Minnesota. By 1917, agricultural high schools were set up in every state of the Union. In these schools, students got actual experience in working the land and caring for farm animals.

A new department of the government. The Department of Agriculture began as an agricultural service of the Patent Office in Washington. In the beginning, its only duty was to distribute seeds throughout farming areas. As the years passed, its work was enlarged. Abraham Lincoln made it a separate organization in 1862, but it did not become an official department of the President's Cabinet until 1889.

An instrument in the U.S. Weather Bureau

A farmer and a rural mail carrier

Duties of Department of Agriculture. The Department of Agriculture cooperates with state agricultural colleges in promoting scientific research. In fact, it is one of the greatest research centers in the country. It studies plant and animal life and investigates the causes and treatment of plant and animal diseases.

Another service of the Department of Agriculture is to preserve our national forests and to work with states to plan and construct improved roads. Nearly every state has an agricultural department of its own. These departments cooperate with the national department to secure the best possible answers to the problems of the farmers. A Bureau of Information publishes pamphlets which are available to interested farmers.

The United States Weather Bureau. An organization on which the farmers greatly depend is the Weather Bureau. It sends out weather information by cable, radio, telephone, and telegraph to every section of the United States, as well as to Canada, Mexico, and Europe. Warnings of rain, frosts, and floods have saved American farmers from many losses.

Rural postal service—a boon to farmers. In 1896, rural postal service over the more important highways began in the United States. It has been extended within recent years, so that there is scarcely a rural family today that does not receive mail at least once a day.

Parcel post service was established between farm and city in 1913. This enabled merchants to send goods directly to the farms, and the farmers to ship some of their produce to their customers.

Financial help for the farmer. Before the United States entered the First World War, the government began giving financial aid to farmers through the system of Farm Loan Banks. Farmers could borrow money from these banks at a low rate of interest and have as long as from five to forty years to pay it back.

There were other bills which were intended to ease the farmer's burden of debt, but farm difficulties remained unsolved. When Franklin D. Roosevelt ran for President in 1932, he made the farm problems one of the leading issues of his campaign. In a later section of this chapter, we shall learn how President Roosevelt tried to put his ideas into practice.

2. Saving and Protecting the Land

The huge task of saving and protecting the natural resources of the United States is not the duty of any one department of the government alone. This vast amount of work is spread through seven different departments of the President's Cabinet.

Natural wealth in the United States. In your study of geography, you have learned that natural resources are those things which exist in nature. In general, these are good soil, forests, water, minerals, and wildlife. The United States has been blessed with a greater abundance of these gifts than any other country in the world. Travelers can see fields of grain, immense forest lands abounding in wildlife, and many fast-moving rivers which furnish water power for our own fac-

Contour-ploughed field
From Ewing Galloway, N. Y.

Old method of plowing
From Ewing Galloway, N. Y.

The land in the foreground has not been irrigated, while the land on the far side of the canal has been irrigated.

tories. The mineral resources and sea wealth, together with those mentioned above, offer many opportunities to Americans.

The need for protecting natural resources. For the most part, frontier peoples waste natural resources. When American pioneers moved westward to find better homes and opportunities for their families, beautiful trees were felled for clearing farms and building homes. Little did the pioneers realize that they were paving the way for disastrous floods in the future.

So much wildlife abounded in these forests that early settlers never thought of sparing it. They never thought, either, of fertilizing their soil. If, in time, it did not yield good crops, they simply moved to another spot. The result was that the soil lost its richness and fertility.

The basic natural resource for farming is soil. Two forces, wind and water, constantly carry soil from one place to another. Oftentimes, too, these two forces destroy the land. For example, soil can be washed away by heavy rains when it is not protected by trees, grass, or shrubs. Sloping land is easily washed away, merely because it is sloping. When soil is unprotected, dust storms frequently blow away good surface soil. The washing away of soil is known as *erosion*. You can see evidences today of how farmers

157

try to keep soil from washing away. One system, called contour plowing, achieves this by plowing hillsides in curves around the hill, instead of up and down.

Conservation. By the end of the nineteenth century, political leaders realized that waste of our natural resources was a threat to the future of America. Theodore Roosevelt was the first President to begin a systematic method of conservation, shortly after taking office in 1901.

Conservation means the wise and thrifty use of natural resources for the benefit of the people. President Roosevelt aided the work of conservation in four ways. First, he enlarged and protected national forests; second, he built irrigation systems for arid, or dry, lands; third, he made plans for improved inland waterways; and fourth, he asked that all the states of the Union cooperate with the national government in furthering this work.

Forests are protected. The first natural resource to be conserved was forest land. Interest in forestry began in the 1890's. Although the United States had agricultural schools, none of these gave special instruction in the care of forests. In 1905, President Roosevelt placed Gifford Pinchot (pin'-show), one of his valued supporters in the conservation policy, at the head of a special forest service. Scientific measures for rebuilding forests and preventing forest fires were seriously considered.

President Roosevelt ordered the

By Ewing Galloway, N. Y.
Gifford Pinchot

Department of Agriculture to set apart large tracts of western land to be converted into National Forests or Parks. A group of men, known as forest rangers, was organized to protect forests from fires. Special information regarding the care of diseased trees and proper methods of lumbering was spread through forest areas. If this wise policy had been adopted a generation earlier, much destruction of timber would have been avoided.

The White House Conference. President Rosevelt's work was so highly thought of by the various states in the Union that, in 1908, it was suggested that a conference be called in Washington to consider a conservation program for the individual states. Governors of thirty-four states, many members of Congress, and members of private organizations were present. The result of the conference was that many states adopted a program of conservation similar to the national one.

Reclamation Act of 1902. Much of the land in our western states is dry. In the latter part of the nineteenth century, an act had been passed which permitted these states to try to improve their land by irrigation. Unfortunately, these states were the least wealthy of all, and lack of funds caused the project to lag. So President Roosevelt endeavored to provide government aid.

In 1902, he secured the passage of the Reclamation Act. *Reclamation* means to make waste land usable by means of irrigation. This act provided for the construction of dams and irrigation systems from the proceeds derived from the sale of public lands. As a result, large tracts of land, formerly worth only a few cents an acre, became worth hundreds of dollars an acre. Fruit could now be raised on land which was previously covered with scrubby grass or sagebrush.

Roosevelt Dam. The Reclamation Act of 1902 resulted in the undertaking of about twenty-four irrigation projects in various parts of the country. Since President Roosevelt was responsible for so much of the reclamation program, it was fitting that the first large project be called

Roosevelt Dam. One of the great projects of the New Deal. What is the value of such dams to the community?   *From Ewing Galloway, N. Y.*

Roosevelt Dam. This dam is located on the Salt River in Arizona, and canals from this reservoir irrigate hundreds of millions of acres of land. This huge project was the forerunner of others about which you will read in this chapter.

3. The Effect of World War I on Agriculture

Throughout the United States during World War I, billboards, magazines and newspapers carried the slogan: "Food will win the War." Do you think food plays any part in helping to win a war?

The farmer prospers during the war. While World War I was raging in Europe, the American farmer was reaping great profit. Our government paid him high prices for food needed for our men in the service. There were millions of acres of good farmland in the United States. In Europe, three thousand miles across the Atlantic Ocean, were more millions of acres of fertile lands. But the war prevented European farmers from cultivating their fields. Consequently, American farmers doubled their crops and were only too willing to sell their surplus to starving Europe. As fast as the money came into their hands, just so fast did many American farmers invest it in more land or in expensive machinery, which would enable them to increase production.

Poor times after the war. The war ended in 1918. European farmers could not immediately attain full-scale production. So Europe was supplied with farm produce from the United States. But, in time, Europe began again to produce enough agricultural commodities. However, American farmers went right on producing as if the war had not ended. Before long, surplus farm commodities became a problem.

Flood and drought. Then two great disasters befell the farmlands in the West. The Mississippi River overflowed its banks in 1927 in one of the most severe floods in the nation's history. Thousands of people were homeless, and agriculture was impeded. Just when it seemed that farming was on the upgrade, another disaster befell the country in the form of a drought, which lasted for many months. Crops were again ruined, especially in the Mississippi Valley.

The government sends help. The farmers of the Mississippi Valley were unable to cope with the situation themselves, so they appealed to the federal government. Army engineers came to their rescue. They constructed floodgates at certain points where the river was apt to overflow. The government paid farmers generously for lands taken for these purposes. Government aid can be valuable, providing that individual ownership of land is not made insecure as a result of it.

When the stock market crashed in 1929 and the great depression followed, the New Deal of President Franklin D. Roosevelt seemed to point towards a period of relief for the farmer.

Homes are destroyed and property is ruined when a river goes on a rampage.

4. What the New Deal Did for the Farmer

We have learned that the New Deal helped industry to rise after the depression of 1929. Now it is time to learn what agricultural laws were passed under the New Deal.

Agricultural Adjustment Act. You will recall that one of the purposes of the New Deal was to revive the prosperity which people enjoyed before the depression. In trying to help the farmers to recover their prosperity, the Agricultural Adjustment Act was passed in 1933. President Roosevelt believed that since an over-production of certain agricultural products, such as cotton, wheat, and corn caused prices to drop, farmers should plant mil-

lions of acres less of these crops. The government then paid the farmers a high price for not raising these crops. The Supreme Court declared this act unconstitutional in 1936. The Justices decided that such upsetting of agricultural practices might harm our trade with other countries. Besides, the court declared that the federal government was taking over powers which belonged to individual states.

Soil Conservation Act. In 1934, the United States suffered a severe drought. Crops failed and cattle died. Communities in the West began to look like groups of ghost-towns. Besides this, dust storms carried tons of soil off and dropped

From Ewing Galloway

The results of a dust storm

it into the Atlantic Ocean. It was obvious that the once thick layer of rich top soil which covered the country was becoming poorer and thinner.

Congress, hoping to find a substitute for the Agricultural Adjustment Act, passed the Soil Conservation Act of 1935. This new act provided for payments to any farmers who would agree to plant some of their acres with soil-enriching crops, such as alfalfa, clover, and soybeans. In this way, surplus production of food-producing crops would be curtailed, or reduced, and millions of acres of soil would be improved.

By 1942, this soil conservation program had proved its worth. Thousands of acres of farm land had begun to produce abundant crops, and at the same time soil was saved from erosion. When 1948 crops were totaled, the farmers discovered that they had raised the largest corn crop in the history of the country, and the billion-bushel wheat crop overflowed its bins and had to be heaped upon the ground. Much of this was sent overseas to feed hungry Europeans.

The Tennessee Valley Authority. The work of reclamation by means of erecting dams in the West, begun during Theodore Roosevelt's administration, was continued by Presidents Wilson and Hoover. Grand Coulee Dam in the state of Washington and Hoover Dam, formerly Boulder Dam, are two of the larger projects.

During the administration of Franklin D. Roosevelt, a further series of dams was also erected.

A flood-control spillway

By Ewing Galloway, N. Y.

Wilson Dam had been built on the Tennessee River during Wilson's administration. The hydroelectric power obtained there was to be used by ammunition plants, but this plan did not materialize. In 1933, President Franklin D. Roosevelt set up the Tennessee Valley Authority. This authority was created to irrigate land in the Tennessee Valley, to control flood waters, and to furnish electric power for homes and factories in this region. **Other attempts to relieve the farmer.** Between 1935 and 1937 other measures were passed by Congress for the relief of farmers. Loans were made to them to enable them to pay off their debts. The tenant farmers, about whom you have read in this Unit, were allowed to borrow enough to purchase small plots of ground. Surplus farm products were distributed to state relief organizations. Electricity was made available in many rural areas, thus making farm life more attractive and easier for American housewives.

Subsistence homesteads. You have learned that rural life is conducive to Christian living. Some bishops in the United States believed that poverty would be relieved when people moved back to rural areas. The government attempted to carry out just such a project in 1932, when it organized *subsistence homesteads*. These homesteads were small farms on which some members of a family worked, while the father and older children labored in factories in the city.

We have learned that because of conditions which the farmer cannot always control, his income is not too reliable. Do you remember what these conditions were? It was hoped that subsistence homesteads would insure a more steady income. The family would have the income from the work in the factory, and would save expenses by raising a sufficient amount of food to supply its needs.

Granger, Iowa, experiments. While some of the subsistence homesteads were not successful, others were of great benefit to farmers. In Granger, Iowa, Monsignor Luigi Ligutti (loo-ee′-jee lee-goot′-tee) became convinced that this government idea could be applied to a community of farms as well as to an individual farmer. In this respect his plan for helping the farmers differed from that of the government.

Most of the people in Granger worked in the mines. Their incomes were low and insufficient. They were compelled to apply for government aid in order to secure what their salaries would not provide. Since the National Recovery Act provided a certain amount of money in loans to aid these people, Monsignor Ligutti used the financial help afforded by this act to convert a portion of the community into subsistence farms.

He helped to place about fifty families on five-acre plots of ground, away from the mines, but near schools and churches. Each farmhouse had its own garden, or-

Brown Brothers

Francis P. Garvan

chard, and pasture. The children of the family helped on the farms. Any surplus farm products were sold, but most of them were used by the family itself. The Granger Plan was very successful. It was a practical application of the wishes of the bishops of this country. Today we find many people living in suburban areas but working in the cities.

Chemurgy. Perhaps you have never heard of the word "chemurgy." It was used first in 1935. It means putting chemistry to work so that surplus or waste farm products can be made into industrial products. For example, plastic is made from soybeans, and rayon is made from cotton pulp.

Chemurgy was begun during the period after the depression of 1929, when farmers had surplus crops. If they could not sell crops as they were, why not convert the surplus into something that could be sold? It was argued that in order to put a pound of food on the market, a farmer often had to grow another pound of material which no one could eat. Chemurgic farming attempts to find uses for this waste. The primary activities which come under the heading of chemurgy are:

1. Development of new, non-food uses for established farm crops.
2. Development of new crops for new or old uses.
3. Discovery of profitable uses for agriculural wastes.

Francis Patrick Garvan. Francis Patrick Garvan, an energetic Catholic, was president of the Chemical Foundation of America. He was a lawyer who had attended Yale University, Catholic University, where he became a trustee, Fordham, and Notre Dame. He was thoroughly interested in the development of chemurgy. Through his influence, Henry Ford called a meeting at Dearborn, Michigan. Three hundred representatives of the leading railroad and automobile companies, college presidents, chemical executives, and influential farmers attended. They set up the National Farm Chemurgic Council, and Francis Patrick Garvan became its first president. It was financed during its first year by the Chemical Foundation.

Unfortunately, the Council was to have Mr. Garvan's able leadership for the short space of two years, for he died suddenly in 1937. This organization, an outgrowth of the depression, has raised the standards of living of the farmer because it enables him to dispose of his surplus crops, as well as agricultural waste.

What is man's relation to the land? Many times we have mentioned that man has God-given rights. One of these is the right to have access to natural resources. The land is perhaps God's greatest natural gift to mankind. It is a source of food, clothing, and fuel. The right to use this gift is necessary for human welfare.

Since man has a right to own land, he also has the obligation to use it to develop his own personality, maintain a decent standard of living for his family, and fulfill his social obligations to the nation. The farmer has a duty to enrich the soil he tills, so that he may, if possible, hand it down to future generations in as good a condition as God gave it to him.

We have mentioned previously how farm life nurtures strong, wholesome, family spirit. The farm is a natural home for a family. Therefore, when a government plans for farm improvement, it will not disrupt or weaken family life. The strength of a nation depends upon the strength of its family life.

The farmer who works on the land has the first right to the fruits of his toil, but he must fulfill his duties and obligations to both the non-working owner and to the state.

Can you explain these words?

agricultural education   erosion
scientific research   reservoir
conservation   irrigation
reclamation   chemurgy
surplus commodities

To test your reading

1. Discuss agricultural education in the United States.
2. Name some services granted to farmers through government aid.
3. What are some ways in which the United States is conserving our natural resources?
4. Why was it necessary to pass laws regarding the protection of our natural resources?
5. What were the achievements of the New Deal in relation to the farmer?
6. Explain what is meant by chemurgy. How has it helped the farmer?
7. What is the Catholic viewpoint regarding man's relation to the land?

Highlights of the unit

I. Catholic Principles to Remember:
1. The land is one of God's greatest natural gifts to man.
2. God gave all men the right to use natural resources.
3. Farmers have a duty to enrich the soil of their land in order to keep it productive.
4. Farmers have the first right to the fruits of their toil.
5. A farmer has the duty to use the land in order to aid human welfare.
6. Men should use the gifts of the earth as God intended them to be used.

II. WHO'S WHO In Unit Three

Franklin D. Roosevelt—
appointed a committee to study farm conditions in 1937
proposed Agricultural Adjustment Act in 1933
replaced the A.A.A. by the Soil Conservation Act in 1935
organized the Tennessee Valley Authority
began subsistence homesteads as part of his relief program for farmers

Bishop Edwin O'Hara—
founder of the National Catholic Rural Life Conference

Theodore Roosevelt—
first President to begin a systematic system of conservation
built first large dam — Roosevelt Dam in Arizona
set aside tracts of land in the West as National Forests or Parks
organized the forest rangers
passed the Reclamation Act in 1902

Gifford Pinchot—
worked with Theodore Roosevelt in his conservation policy
became first head of a special forest service

Monsignor Luigi Ligutti—
head of the Granger, Iowa, Experiment

Francis Patrick Garvan—
did outstanding work in the National Farm Chemurgic Council

III. Ways of Improving the Lot of the Farmer

Consolidated schools—
permit better education for rural children

The Granges—
improved social life of the farmer

The Populist Party—
the only political party ever organized by farmers
no longer in existence

4-H Clubs—
give rural youth the opportunity to learn better methods of farming
were given permanent recognition by the Department of Agriculture in 1914

Farmers' Cooperatives—
organizations in which farmers work together
a possible means of teaching Christian social living

Inventions—
gave farmers more leisure time

IV. Government Attempts to Help the Farmer

Interstate Commerce Act of 1887—
attempted to secure fair railroad rates for farmers

The Morrill Law—
passed in 1862
first law to encourage agricultural education

Department of Agriculture—
officially adopted in President's Cabinet in 1889
one of greatest research centers in country
studies soil, and plant and animal life
preserves national forests

The Weather Bureau—
gives warnings to farmers of weather conditions

Rural Postal Service—
improved mail service between city and farm

Agricultural Adjustment Act—
the New Deal measure to help the farmer recover from the depression of 1929
declared unconstitutional in 1936

Soil Conservation Act—
   paid farmers who agreed to plant
   some of their acres with soil-enriching crops
   hoped to reduce surplus production of crops and to improve the
   soil
Tennessee Valley Authority—
   irrigated land of the Tennessee
   Valley
   controlled flood waters in the
   region
   furnished electric power for
   homes and factories
Reclamation Act of 1902—
   began the construction of a series
   of dams
Farm Loan Banks—
   organized by Government to give
   financial aid to farmers at low
   rate of interest
Subsistence Homesteads—
   organized as part of the New
   Deal project
   farms on which some members
   of the family worked while
   others worked in the city

V. Terms to Remember
rural life—
   life in the country
tenant farmers—
   those who work farms but do not
   own them
natural resources—
   things which exist in nature
   soil, forests, water, minerals,
   wildlife
erosion—
   washing away of soil
conservation—
   wise use of natural resources
reclamation—
   making land usable by irrigation
chemurgy—
   a scientific way of using surplus
   farm products

forest rangers—
   men who protect the forests

VI. The Work of the Church for the Farmer
   National Catholic Rural
   Life Conference—
      the most active Catholic organi-
      zation for helping the farmer;
      purpose — to develop in youth
      an appreciation of the blessings
      of living in rural areas
   Religious vacation schools
   Gives special education to priests
who will work in rural districts
   Believes that ownership of the land
is one solution to the farm problem

Clinching the highlights through activity

1. Make a poster that might have
   been used to encourage farmers to
   plant soil-enriching crops.
2. Write a newspaper account of the
   value of the Tennessee Valley Project.
3. Make a set of diagrams depicting
   the changes brought about in life
   on a farm as a result of advances
   in science, industry, and education.
4. Draw a large map of the United
   States, showing the location of our
   national parks. Have a number of
   pupils give oral reports on them.
   Isabelle F. Story has edited a book
   entitled *Glimpses of Our National
   Parks.*
5. Have a debate. Resolved: Greater
   opportunities for Christian social
   living are found in rural areas
   than in cities.
6. Draw a series of pictures illustrating the problems against which
   the farmers must cope. Include:
   floods, drought, insect plagues,
   surplus products, high railroad
   rates, erosion of land, etc.

A final check-up

I. Number a paper from 1 to 25. If a statement below is true write X after the number; if false, write a — sign.

1. The Department of Agriculture became a department of the President's Cabinet during the Civil War.
2. The development of big business had little effect upon agriculture.
3. The life of the farmer was improved socially by the invention of modern farm implements.
4. Rural life has the possibilities of strengthening a good Christian family spirit.
5. The United States in the twentieth century is at last free of the misfortune of tenant farming.
6. Cooperative farming is contrary to Catholic principles.
7. The purpose of the Grange meetings was to benefit farmers socially and educationally.
8. Farmers' organizations never became involved in political difficulties.
9. One purpose of the 4-H Clubs is to teach rural youth productive methods of farming.
10. The National Catholic Rural Life Conference is a Catholic organization which believes that American problems will be solved when all people go back to the farms to live.
11. There is still in existence an agricultural political party.
12. Twentieth-century United States has developed an interest in agriculture partly because of the founding of agricultural colleges.
13. Besides the National Department of Agriculture, each state has its own department of agriculture.
14. Farm Loan Banks gave loans to farmers at a very low rate of interest, with a long term to pay back the loans.
15. The New Deal program of Franklin D. Roosevelt accomplished very little towards helping the farmer.
16. The Department of Agriculture is solely responsible for the protection of our natural resources.
17. From early days, people in the United States have been aware of the necessity of conserving natural resources.
18. The income of a farmer is not too reliable because of conditions which he cannot always control.
19. By plowing hillsides in level curves around the hill, scientific farmers have discovered a way to keep good soil from washing away.
20. The Reclamation Act of 1902 provided for the irrigation of hundreds of acres of arid land in the West.
21. One of the weaknesses of our agriculture system is the accumulation of waste material.
22. Government aid to farmers is valuable as long as it does not make individual ownership of the land insecure.
23. The right to use natural resources is one of God's greatest natural gifts to man.
24. Immediately after the First World War, the United States suffered from a lack of agricultural products.
25. The disastrous floods which have swept over some sections of the United States in recent years were partly due to lack of conservation of natural resources.

A completion test

II. Can you complete these statements without the help of a list of words from which to choose?

1. Life in the country is spoken of as ....life.

2. People who work on a farm for the owner and who often have to move from place to place to find work are called................farmers.

3. In the eyes of the Church, one solution of the farm problem is ....of the land.

4. The only political party ever formed by farmers' organizations was the................................

5. In order to learn the most efficient methods of farming, thousands of American boys and girls belong to................................

6. By working together in...................., farmers have the opportunity of living Christian social principles.

7. The most active Catholic organization which helps the farmer is the................

8. In 1887, Congress passed the............ ....in order to solve some of the railroad problems of the farmers.

9. The first law which encouraged agricultural education was the ....passed in 1862.

10. Two government services which have greatly aided the farmer are the .... and the ....

11. The wise and thrifty use of natural resources is known as................

12. In order to rebuild our rapidly diminishing forest land, President Theodore Roosevelt established................................

13. ....means to make land usable by means of irrigation.

14. The................................Act of the New Deal was declared unconstitutional because it gave the Government powers which really belonged to the individual states.

A matching test

III. Here are ten sets of matching words or phrases. On your paper write the letter from Column II after the number in Column I which it best matches.

Column I	Column II
1. Tennessee Valley Authority	a. Populist Party
2. Soil Conservation Act	b. Monsignor Ligutti
3. The Granger Experiment	c. soil-enriching crops
4. chemurgy	d. Department of Agriculture
5. Bishop Edwin O'Hara	e. Reclamation Act of 1902
6. political organization of farmers	f. Theodore Roosevelt and Gifford Pinchot
7. scientific research	g. The Granges
8. irrigation projects	h. New Deal aid for farmers
9. development of conservation	i. greatest irrigation project in the United States
10. subsistence homesteads	j. use of agricultural wastes
	k. National Catholic Rural Life Conference

Mary's Perpetual Virginity

HISTORY. The Blessed Virgin Mary is the Mother of God. Feasts which remind us of Mary's Perpetual Virginity are the Purification, February 2, and the Annunciation, March 25. This dogma was solemnly defined by the Council of the Lateran in the year 649 A.D.

BELIEF. Catholics believe that Mary was a virgin before, and remained a virgin during and after the birth of her Divine Son. This means that Jesus had no earthly father but was conceived miraculously by the power of the Holy Ghost; Mary remained a virgin though bearing a son, and though married, she preserved her virginity till death.

Prayer

MAY we be assisted, we beseech Thee, O Lord, by the worshipful intercession of Thy glorious Mother, the ever-Virgin Mary; that we, who have been enriched by her perpetual blessings, may be delivered from all dangers, and through her loving kindness made to be of one heart and mind: Who livest and reignest world without end. Amen.

An indulgence of 3 years. A plenary indulgence on the usual conditions if this prayer is recited every day for a month (See "The Raccolta," the official book of indulgenced prayers, page 254).

DOGMA. Mary's Perpetual Virginity is a dogma (a truth solemnly declared by the Church to be an article of Catholic faith), and was defined by the Council of the Lateran in 649. It is one of the five great truths pertaining to Mary. The other four are: Her Immaculate Conception, her Assumption, her Divine Motherhood, and her Plenitude of Grace.

Courtesy of Rev. J. B. Carol, O. F. M.

UNIT FOUR

AMERICA'S MARCH OF PROGRESS

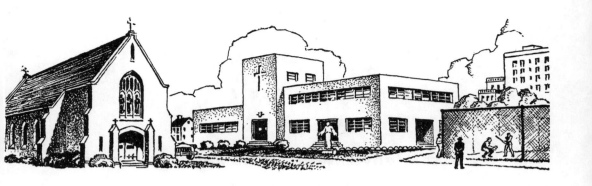

UNIT FOUR

AMERICA'S MARCH OF PROGRESS

As THE social and economic conditions of a country change, so the government changes. The United States government in the complex industrial twentieth century is in many ways different from what it was in early days. When our nation was composed of small farmers and traders, Americans believed that the government should have no further burden than to maintain peace and order. The Industrial Revolution helped to change this view. There were, of course, other important factors.

The possibility of changing our Constitution, when there is a genuine need, allows us to alter our basic law to meet needs as they arise. In the course of the first fifty-one years of the twentieth century, seven amendments have been added to the Constitution, the last one becoming effective in 1951. Some of these amendments had to do with political problems and some with social problems.

An important factor which aids in the progress of a nation is education. It, too, experienced considerable change in the twentieth century. Public schools tried out many new ideas in education, but not a few of them were soon discarded for more stable, or sound, methods of instruction. New types of education, such as adult education and vocational education, had their beginnings in this century. The Catholic University of America, established in the latter part of the nineteenth century, grew rapidly. It has become the leader in spreading Catholic principles of education.

Progress in America has also been hastened by cultural and scientific contributions. American contributions to literature, art, and music have been noteworthy. Radio and television have encouraged talent. The scientific experiments made in the United States have been so numerous that everyday life has taken on a different aspect.

CHAPTER I

THE FEDERAL GOVERNMENT ASSISTS AMERICAN PROGRESS

Important points to learn. Progress means change—change in customs and in laws. We know that the Constitution is the supreme law of our land. As the country changes, the Constitution also may need to be changed. When it does, an amendment is added.

Even the Supreme Court went through a period of change. When Franklin D. Roosevelt's New Deal program was inaugurated, the chief judicial body of our land felt its effects.

The government passed laws which aided American progress. One of these laws affected the people who wished to hold government positions. By requiring these citizens to take civil service examinations to determine their fitness for the work, better service for the nation was secured.

In this chapter, three points will be studied: (1) Amendments Change the Constitution, (2) The Supreme Court Undergoes a Change, and (3) The Government Improves Social Conditions.

1. Amendments Change the Constitution

Frequently, the Constitution of the United States has been referred to as the "framework" of our na-

tional government. The fact that not all leaders were in complete agreement, even on the original part of it, led the framers of the Constitution to provide a method of changing it when the need arose. This method took the form of amendments. By inserting amendments from time to time, the government has been better able to solve problems that have arisen.

A brief review of early amendments. The first ten amendments are known as the Bill of Rights. These define some liberties which all Americans are entitled to enjoy. The Bill of Rights guarantees, or pledges, to citizens freedom of speech and of religion, the protection of the law, and it provides for trials by jury.

The amendments passed during the nineteenth century concerned political practices and the status of Negroes. The Thirteenth Amendment had abolished slavery. The Fourteenth made the Negro a citizen. The Fifteenth declared that a citizen was not to be denied the right to vote merely because of his color.

Twentieth-century amendments. Between 1913 and 1951, seven amendments were added to the Constitution. Their general purpose was to promote democratic principles in America and to facilitate the passage of laws which would promote the common welfare. We shall study these amendments in the following paragraphs.

Federal income tax. During President Cleveland's administration, an income tax law was passed to increase the government's revenue. The Supreme Court declared this law unconstitutional because the Constitution did not give Congress the right to collect such a tax. The money was necessary, so what was to be done? The solution to the problem was to amend the Constitution. Therefore, the Sixteenth Amendment was passed in 1913. From that time on, Congress had the power to tax the incomes of individuals and business corporations.

The justice of taxation. Do you know what the government does with the money which it raises through taxation? You ride bicycles along nicely paved streets. Have you ever wondered who pays for these roads? Your parents and other citizens of our cities, counties, or states pay for them through taxation.

Good roads are only one of the many benefits citizens receive in return for the payment of taxes. Fire and police protection, public parks and recreation facilities, the huge projects for conservation and irrigation about which you have read—all of these are made possi-

Brown Brothers

By Ewing Galloway, N. Y.

Firemen, policemen, and postmen perform essential services.

By Ewing Galloway, N. Y.

ble because of the taxes which the local, state, or federal government collects. No citizen could provide such projects by himself. The taxes which all contribute, however, enable everyone to use these conveniences.

Do you think it is just, then, for the government to require citizens to pay taxes? Do you think the Sixteenth Amendment requiring income tax follows the principles of social justice? Why?

The Seventeenth Amendment. The Seventeenth Amendment, which was also passed in 1913, gave the Constitution a more democratic character than it previously had. Originally, the Constitution provided that United States Senators be elected by the state legislatures. If the state legislature were controlled by a particular group, such

as the capitalists, then senators favoring big business would be chosen. Can you see how easy it would be in this type of election for a favored group to control the lawmaking of the federal government?

This was contrary to just principles. The people declared that if the Senators would be directly elected by them, any legislation passed by the federal government would be more for the welfare of the public than for one particular group. The Seventeenth Amendment provides for this direct election.

Women become voters. Women began crusades for the right to participate in politics in the middle of the nineteenth century, but not until 1920 was *Woman Suffrage,* or women's right to vote, nationally recognized by the Nineteenth Amendment to the Constitution.

Since the passage of this amendment, women have taken an active part in politics. Some have become mayors of cities, some have become members of state legislatures, and some have been elected to Congress. One, Frances Perkins, became a member of Franklin D. Roosevelt's Cabinet. Would the Constitution permit a woman to become President or Vice President?

Twentieth Amendment. At some time or other you might hear the expression "Lame Duck Amendment." This refers to the Twentieth Amendment, which was passed in 1933. It changed the dates for the opening of Congress to January 3 and the inauguration of President

"Suffragettes" urging votes for women.

Brown Brothers

and Vice-President to January 20 instead of, as before, March 4.

Before this new arrangement, Congressmen, defeated in the November elections, would remain in office until March of the following year. Frequently, these "Lame Duck" Congressmen would block the passage of legislation favored by the voters.

Two social amendments. During the opening of the West, the saloon became a popular meeting place. The sale of intoxicating liquors in these places led to many types of crime. State-wide movements, generally called prohibition movements, forbidding the sale of intoxicating liquor, were started in many of the Middle-Western states. Eventually, various groups attempted to induce Congress to amend the Constitution, and make prohibition nationwide.

In 1920, the Eighteenth Amendment was passed. It prohibited the manufacture and sale of intoxicating liquor in the United States for mere purposes of pleasure.

The Church has always been opposed to extreme use of intoxicating drink. She knows that intemperance, or drunkenness, is sinful, and not only weakens the will and leads to further sin, but impairs health. However, the Church does not favor laws prohibiting the use of liquor, for it is not just to deny its use to those who drink moderately and within reason.

The Prohibitionists or "Drys," as they are sometimes called, thought the Eighteenth Amend-

Bettmann Archive
A cartoon against the Volstead Act.

ment would improve social conditions. A glance into the history of the thirteen years it was in effect proves the contrary. When men could not purchase liquor legally, some began to make and sell it secretly. These men were known as bootleggers. They not only violated the law, but many of them amassed great wealth unjustly. Often the liquor they sold was poisonous, and it endangered the lives of the citizens who purchased it. Rival gangs of bootleggers also fought with each other for the control of the illegal liquor trade. Since the prohibition law was widely disregarded, disrespect for law grew in many minds.

Something had to be done to check this lawlessness. The Republicans believed that stricter enforcement of the amendment would be the answer. The Democrats felt the only way to cure the ills it caused was to repeal the amendment. In

1933, the Democrats were victorious when the Twenty-first Amendment, repealing prohibition, was passed. This has been the only instance in the history of the United States of the repeal of an amendment to the Constitution.

The Twenty-second Amendment. George Washington established the tradition that an American President serve no more than two terms. Until 1940, when Franklin D. Roosevelt was elected, the tradition remained unbroken. There had never been any law against a President's serving more than two terms. Although the tradition was strong in America, it was not strong enough to prevent Roosevelt being reelected three times. Since 1951, the limitation of two terms has no longer been a matter of tradition. In that year the last needed state ratified the Twenty-second Amendment, and made obligatory the limitation of two elected terms, plus not more than two years of the predecessor's term.

2. The Supreme Court Undergoes a Change

The Supreme Court is the most dignified and important Court in the United States. It is comprised of a Chief Justice and eight associate Justices. The Justices convene, or meet, in one of the most beautiful buildings in Washington, D. C.

Duties of the Supreme Court. You have already learned about two laws which the Supreme Court determined were unconstitutional. Do you recall them? One was the Agricultural Adjustment Act and the other the National Recovery Act of the New Deal.

It is one of the duties of the Supreme Court to rule whether or not laws are in accordance with the meaning of the Constitution. Another duty is to hear and decide on certain cases which have been appealed from the decision of lower courts. The trial of a United States ambassador or certain high public officials would also take place before this Court.

For many years, this body of men has been the determining factor in very important law suits. Recently, it seems that the Justices have changed their interpretation of some very fundamental principles contained in the Constitution. One in particular is worthy of note. The First Amendment states that "Congress shall make no law respecting an establishment of religion or prohibiting the free exercise thereof." In 1948, the Supreme Court declared unconstitutional a certain arrangement of released-time for teaching religion in public-school buildings. Up to this time, our Constitution was interpreted to mean that the federal government could aid religion if it did so without discrimination.

When the Supreme Court made this decision in 1948, many thought it was a dangerous attempt to overrule the will of the American people, as expressed in the Bill of Rights, and a reversal of all previous American policy and action. In 1952 the Court declared that released-time for religious instruction

"Equal Justice under Law." This motto is carved over the portal of the Supreme Court
Building in Washington, D. C.

of public-school children was constitutional if the parents freely desired it, and if the instruction was
not given in public-school buildings.

Since the Supreme Court makes
the final decision on some very vital
problems which arise in the United
States, it is essential that only highly intelligent, honest men of sound
principles be appointed to this body.
**The New Deal and The Supreme
Court.** We have learned that some
of Franklin D. Roosevelt's New
Deal legislation was declared unconstitutional by the Supreme
Court. The President believed his
policies should be approved and, in
order to accomplish his purposes,

he advocated a change in the organization of this court. He wanted
it enlarged from the traditional nine
judges to fifteen judges. By this
means, he hoped to appoint men
who were more favorable to his
New Deal plans.

At the time of his reelection in
1936, President Roosevelt was fairly confident that his plan would not
be opposed. However, the Senate
voted against the change. It feared
that if this plan succeeded, the Supreme Court would thereafter be
dependent upon the will of the
President, thus forfeiting, or giving
up, the independence which the Supreme Court has always enjoyed.

3. The Government Improves Social Conditions

Social conditions are those conditions of living which arise because people depend upon one another. Unfortunately, there are some people who do not live in comfortable surroundings for one or another reason. Perhaps they are not paid a just wage. Do you remember what a just wage is? Perhaps they are not good managers of what they possess. The government has done valuable work in attempting to remedy unfair social conditions.

Reform needed in government positions. As far back as the days of Andrew Jackson, a vicious system, known as the Spoils System, existed in politics. Under this system, the party that won an election gave government jobs to those who aided in that election. Often important positions were given to dishonest or incapable men.

Many good citizens saw the injustice of this and demanded reform. The incident that brought the reform movement to a climax occurred in 1881. A half-crazed and disappointed office-seeker shot President Garfield when he was boarding a train in Washington, D. C. The President died several months later, and the Vice President, Chester A. Arthur, succeeded him. President Arthur was determined that he would abolish the Spoils System.

The Pendleton Act. In 1883, therefore, Congress passed the Pendleton Act. This act provided for a system of examinations to determine the fitness of an applicant for a government position. These examinations are known as *Civil Service Examinations.* The Pendleton Act also provided for a Civil Service Commission of three men who were to prepare the examinations. The law provided, finally, that no civil service employee would lose his job because he belonged to the party which was leaving office.

Civil service examinations are required today for many more public offices than formerly. This system, frequently called the *merit system,* is an aid in keeping American democracy alive, because unworthy and inefficient applicants will be less likely to find a place in government positions.

Public health—a matter of justice. We have just learned how the government took wise steps in reforming the manner of securing political positions. This reform was also extended to the field of public health.

As Catholics, we know that according to the law of God we are bound to care for our own health. It is a matter of justice for the government, too, to be concerned about the health of American citizens.

The passage of the Pure Food and Drug Act in 1906 was an important step in protecting the health of American citizens. Investigations made during the presidency of Theodore Roosevelt had brought a number of careless practices to light. Canning and baking companies were not always using proper methods in preparing foods. Meats were not thoroughly in-

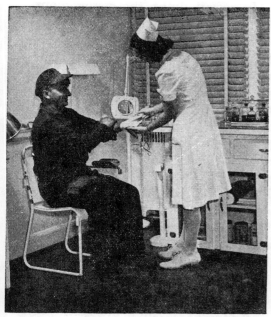

A Factory Dispensary

Workers use safety devices.

spected. This act of 1906 provided careful inspection by the government to make sure that harmful and unsanitary conditions would be abolished.

Care of health in industry. Public health is also a matter of concern in our complex system of manufacturing. Most of the large factories in the United States have their own doctors and nurses to care for any emergencies which might arise. Some industries have wards set aside in hospitals to handle cases which might need long treatment. Much machinery in modern factories is equipped with safety devices which lessen the possibility of injuries.

Unhealthful working conditions have decreased in most of our factories. But there are some types of occupations which in themselves are dangerous to the health of the worker. For example, a man may develop lung trouble from inhaling tiny metal scrapings; he may be exposed to skin diseases as result of working with certain chemicals. Throughout various states, laws have been passed to protect workers against these diseases, which are known as *occupational diseases*. It frequently happens that an entire industry is moved to a different section of the country where centers of population will not be exposed to injurious fumes from factories.

Public health services. Public health services are performed by all types of government — local, state, and federal. Health boards inspect restaurants, hotels, bakeries; they look into unhealthy living conditions in slums; and they check on epidemics and disease. Motor X-ray units examine employees in industrial plants and children in schools, to prevent the spread of tuberculosis. This service is often provided free by governmental or voluntary agencies. Such preventive services have greatly increased the general health of the nation. Inspection of water, cleaning of streets, and the disposal of garbage by local governments have also aided in controlling disease.

Better living conditions — better citizens. For many years little concern was shown for proper housing for American families. As the years passed, great slum districts arose in all large cities. There were no places in these districts where children could grow up in healthy surroundings. Tall, closely-built tenement houses deprived them of God's sunshine and air.

A modern housing project.
From Ewing Galloway, N. Y.

In recent times, the government has realized that such conditions were unhealthful and at times a violation of social justice. Projects for clearing away slum areas were begun in all large cities. As you travel through these cities, you will see many such housing projects.

You have already learned about subsistence homesteads, which were established during the New Deal. Do you recall what they were? President Roosevelt also attempted to improve housing conditions by establishing the Federal Housing Administration in the 1930's. Through this bureau, the national government assisted families to improve their old homes or to purchase low cost new ones.

The United States is a nation of families, and adequate housing is one of the requisites for keeping family life intact.

The Social Security Act. The Social Security Act, which President Roosevelt signed in 1935, was a measure designed to relieve the poverty caused by depressions and, at the same time, care for the aged of the United States.

According to this act, a tax is placed on the payrolls of employers and the salary of every employee. The money derived from this taxation is put into a fund to be used for old-age pensions. The amount each individual receives depends upon the number of years he contributed to the fund and upon the salary he received while working.

The Social Security Act also provides for unemployment insurance, which aids an employee who loses his job. If a state offers this type of insurance, the federal government repays about ninety per cent of this money to the state. By the year 1941, all states had both old-age pension and unemployment insurance laws.

Explain the meaning of

direct election of Senators	occupational diseases
"Lame Duck" Amendment	income tax
intemperance	woman suffrage
associate justices	repeal
Civil Service Examinations	Spoils System
	social security
	Chief Justices

Think before you answer

1. How did the amendments discussed in this Chapter add to "America's March of Progress"?
2. Why was the Seventeenth Amendment passed?
3. Discuss the justice of taxation.
4. Discuss the reactions of American citizens to the Eighteenth Amendment.
5. What instance mentioned in this Chapter shows the necessity for serious consideration before an appointment to the Supreme Court is made?
6. In what ways did the Pendleton Act promote just principles?
7. How did the government meet its obligations regarding the health and welfare of American citizens?

Fill the blanks

Choose a word or group of words from the following list to make each statement below correct.

Woman Suffrage	amendment
income tax	Pendleton Act
repeal	unemployment
nine	Bill of Rights
pension	twelve
Theodore Roosevelt	
Twentieth Amendment	
interpret the Constitution	
occupational disease	
Franklin D. Roosevelt	
Pure Food and Drug Act	
Eighteenth Amendment	

1. The only way the Federal Constitution may be changed is by passing an................
2. The part of the Constitution which defines the basic liberties to which all Americans are entitled is called the................
3. The Sixteenth Amendment gave Congress power to................
4. ....gave women the opportunity to vote.
5. The .... attempted to correct intemperance.
6. The passage of the Twenty-first Amendment is the only instance of the................of an amendment.
7. At the present time there are ....justices in the Supreme Court.
8. One of the important duties of the Supreme Court is to................
9. President .... tried to change the number of justices in the Supreme Court.
10. The appointment of incapable and dishonest men to government positions was checked by the.......
11. An................is the result of injurious working conditions found in certain types of industry.
12. The government has the right to inspect foods since the passage of the................
13. The Social Security Act provides for a................for the aged and................insurance.
14. The expression "Lame Duck" refers to the................

CHAPTER II

CULTURE AND SCIENCE CONTRIBUTE TO AMERICA'S PROGRESS

Introducing a new chapter. No story of a nation would be complete without mentioning something about its cultural achievements. Cultural achievements are those which result from learning. The teacher's effort to educate people, an author's or an artist's attempt to give them enjoyment, and the scientist's search for new ways of making life safer and more convenient are cultural achievements. All of these play a very important role in the progress of a nation.

We must be aware at all times, however, that without God's enlightenment, none of the things which make life fuller and richer can be attained. As a result, education, literature, art, and science should give glory to Him Who inspired human beings to expand these fields of learning.

The three points we shall study in this chapter are: (1) Education Strengthens Life in a Democracy, (2) The Fine Arts Flourish in the United States, and (3) Scientific Progress Advances American Prestige.

1. Education Strengthens Life in a Democracy

Our founding fathers knew that if the United States was to succeed as a democracy, people would have to be educated to decide wisely the questions and problems presented to them. They knew an ignorant people would be incapable of self-government. However, as the nineteenth century dawned, only the privileged class could acquire an education.

Reviewing early education. You probably recall from your previous study of history, that education for all the children of all the people did not begin in the United States until the middle of the nineteenth century. Since the days of Horace Mann, the "Father of the American Public School System," public education has progressed. Horace Mann established the first teacher-training school in this country. His work was not confined to his native state of Massachusetts but spread throughout all states of the Union.

Who controls the public schools? Each state exercises control over its own system of education. The Constitution does not grant the federal government any control of education except in the District of Columbia and our territories. There have been people who favor the establishment of a Department of Education, just as we have a Department of Commerce, or a Department of Labor. Others oppose this view.

From time to time, however, the government has passed laws which have been in the interests of education. Do you recall the name of the act which provided for the establishment of agricultural colleges? The government has been interested in adult education of immigrants, and has granted many opportunities for education to men who have served in our armed forces. The deplorable amount of illiteracy brought to light at the time of the First World War caused Uncle Sam to take more thorough means to improve our standards of education.

In spite of this, there is still a lack of suitable educational facilities, especially for Negroes and Indians. **Modern public school education.** Today the public school in the United States provides for the education of a child from the time he enters the kindergarten to young adulthood. Nearly every large community has its elementary, junior high and senior high schools. The *vocational school* has become popular in many cities in recent years. In schools of this type, students learn special trades which help them earn a living as adults. Trades

Students in a manual training school learn woodworking. Vocational Schools like this are important today. Can you tell why?

By Ewing Galloway, N. Y.

Education for GI's.

are important occupations in these days of highly mechanized industries.

After a student completes high school, it is possible for him to attend a *junior college,* which includes the first two years of college work, or a regular college, and finally the university.

An American school divorced from religion. From the beginning of the public school system, education was the concern of the individual states, and most Americans agreed that religion was necessary in school because it is the foundation of morality.

Very soon, however, a problem arose. Children of various Protestant denominations attended the public schools. Which religion was to be taught? When Catholic immigration began, the problem in-

creased. The Protestants did not want the Catholic religion to be taught to their children, any more than the Catholics wanted their children taught Protestantism. The solution finally arrived at was to limit state support to publicly controlled schools and also to exclude religion from public schools. This was not a good solution because there is no true education apart from religion.

Children in public schools are prepared for living in the world today. No provision is made, however, for the welfare of a child's soul. It is this very vital need that the Catholic schools supply, in addition to giving American children proper training for meeting the problems of everyday life.

Increase in college and university attendance. After the Second World War, which ended in 1945, the attendance at institutions of higher learning increased sharply. There were several reasons for this increase. *First,* college education was made available to ex-servicemen and women at government expense. *Second,* there was a period of prosperity following the war, which enabled people to further their education. *Third,* there are ever-increasing educational requirements for professions and business. College training is fast becoming as necessary today as high-school training was in the beginning of the twentieth century.

Prominent public school educators. The United States has had some outstanding public school authorities in the twentieth century. Dr. Nicholas Murray Butler organized Teachers College at Columbia University and was also responsible for the introduction of manual training into the public schools.

One of the outstanding educators of the twentieth century, Dr. Robert Hutchins, former President of the University of Chicago, expressed his belief that education must cultivate moral qualities as well as intellectual ability.

In public-school education, John Dewey has been considered one of its greatest men. However, John Dewey introduced some erroneous ideas into the public-school system. Like many other philosophers, or thinkers, of today, he depended too much on human reason and failed to consider the fact that there is a life hereafter towards which all human beings must strive.

The Church's stand on education. In previous chapters of this book, we have learned that the Church has always been active in social and economic guidance. The field of education is no exception. The Church is greatly interested in this particular activity because she looks to the youth of the world for the future. In 1929, Pope Pius XI wrote an outstanding encyclical, *On the Christian Education of Youth*. In this encyclical he set forth the Church's teaching on the basic principles of education. Among these principles are:

1. Parents have a right and duty to care for the education of their children.

2. The Church has a supernatural right to guide and control the education of her children.
3. The state has the right to demand that children be prepared to be worthy citizens.

A brief review of Catholic education. We have already learned that every parish in the United States was required, after the Third Plenary Council of Baltimore in 1884, to build a parochial school. Previous to that time, there were many parochial schools, but their number was greatly increased after the American hierarchy made this decision.

Each diocese has its own schools. They are centrally guided by a superintendent appointed by the bishop. Supervisors, who are usually members of Religious Communities teaching in the diocese, visit these schools and keep the superintendent and the school system closely connected.

The following numbers will give you an idea of the extent of our Catholic school system. Almost three million children are in Catholic elementary schools; the schools number almost 9,000. There are over 2,400 high schools and 233 colleges and universities for men and women. A faculty of 82,000 Sisters teaches in elementary and high schools. The faculties of our colleges consist of priests, Brothers, Sisters, and lay people.

Catholic institutions of higher learning. Most of our Catholic colleges and universities for men were established by the end of the nine-

An aerial view of the University of Notre Dame, a famous center of learning.

teenth century. Colleges for women began early in the twentieth century. The Jesuits have long been noted for their colleges and universities. Georgetown University in Washington, D. C., founded in 1789, is the oldest Catholic university in the United States. Some other Jesuit schools are Fordham, Loyola, Boston College, and Marquette.

Besides the Jesuits, there are other priests who devote their lives to teaching. Some of these are the Sulpicians, Franciscans, Augustinians, and Benedictines. Almost every American has heard of the University of Notre Dame, of football fame. This school in Indiana was founded by the Holy Cross Fathers in 1842. One secret of its success lies in the deep devotion of its students to Our Lady.

Near Notre Dame is situated St. Mary's College for Women, conducted by the Holy Cross Sisters. Other colleges established in the latter nineteenth century for women are Manhattanville College of the Sacred Heart in New York, Trinity College, Washington, D. C., and Seton Hall College in Pennsylvania. There are many other Catholic colleges for either men or women or both.

The Catholic University of America. At the same time the bishops of the United States were urging the formation of parish schools, they established a center for Catholic learning in this country. This is the Catholic University of America in Washington, D. C. Grouped about it are many houses of study, owned or operated by Religious Orders from various parts of the country.

The Catholic University is the pride and hope of the American Church. Three great men took an active part in its foundation. They are James Cardinal Gibbons, Bishop John Keane, and Bishop John Lancaster Spalding. If any one man can be called the founder, that man is Bishop Spalding because he was the most active in its establishment. **Catholic teacher training.** The training of Sisters and Brothers for the teaching of Catholic youth was formerly conducted by each individual Religious Community. Although this method is still followed in most instances, *diocesan teacher training institutions* have been established in some dioceses.

The first teacher training institution not under Community control was the Catholic Sisters' College established in 1911 in connection with the Catholic University. The man responsible for the development of this college was Dr. Thomas Shields. His work as an educator marked a turning point in the development of Catholic schools. As we have learned, state

Modern buildings on the campus of Georgetown, the oldest Catholic university in the U. S., founded in 1789, by Archbishop Carroll. *By Ewing Galloway, N. Y.*

Two Catholic leaders in Education. Top: Archbishop McNicholas. Bottom: Monsignor George Johnson.

control of public schools soon resulted in the elimination of religion from the classroom. Dr. Shields feared that this *secularism,* or disregard of religion, might even come into Catholic schools by way of textbooks. He insisted that textbooks used in Catholic schools be based on sound Catholic principles.

In 1950, the Catholic University took over Catholic Sisters College which ceased to exist as a separate institution for granting degrees.

The National Catholic Educational Association was formed in 1904 to unite all Catholic educators and to encourage and safeguard Catholic educational interests in the United States.

The Commission on American Citizenship. The formation of the Commission on American Citizenship is another example of the Church's interest in education. One of the aims of the Catholic school is to form good citizens for our country. Pope Pius XI was deeply interested in Catholic education. He appealed to the Catholic hierarchy of the world to organize a program of Catholic social action, which would help children develop into good citizens. The American hierarchy rallied to his appeal and, in 1938, asked the Catholic University to prepare a program designed to "make men respect their own rights and the rights of their fellow-citizens."

In order to carry out this program, the Catholic University organized the Commission on American Citizenship. This commission has worked diligently to improve the curriculum and text books of Catholic schools.

Noted Catholic educators of the twentieth century. Pope Pius XI said that "education consists essentially in preparing man for what he must *be* and for what he must *do* here below, in order to attain the sublime end for which he was created." All Catholic educators have this aim in view.

You have already read about the work of Dr. Shields. Outstanding among the Catholic educators was Archbishop John McNicholas of Cincinnati, President of the N.C.E.A. for many years until he died in 1950. Monsignor George Johnson, for many years connected with the Catholic University, also did excellent work as director of the Department of Education of the National Catholic Welfare Conference.

Catholic education is a monument, not only to those men who have gained national reputations as leaders in education but also to the many holy women who labored in the cause of education in the United States.

2. The Fine Arts Flourish in the United States

The fine arts which we shall consider in this section are literature, art, and music. They add beauty and enjoyment to men's lives.

What twentieth-century America reads. Since very early days in our country, the newspaper has been a powerful means of influencing public opinion. In the twentieth cen-

tury, the majority of people obtain much information from newspapers and magazines. Most American homes have at least one newspaper; for us, as Catholics, there should be two—a good daily paper and the Catholic diocesan paper.

A newsman gathers news. There could be no newspapers unless men were willing to collect the news. You are familiar with these individuals whom we call press reporters. The work of the newsgatherer is frequently very dangerous and difficult. As soon as a fire occurs, an airplane crashes, or a tornado sweeps a section of the country, the newspaperman braves the danger and gets information for his paper.

Since news is important to people living in a democracy, it is necessary that it be true. If American citizens are to vote intelligently and do their part in the social and political life of their country, essential facts must be available to them.

Press services. In the nineteenth century, some of the large newspapers in the United States began sending their reporters to various parts of the country to gather important news. In 1848, a news-gathering agency, called the *Associated Press,* was organized in New York City. The reporters collected the news items and this agency dispatched them to member papers throughout the United States. Later, other agencies, such as the *United Press* and the *International News Service,* were founded. Through these agencies and

Newspaper reporters covering a story

through the use of the telephone, telegraph, and later the radio, our newspapers are able to print news and pictures of events almost as soon as they have happened. No place in the world is too far distant for the news reporter to go.

Freedom of the Press. One of the freedoms guaranteed by the First Amendment of the Constitution is "freedom of the press." This means that anyone is free to express honest opinions in printed form. Sometimes this freedom is abused and false news, or slanted news, is printed by certain individuals or organizations to accomplish selfish ends. Such news is termed *propaganda*. Propaganda is common today, especially in those countries which are governed by dictators, who take every means to control what is printed in papers and magazines. Propaganda, in this sense, violates the virtue of truth and is, therefore, contrary to Christian principles. Perhaps you are wondering how it is possible, then, to decide what is true and what is not. One dependable way is to read Catholic newspapers and periodicals.

Early history of the Catholic press. The beginnings of the American Catholic press date back to colonial days—before George Washington became President. During those days, the main purpose of a Catholic press was to defend Catholicism from the vicious attacks upon it.

Between 1840 and 1850, the Catholic press grew rapidly. With the coming of the Civil War, however, no new Catholic papers were started, and some of those already being published failed for lack of support. Immediately after the war, there was renewed enthusiasm for providing Catholic news. In about a twenty-year period, 120 Catholic newspapers and forty Catholic magazines made their appearance, some of which are still being published.

Twentieth-century progress of the Catholic press. In the early twentieth century, the Catholic press developed rapidly, due in large measure to the *N.C.W.C. News Service,* established in 1919 as a department of the National Catholic Welfare Conference. This is the only religious news service which has had the privilege of admission to the press galleries of Congress and the White House press conference.

Catholic newspapers. Two strong Catholic newspaper chains developed in the twentieth century. One is the *Register,* which began as a system in 1929. By midcentury, this chain had spread to thirty-two dioceses, and in less than twenty years had a circulation of more than 800,000 papers. The other important system is that of *Our Sunday Visitor.* This chain reports a circulation of over 700,000 in national and diocesan editions.

The Catholic press still lacks, however, a vigorous Catholic *daily* paper in the English language. There are four daily papers pub-

lished in foreign languages, however, which do much to advance the cause of Catholicism in America.

Catholic magazines. *America* and *Commonweal* are weekly publications. These two magazines have always been written in a rather serious style.

The Catholic World, the *Sign,* the *Ave Maria,* the *Messenger* of *the Sacred Heart* and the *Catholic Digest* are monthly magazines, at least one of which should be found in every Catholic home. The last has been edited in nine languages, and there is even a Braille (brail) edition for the blind.

There is no better way in which to learn the truth of what is happening in the world today than by reading the Catholic press. You have a wide selection to choose from because there are nearly 145 week-

A book printed in Braille.
By Ewing Galloway, N. Y.

ly and over 400 monthly newspapers and magazines.

Religious best sellers. The term "best-seller" in connection with books is, no doubt, a part of your vocabulary. In the past few years, many Catholic books have made the best-seller list.

Whether or not the American people were hungry for the basic truths of religion, the fact remains that, in the years between the First and the Second World Wars, and particularly since World War II, Catholics and non-Catholics bought and read more religious books than ever before.

Some American authors of note. Freedom of the press has enabled American authors to criticize anybody and anything, sometimes more than the law of God permits. After the First World War, there was a

Joyce Kilmer

Brown Brothers

trend to write critical novels, that is, stories in which authors criticized the shortcomings of America or the social ills of the day. One of the most famous of such critical novels was *Main Street*, written by Sinclair Lewis. The popularity of historical novels increased also. A historical novel attempts to make past history live again in the minds of the readers.

One of the prominent women writers of America is Willa Cather, who has recorded the lives of the immigrant pioneers in the Middle West. Carl Sandburg has won fame not only as a poet, but as the biographer of Lincoln. Edna Saint Vincent Millay and Robert Frost are two outstanding poets of the twentieth century.

As Catholics, we can be justly proud both of the heroism and the noble thoughts of the soldier-poet, Joyce Kilmer, a convert to Catholicism. Kilmer found inspiration for many of his poems in the doctrines of the Church. His joy in living and his respect for humanity are expressed in a quotation from a postcard, which he wrote from France while he served in the First World War. It reads: "Nice war, nice people, nice country, nice everything." Joyce Kilmer was a man who saw beauty in all of God's creation. While the poem *Trees* is not his greatest, it is his most loved. It has even been set to music. The life of this promising young poet was brought to an end when he was killed in action.

In the field of serious religious

Bishop Fulton J. Sheen

books, an outstanding twentieth-century author is Bishop Fulton J. Sheen. His works have inspired many Catholics as well as non-Catholics.

Book clubs. Reading in the twentieth century has been promoted to a great extent by the organization of book clubs. Many Americans belong to the Book-of-the-Month Club, which mails to its members the book that has been judged the "best" for the month. It frequently happens that some of these books violate principles which Catholics and sincere Christians cherish.

In order to procure good books, many Catholics have joined Catholic book clubs. Some of these clubs are the *Catholic Book Club*, the *Spiritual Book Associates*, and the *Catholic Literary Foundation*. There is also a *Catholic Children's Book Club*, which aims to put into the hands of young readers books that will both interest them and influence them for good.

By belonging to such clubs, a person can build a good Catholic library right in his own home.

As you grow older, you should guide your reading by consulting Catholic book reviews, which are printed in Catholic magazines.

American architecture. Architecture also has contributed to American culture and progress. Up to the twentieth century, Americans were chiefly imitators of European styles in architecture. Public buildings followed the Greek and Roman style. Then appeared the most important contribution of America to the art of building—the skyscraper.

The idea of the skyscraper occurred to Louis Sullivan, a native of Boston, who carried his plan to completion late in the nineteenth century. Sullivan declared that the style of buildings should change according to the needs of the time. He became convinced that the congested living conditions, the increasing amount of industrial activity, and an ever-growing population pointed towards the advisability of tall buildings. The fact that America had the tools and the valuable natural resources needed to erect such buildings has given the large cities of the United States the interesting skylines which they possess.

The homes which have been erected in the modern United States follow the principle of convenience as well as that of beauty. While public buildings grew taller, residences took the opposite direction. The old-fashioned large house has given place to the one-story rambling home, beautiful in its simplicity, and characteristic of modern American life.

There are two things which have made modern buildings possible—structural steel and reinforced concrete. In former days, these items were not available to builders, with the result that homes and public buildings were limited in size and height. The use of these products has also decreased the costs of "building," since even complicated designs can be executed swiftly and accurately.

We should remember that without these two important items modern structures like the Empire State Building could not be constructed.

Structural steel and concrete are tributes to American invention and production.

The art of sculpture. As in the realm of architecture, so in the field of sculpture, American artists have created many beautiful objects. By the beginning of the twentieth century, a distinctly national type of statuary had developed. Public parks throughout the United States have been beautified by hundreds of statues carved by Americans.

One of the American sculptors of the twentieth century was Gutzon Borglum, a Catholic of Danish ancestry. On one of the cliffs of the Black Hills in South Dakota he carved the features of Washington, Jefferson, Lincoln, and Theodore

By Ewing Galloway, N. Y.
The Empire State Building, N. Y.

Roosevelt. The original plans of Borglum included a huge tablet, 80 feet by 120 feet in size, on which would be carved a history of the United States from 1776 to the completion of the Panama Canal. These plans are being carried out by Borglum's son who, like himself, is a sculptor.

A great monument to the American spirit. Mount Rushmore National Memorial in the Black Hills of South Dakota, the work of the American sculptor Gutzon Borglum.

Gutzon Borglum did not intend this project to be a monument to the individual men whose features appear in the rock of Mount Rushmore. It was rather a monument to the spirit of the United States government as exemplified by those men.

Other well-known sculptors are Daniel Chester French and Augustus St. Gaudens.

American painting. American art has developed steadily throughout our history. Early American artists were influenced by European art but, as time passed, they learned that they must paint the life they knew if they would be truly American. After World War I the American artist began to turn more to the fields, the factories and the cities for his subject matter. This made the American people more interested in art because the subjects were familiar to them—something they knew and loved.

No doubt, you have seen churches, libraries or other public buildings with large pictures painted on the walls. This type of art is called *mural painting*. It is not new, having been done in a crude form by the cave men on the walls of their caves. Mural painting, today, has reached a high point of progress and has beautified the walls of many modern public buildings.

Poster painting. The American

By Ewing Galloway, N. Y.

A modern mural. This huge painting depicts the state history of Tennessee.

poster is used for advertising purposes. This type of illustration had its beginnings in theatrical and circus advertising late in the nineteenth century. Not until 1923, however, did a real study of this type of commercial art begin. It is called "commercial art" because its purpose is not merely to be enjoyed for its own sake, but to help to sell a commercial product. This type of art has come to occupy a place of primary importance in American advertising and wields a strong influence in determining the buying habits of the public.

Music in America. Until not so very long ago, it was fashionable to make a remark like the following in regard to music: "Yes, we have our Stephen Fosters, MacDowells, and Thomases, but have we ever produced a Bach or a Beethoven?" The latter two men were European geniuses in music, and people wondered when America would produce such men. This type of criticism has become rarer in more recent years because American interest in music has grown by leaps and bounds. American music has been enriched by folk music, symphonic compositions, patriotic songs, and Negro spirituals. All are a part of America's exciting coming-of-age as a nation in the musical world.

Twentieth-century America can boast of many conservatories or

A symphony orchestra. There are orchestras like this in many of our American cities.
Can you identify any of the instruments?

schools of music, and choral groups. Nearly every large city has a symphony orchestra; there are about one hundred sixty in all. There was even a symphony orchestra for children which was started by Walter Damrosch in New York City. There are also about thirty-seven opera companies in the United States, the best-known being the Metropolitan Opera Company of New York. Theatres, radio, and television have all played important roles in bringing the best in classical as well as popular music to the widest audience.

A typical form of American dance music is that known as jazz. It became prominent early in the twentieth century. Jazz musicians usually did not follow any written music, but made up their own harmony and variations as the mood struck them. Jazz grew out of Negro spirituals of the South. It was not long before it spread all over the world.

American composers. Although American composers have not reached the heights of European composers, they have produced some fine music. The first popular and American opera is *Porgy and Bess,* composed by George Gershwin. Gershwin believed that jazz and classical music could be combined if done skilfully. Consequently, *Porgy and Bess* is a clever combination of the two types of music. Gershwin's *Rhapsody in Blue* made him the leading composer of jazz in the twentieth century.

Probably the most outstanding American composer of opera today is Gian-Carlo Menotti. His operas, *The Medium* and *The Telephone,* have received wide acclaim. He is also the first to compose an opera for television, *Amahl and the Night Visitors,* which made its first appearance in 1951.

The American people have shown great interest in the operetta, which is a form of light opera. Victor Herbert holds a supreme place as the composer of light opera in the United States. Some operettas, like *The Student Prince,* by Sigmund Romberg, have played as many as 600 performances in succession in one theatre.

Music and the theatre. The American theatrical world has captured music and made it lovable for the common people. Operettas have not only been performed on the stage, but have had extraordinary success as motion pictures. The motion picture industry can improve on the operetta because of the fact that many more beautiful and artistic scenes can be employed than would be possible on a stage.

Catholic contribution to music. American Catholics have contributed a great deal to their country's cultural development in music. There have been many Catholic instrumentalists and singers. There are also some Catholic composers of note, among whom may be mentioned Paul Creston, whose symphonies have been performed by the leading American and foreign orchestras.

It is also of interest that the first American city to have an opera house was Catholic New Orleans.

An outstanding church choir is the Paulist Choir in New York. This choir was begun by Father William J. Finn, C.S.P., in Chicago, in 1904. The previous year, Pope Pius X had issued his famous encyclical on church music, urging that Gregorian Chant be sung in churches. While this is the official music of the Church, it had been too frequently replaced by a less appropriate and less spiritual kind of music in the United States and elsewhere. Father Finn organized his Paulist Choristers in order to comply with the Pope's wish to make this beautiful music known to Americans.

Father William J. Finn, C.S.P., founder of the Paulist Choristers, directs his choir on a Catholic Hour broadcast.

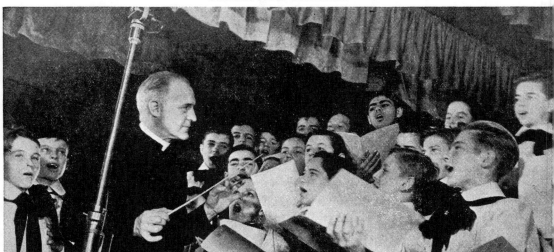

The example of Father Finn led to the formation of the Pius X School of Liturgical Music in New York City. The purpose of this school is to educate Catholics in *liturgical music,* that is, the music of the Church, so they might appreciate it and, by singing it, participate in the services of the Church.

Gifts of other lands to American life and culture. America is indebted to other countries for many benefits enjoyed by her people today. We Americans speak English rather than another language, because of the predominence of English-speaking people among those who came early to our shores.

Our earliest colleges were patterned after those in England. Our ideals of law and government always resembled those held by the English. We adapted their idea of common law to suit our own needs.

The influence of the Spanish is seen most clearly in our Southwest. We have taken as our own many words from their language, which reflect Spanish culture. Among these are *adobe, broncho, rodeo, tango,* and *barbecue.*

French influence is to be seen in the architecture of the Capitol building in Washington. Many American artists have learned from French teachers abroad how to improve their techniques.

German musicians have provided much beautiful music. Their educators have contributed to our educational system, and their scientists have given much to daily living.

Many other immigrant groups, among them the Italians, Swedes, Poles, Dutch, and Bohemians, have also enriched American life and culture.

3. Scientific Progress Advances American Prestige

In this chapter, we have been attempting to find out what has caused America to become great. In addition to what we have already studied, the progress made in the realm of science and invention has been so outstanding that the United States has earned a place among the leading scientific nations of the world.

Man flies at last! Although men had long attempted to build a machine which would travel in the air,

The Wright Brothers first flight at Kitty Hawk, North Carolina. Orville is prone in the plane; Wilbur is running alongside.

Brown Brothers

The "Spirit of St. Louis" and Col. Lindbergh, just before the history-making flight over the Atlantic.

it was not until 1903 that the first successful flight was made. Wilbur and Orville Wright were bicycle manufactures in Dayton, Ohio. Like a number of other people who had been interested in air travel, they experimented with various kinds of machines. Where others had failed, these brothers succeeded. They flew the first heavier-than-air machine in history over the sand hills of Kitty Hawk, North Carolina. The first flight of the Wright brothers lasted for only a period of seconds. But this was the beginning of an achievement which has changed the customs of the entire world.

Progress in aviation. Orville Wright lived until 1948. During his lifetime, he saw the airplane develop from doubtful beginnings to unimagined success. Up to the year 1914, when the First World War broke out, the airplane was still considered by many a novelty. It was during this war, however, that every nation set its engineers to work to improve aircraft. In fact, air supremacy became an important element of the war.

The United States government enacted the first federal legislation for aviation in 1926, when it passed the Air Commerce Act. This act established a Bureau of Air Commerce and charged it with the duties of licensing pilots, making flying safe, mapping airways, and furnishing flight information. Throughout the United States today, giant airline companies render valuable service to American citizens.

Famous American flights. The

United States did not really become "air-conscious" until Charles A. Lindbergh made his non-stop solo flight from New York to Paris in 1927. Lindbergh was not the first to fly across the Atlantic Ocean, but his flight was sensational because it was the first solo flight over such a large body of water.

Lindbergh climbed into his plane, the *Spirit of St. Louis*, on May 20, 1927, and covered a distance of 3600 miles in a little over thirty-three hours. Today, a passenger plane can cover this same distance in about nine hours. Lindbergh's feat began a series of flights which resulted in the beginnings of nation-wide and, later, international air-routes for passengers and mail.

Lieutenant Richard E. Byrd of the United States Navy made two remarkable flights. In 1926, he flew over the icy waters of the North Pole, and in 1929, with a group of scientists, he went to the South Pole. Byrd and his party spent two years exploring the land.

Life in an air age. The airplane has so changed ways of living that the second quarter of the twentieth century has been spoken of as the "air age." Today, commercial airways have been established throughout the world, just as railroad lines and good roads have been built. Regular service for both passenger and freight can be obtained twenty-four hours a day.

One safety device is *radar*, which was developed during the Second World War. Radar helps pilots see through fog, storms, and smoke, and gives warning of unseen moun-

A modern passenger plane. Aviation has come a long way since the days of the Wright Brothers.

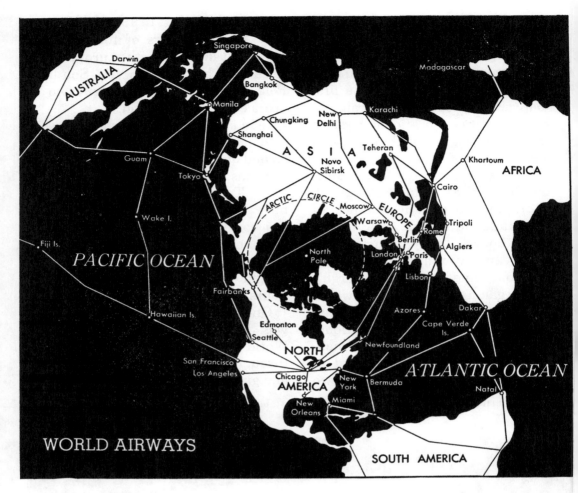

WORLD AIRWAYS

tains or obstacles ahead. Huge beacon lights also guide the aviator on night trips.

Air-mail has become an almost necessary type of postal service, especially between far-distant cities. Travel by air has become less expensive than formerly, thereby enabling the general public to use this form of transportation. Continents are no longer separated by days of ocean travel, but are drawn together by a matter of a few hours' journey. Since the people of the world are in closer association be-

cause of the airplane, it is important that all nations understand and generously cooperate with each other in order to fulfill their obligations of justice and charity towards one another.

Science for destruction? Unfortunately, as in the case of many inventions, the airplane was almost at once put to destructive uses. Modern science has developed hundreds of mechanical weapons which have made it nearly impossible for civilians to escape the horrors and suffering caused by war. While the airplane has contributed notably to the progress and convenience of the world, its military use has hung like a pall of fear over many countries.

The justice of war and the use of bombs will be discussed in a later chapter. But the Church's view of science must be mentioned at this time. This view was expressed by the Vatican Council as follows:

> The Church . . . far from hindering the pursuit of the . . . sciences, fosters and promotes them in many ways. For she is neither ignorant nor unappreciative of the many advantages which flow from them to mankind. On the contrary, she admits that just as they come from God . . . if rightly used, with the help of His grace they lead to God.

The Church, then, desires that science be developed for the good of mankind. But when scientists fall into the error of opposing divine doctrine and truth, the Church must condemn their ideas for having overstepped their proper limits.

Progress in other forms of transportation. We have learned something about the most modern means of transportation, the airplane. From experience, we know that everyone does not travel by airplane. The most common form of transportation is the automobile. You recall from Unit Two that the automobile was popularized and made available to the general public by Henry Ford. In its fifty years of existence, the automobile has made a great contribution to the progress of the United States.

By making it possible for people to enjoy the pleasant surroundings of a home on the outskirts of a city, and drive back and forth from their homes to work, the automobile has caused the growth of suburban areas. The automobile has also changed the lives of the farmers. Trucks solve many problems of the transportation of farm produce. But one of the greatest benefits the automobile has brought to the farmer is the possibility of a better education. In bygone years, if children had to walk many miles to a school, they frequently did not receive an education. This has been changed because school buses daily set out from consolidated schools to gather children from neighboring districts.

The automobile, the airplane, and streamlined trains which speed across the country have all made it

A streamlined train
Bettmann Archive

Marconi in his laboratory

other countries, such as England and Newfoundland. Many scientists took up Marconi's invention and tried to perfect it in their own countries. In the United States, the most important single figure in radio was Lee de Forest, the inventor of the vacuum tube which has made modern radio and television sets possible.

The first radio station in the United States, KDKA, was set up in East Pittsburgh by the Westinghouse Company in 1920. In that year, the returns of the presidential election were broadcast over radio. Radio had at last come of age as a means of communication. From that time on, radio developed rapidly. Networks of radio stations, such as the National Broadcasting Company, the American Broadcasting Company, the Mutual Broad-

possible for Americans to become acquainted with various parts of their native land. This tends to broaden people's interests and gives them a better understanding of this Land of Our Lady.

The miracle of radio. In the preceding paragraphs we have learned how constant improvements in ways of travel helped the United States to conquer distance. The twentieth century has seen just as important improvements in ways of communication as in means of travel. One of the chief means of communication is the radio.

The radio has developed from another invention known as the wireless telegraph, which was invented by Guglielmo Marconi (gool-yel′-moe mar-koe′-nee) in 1896. Marconi was born in Italy, but did a great deal of his experimenting in

An early crystal-set radio

By Ewing Galloway, N. Y.

A radio broadcast. This studio in Radio City, New York, seats 1200 persons. The control room is at the left.

casting Company, and the Columbia Broadcasting Company came into existence.

Uses of the radio. The radio, although few Americans realized it, was destined to equal, if not surpass, the printing press in importance. The radio became a dispenser of knowledge, culture, and information, as well as an instrument for spreading propaganda. Do you recall what "propaganda" is? In the United States, freedom of speech has guaranteed everyone the right to impart ideas, and the radio, like the printed page, is, therefore, a means of communication which can be used either for good or evil.

The messages which come through radio can reach millions of people, and it is important that only true information be broadcast. In many countries, especially those which are ruled by dictators, the people, unfortunately, do not hear the truth. In America, the people must ever be on their guard that no twisted or partly true information is imparted by radio. Such violation of truth would be harmful to our democratic way of life.

There are almost 99,000,000 radios in use in 41,600,000 American homes. People, today, can hear political or religious speeches, fine music, and all kinds of entertaining programs simply by turning a dial. Nearly every home, office, school, and hospital in the country has a radio today. Many automobiles are equipped with them. Ships at sea, and airplanes in flight depend upon the radio in case of any emergency. The ends of the world have been brought into almost instant communication with one another by the marvel we call radio.

Television. Swift progress marked radio's development. By 1924, the first photographs were transmitted across the Atlantic Ocean by radio. Since then, inventors have been

A television studio

producing television sets, through which programs can be seen as well as heard.

Television became a commercial industry in July, 1941. The first commercial television station was set up atop the Empire State Building in New York City by the National Broadcasting Company. At first, progress was slow and was interrupted temporarily because of the Second World War. Regular television programs were resumed in 1944. After the war, television became one of the fastest growing industries in the United States. The number of television sets in the United States in 1949 reached, in round numbers, 3,250,000. The number is now about 15,000,000. On June 25, 1951, color television made its formal bow in the United States. An hour-long program, which originated in New York City, was broadcast by the Columbia Broadcasting System.

The motion picture industry. Another brain-child of twentieth century inventors is the motion picture. In 1903, the Edison Laboratories at West Orange, N. J., produced "The Great Train Robbery," the first picture which really had a plot. From that time on, the motion picture industry flourished in the United States. It has made such rapid strides that it ranks among the largest industries in the country. The first pictures were black-and-white, and the words spoken by the actors were flashed on the screen for the audience to read. Later, sound and color were added, thereby making an interesting form of amusement doubly attractive.

The motion picture has a great influence in spreading ideas in America. Approximately 100,000,-000 Americans attend motion pictures each week. Because of this large attendance and the effect which motion pictures were bound to have on the thinking of old and young Americans, the bishops of the United States organized the National Legion of Decency. This movement has accomplished valuable work in fostering the production of decent pictures which will give Americans a true sense of values.

Besides furnishing amusement for millions of Americans, motion pictures have tremendous educational value. By combining sight, sound, and color, the "talkies" of today convey ideas, whether entertaining or educational, with very little effort on the part of an audience. These ideas make a lasting impression either for good or evil. **The Pope speaks about movies.** Pope Pius XI wrote an encyclical on motion picture entertainment in 1936. In this encyclical, he stated that it is the obligation of Catholics who hold key positions in this industry to use their influence for the promotion of principles of sound morality. He also emphasized the fact that it is especially during times of recreation that it is necessary to safeguard the morals of men. Catholics who are fearless in their efforts to keep movies clean win the approval and cooperation of all right-thinking men, whether Catholic or non-Catholic. They can direct the motion picture into paths which promote the highest ideals and the truest standards of living. **Medical progress.** For a nation to progress, its citizens must be healthy enough to accomplish the things which tend towards progress. Since the middle of the nineteenth century, the results of medical research in the United States have been most important.

Twentieth-century America has seen remarkable developments in the use of antiseptics which prevent infection. Each year, scientists discover more about the germs which cause disease. Modern "wonder-drugs" have been discovered for the conquering of bacteria. Some of these drugs are the sulfa drugs, penicillin, and aureomycin (aw-ree-o-my′-sin). Although some of these drugs were first discovered in other countries, the United States succeeded in attaining large-scale production of them through the tireless efforts of our scientists.

X-ray, which was invented by a German scientist, was first discovered to be valuable in killing germs by Dr. William Coolidge, an American, in 1913. Since that time, a type of X-ray treatment has been used for treating cancer. The X-ray has proved a definite aid in America's progress because through it many diseases which frequently cause death can be quickly detected and treated.

Often on the field of battle, daring feats of surgery have been attempted which would not have been risked in other situations. Out of these risks have come new ideas. One such idea is the use of blood plasma. Blood transfusions had for a long time been administered in hospitals, but the use of plasma was a more convenient way to supply lost blood on the battlefield. It saved many lives.

New household conveniences. Fifty years ago, the interior of a house presented quite a different appearance than it does today. The man who deserves a great deal of credit for transforming the home and the routine of household duties is Thomas A. Edison. Through his efforts electricity began to play a very important part in American homes. The electric light not only provided convenient illumination but it paved the way for the application of electricity to many house-

By Ewing Galloway, N. Y.
A modern kitchen

hold utensils. Electricity makes toast and coffee for our breakfasts, washes and irons clothes quickly and easily, preserves food in refrigerators, and keeps our homes clean by means of vacuum cleaners.

Edison's electric filament bulb met a competitor in the fluorescent (floo-o-res'-ent) light. These lights have become popular in schools, public buildings, stores, and theatres, and even in many of the newer homes.

Automatic devices have made heating an easy problem in American homes, and air conditioning keeps modern homes and buildings comfortable.

Chemistry makes fabrics. Years ago, the finest material which ladies could buy was silk. Because of its expense, scientists began experimenting to see whether or not a cheaper material, similar to silk, could be made. The first substitute for silk was rayon. It was made from either wood pulp or cotton pulp. Then followed a finer type of silky material known as nylon. Nylon was developed by the Du Pont Company.

Nylon is made of by-products of coal, combined with water and air under a certain amount of heat and pressure. This material is woven into fabrics and used for clothing. It has also been used for bristles in tooth-brushes and for tennis-racket strings. Nylon is stronger than silk, wool, cotton, or rayon, and will not burn under normal pressing heat. When a flame strikes it, it does not blaze, but melts!

The world of plastics. You have seen plastic umbrella handles, plastic lamp bases, plastic combs, and

Plastics have many uses
By Ewing Galloway, N. Y.

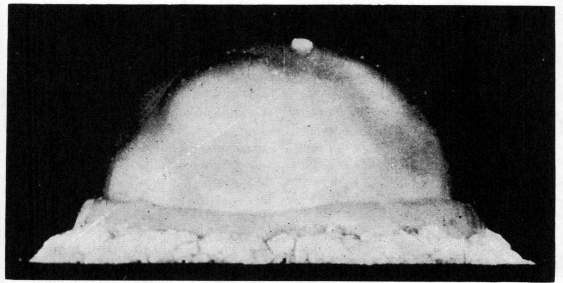

A world-shaking event in more ways than one. The first test of the atomic bomb in the New Mexico desert.

plastic steering wheels in automobiles. Plastics have a multitude of uses. The entire plastic industry began in Albany, New York, as long ago as 1868, with a billiard ball! Up to this time, billiard balls had been made of ivory, which was very expensive. John Wesley Wyatt of Albany discovered that he could make a material resembling ivory from cotton. This material he called *cellulose*. From cellulose, John Wyatt developed another material which he named celluloid. In his estimation, this was just the right substitute for the ivory billiard ball!

The celluloid industry flourished, and in 1872 the Celluloid Corporation was founded. From this time on, thousands of uses for celluloid were discovered. It played a vital part in the development of photography, motion pictures, and X-ray films.

As experiments continued, a form of hard rubber was obtained from celluloid, which eventually gave way to the modern plastic.

Atomic energy. One of the greatest scientific achievements of the twentieth century was the development and use of atomic energy or power. Do you know what an "atom" is? Most people say that it is a very small particle of matter—so small that it cannot be seen except through a powerful miscroscope. That is true, and yet scientists have proved that it is possible to break an atom up into even smaller parts. The sudden breaking up or shattering of the atom is called *atomic fission*. It is this principle which is the basis for the production of the destructive atomic bomb.

The Atom Bomb and the H-Bomb. When the United States was drawn into World War II, many facts regarding the making of an atomic bomb were already known to scientists throughout the world. Immediately after the Pearl Harbor disaster, the United States government took complete control of the development of atomic energy in this country as a possible means of defense. At last an atomic bomb was made. In the summer of 1945, the first experimental bomb was successfully exploded in New Mexico. It is said that the explosion was so violent that it knocked down men at the control center six miles away.

In November, 1952, news that the United States had exploded the new and more powerful H-bomb, or hydrogen bomb, was given to the world.

Controlling atomic energy. It was easily seen that atomic weapons could be a means of endangering the civilization of the entire world, if not controlled. Consequently, in 1946, Congress passed the Atomic Energy Act, which gave the control of all atomic energy activities to an Atomic Energy Commission consisting of five men. This act charged the Commission with promoting the use of atomic energy for peaceful ends.

Peacetime uses of atomic energy. Probably the first peacetime use of atomic energy was the development of a type of fuel that could be used in regions which are isolated from sources of coal or water power.

Atomic energy also aids scientific research. Frequently certain scientific projects require extremely high temperatures. Higher temperatures can be reached by using atomic energy than by using any other types of fuel. In the field of medicine, atomic energy has been a means of locating brain tumors with extreme accuracy.

A dangerous attitude towards science. You have learned a very small part of the wonderful progress science has made in the past fifty years. The work accomplished by American scientists has equalled, if not excelled, that of the scientists of any other country. But there is one danger which all scientists must avoid. This danger lies in the fact that there is a trend to be too much concerned with material things.

Some words and phrases to remember

cultural achievements
vocational schools   operetta
secularism   liturgical music
propaganda   radar
journalism   bacteria
historical novel   blood plasma
mural painting   atomic fission

How well can you answer these questions?

1. Explain how religion has been gradually excluded from public schools.
2. Name some of the educational opportunities an American has.
3. What caused an increase in higher education after the Second World War?
4. What other Catholic universities can you name besides those mentioned in this chapter?
5. What important contribution to education did each of the following men make:
Horace Mann

Dr. Nicholas Murray Butler
Dr. Thomas Shields
Bishop John Lancaster Spalding

6. Name the encyclical which states the Church's views toward education. Which Pope wrote this encyclical? What important points from this encyclical should you remember?

7. In what ways do Americans get information? How important is the work of the news reporter? In discussing these questions be sure to mention the terms "propaganda" and "freedom of press."

8. What organizations have promoted the wide reading habits of the American public? As you grow older, to which one would you wish to belong?

9. For what reasons did Gutzon Borglum select the features of Washington, Jefferson, Lincoln, and Theodore Roosevelt for his monument on Mount Rushmore?

10. How would you defend this statement: "The United States has become music-conscious in the past fifty years?"

11. Explain how each of the following inventions has affected American ways of living: airplane, radio, automobile, movies.

12. What did Pope Pius XI say in regard to motion pictures?

13. How have recent medical discoveries aided American progress?

14. What danger often lies hidden in the field of science?

Meet this challenge

From the list of words below, choose the one which correctly fills the blanks in the sentences which follow:

Georgetown University
Bishop John Lancaster Spalding
Dr. Thomas Shields
Monsignor George Johnson
Charles Lindbergh

Pope Pius XI	skyscraper
Book Clubs	mural painting
atomic energy	Richard Byrd
Joyce Kilmer	Walter Damrosch
sulfa, penicillin,	X-ray
aureomycin	nylon

KDKA manual training
blood plasma radar
Victor Herbert Sinclair Lewis
Gutzon Borglum book clubs
George Gershwin
John Wesley Wyatt
Guglielmo Marconi
Father William Finn
Thomas A. Edison
Edison Laboratories
Wilbur and Orville Wright

1. ....did outstanding work on the Commission of American Citizenship.

2. The first radio station in the United States was.............in East Pittsburgh.

3. The critical novel, *Main Street,* was written by..............

4. .... discovered during World War II is valuable in supplying blood on the battlefields.

5. The Du Pont Company has produced............a material which is stronger than silk, wool, or cotton.

6. The experiments of............led to the ever-growing plastic industry.

7. ....has proved to be a great help in the treatment of cancer.

8. ....have been called "wonder-drugs" because of their success in killing bacteria.

9. ....more than any man can be called the founder of the Catholic University of America.

10. The oldest Catholic university in the United States is........................... .

11. *Trees* is the best-loved poem written by the soldier-poet.............

12. ....made the first solo flight across the Atlantic Ocean in 1927.

13. The most noted composer of light opera in the United States was ....

14. An Italian named............................... invented radio.

15. The first motion picture with a plot was produced in 1903 by ....

16. The greatest original contribution to American architecture was the..........................., a product of the mind of Louis Sullivan.

17. The United States has been educated to the beauty of liturgical music through the efforts of......... ...., organizer of the Paulist Choristers.

18. The first heavier-than-air machine in history was successfully flown by............................... .

19. ....which beautifies the walls of public buildings has become a popular type of art in the United States.

20. The first children's symphony orchestra in America was organized by................................ .

21. *Rhapsody in Blue* by........................

was an attempt to prove to the musical world that jazz and classical music could be combined.

22. ....named the land which he found at the South Pole, Little America.

23. The inventions of............................ paved the way for the use of ....in the home.

24. The obligations of Catholics in regard to the education of children are found in the encyclical *On the Christian Education of Youth* written by.................... .

25. ....was introduced into American public schools by Dr. Nicholas Murray Butler.

26. American interest in reading has been greatly increased by the formation of.............................. .

27. ....helps the pilot of an airplane to detect unseen obstacles, thereby insuring safer air travel.

28. Better training of Sisters who are preparing to teach was begun by ....when he organized the Catholic Sisters College in connection with the Catholic University of America.

29. A great American achievement in sculpture was carved in the Black Hills of South Dakota by ....

30. Industry, scientific research, and medicine have benefited by the development of ....

Highlights of the unit

TWENTIETH CENTURY HALL OF FAME	
Famous Person	*Contribution to American Progress*
Dr. Nicholas Murray Butler	Introduced manual training into public schools
Bishop John Lancaster Spalding	Laid the foundation for the establishment of the Catholic University

Dr. Thomas Shields	Catholic Sisters College in Washington
Pope Pius XI	Encyclical, *On the Christian Education of Youth*
Sinclair Lewis	Author of *Main Street*
Willa Cather	Prominent woman author—recorded lives of immigrants in Middle West
Joyce Kilmer	Soldier-poet; *Trees* and other poems; convert
Louis Sullivan	Originated the skyscraper
Gutzon Borglum	Famous sculptor—features of four presidents in the granite hills of South Dakota

Making connections

Without using a textbook, give the topic which each of the words below suggests to you. *For example*: Newlands Act — irrigation projects in the West.

1. Nineteenth Amendment
2. Supreme Court
3. Pendleton Act
4. Pure Food and Drug Act
5. occupational diseases
6. Federal Housing Administration
7. Social Security Act
8. Third Plenary Council of Baltimore
9. National Catholic Educational Association
10. Commission on American Citizenship
11. Paul Creston
12. Atomic Energy Commission
13. Air Commerce Act
14. Guglielmo Marconi
15. Edison Laboratories
16. Du Pont Company

More points to remember

1. The Bill of Rights guarantees freedom of speech, religion, and the protection of the law to all American citizens.
2. The government has a right to levy taxes because they contribute to the general welfare.
3. The welfare of a group should be the concern of every individual rather than his own personal gain.
4. The Seventeenth Amendment provides for direct election of Senators by the people. This promotes the general welfare and not the welfare of a particular group.
5. The Twenty-first Amendment is the only instance in the history of the United States of the repeal of another amendment. This amendment repealed prohibition.
6. One of the important duties of the Supreme Court is to interpret the Constitution. Justices, therefore, should be guided by principles of justice and charity.
7. Civil Service Examinations aid democracy by making it difficult for unworthy and incapable men to obtain government positions.
8. The passage of the Pure Food and Drug Act in 1906 was an important step made by the government in protecting the health of American citizens.
9. Government agencies provide services which prevent the spread of contagious diseases,

thereby increasing the general health of the nation.

10. The government has cared for the public health of the nation by improving housing conditions.

11. Education, literature, art, music, and science should strengthen and not weaken American democracy. These cultural achievements will accomplish this end if they give glory to God.

12. Each state in the United States controls its own system of education. The federal government controls education only in the District of Columbia and our territories.

13. The public school provides for the education of a child in every respect except the most important one, the welfare of his soul.

14. Since the days of Horace Mann, education is possible for every child in the United States. State control of schools, however, has divorced them from religion.

15. After the Second World War, there was a great increase in college attendance due to educational benefits given to service men and to higher requirements for professions and business.

16. Georgetown University is the oldest Catholic university in the country.

17. The chief center for Catholic learning in the United States is the Catholic University.

18. The Catholic Church is interested in the education of youth because she believes that it is through the youth of the present that the future will be insured.

19. The majority of people in the twentieth century obtain information from newspapers, magazines, and the radio.

20. Because of freedom of the press, either true or false news can be spread through the printed page. As Catholics, we must watch our reading.

21. By means of propaganda, unprincipled men often spread false doctrines.

22. The Catholic press dates back to colonial days.

23. The most important Catholic news agency is the National Catholic Welfare Conference (N.C.W.C.) News Service.

24. Two important Catholic chain newspapers are the *Register* and *Our Sunday Visitor*.

25. More religious books have been published and purchased since World War I than ever before.

26. Reading in the twentieth century has been promoted greatly by the organization of book clubs.

27. The chief contribution to architecture in the first half of the twentieth century was the skyscraper.

28. American public buildings have been beautified by mural paintings.

29. By 1950, nearly every large American city had a symphony orchestra.

30. American interest in light opera has extended its production to motion pictures.

31. Plain Chant (Gregorian Chant) is the official music of the Catholic Church.

32. The airplane has changed both passenger and freight travel in the United States.

33. The Church approves of scientific advancements as long as they do not oppose divine doctrine and truth.

34. Modern inventions, properly used, tend to develop mutual understanding between nations and races.

35. Information imparted over radio or through printed material must be true or it will be harmful to our democratic way of life.

36. Television became a commercial industry in 1941.

37. Motion pictures have a tremendous educational value.

38. Pope Pius XI, in his encyclical on motion pictures, said that it is especially during times of recreation that it is necessary to safeguard the morals of men.

39. The United States succeeded in producing large-scale quantities of such "wonder-drugs" as sulfa, penicillin, and aureomycin. These drugs fight bacteria.

40. Twentieth-century American homes contain such modern inventions as fluorescent lighting, automatic heating devices, and air conditioning.

41. One of the greatest scientific achievements of the first half of the twentieth century was the development of the use of atomic energy.

42. American scientific research in the first half of the twentieth century equaled, if it did not excel, that of European scientists.

Clinching the highlights through activity

1. Draw a series of illustrations to show how modern inventions have drawn the nations of the world closer together.

2. Write a news reporter's account of one of the inventions mentioned in this Unit.

3. Impersonate one of the amendments mentioned in this Unit. Tell in detail how it contributed to the progress of the U. S.

4. Hold a debate on:
   a. *Resolved:* The press, the radio, and the motion picture are helping to build a better United States.
   b. *Resolved:* Catholic education contributes more to American progress than public school education.

5. Give a radio speech on the development of music in the U. S.

A final check-up

I. IDENTIFICATION TEST. Copy the following list of names. After each name there are three groups of words or phrases. Choose the word or phrase with which the person named was connected and write it after his name on your paper.

Horace Mann	state control of schools	building of schools	vocational schools	junior colleges
Wright Brothers	radio	nuclear physics	atomic fission	airplane
Sinclair Lewis	novelist	scientist	inventor	educator
Louis Sullivan	sculpture	music	literature	architecture
Gutzon Borglum	New York	Washington, D. C.	Mt. Rushmore	New Orleans
George Gershwin	chant	Paulist Choristers	"Rhapsody in Blue"	"Student Prince"

Richard E. Byrd	Alaska	Exploration of the Poles	discovered radar	first flight across Atlantic
Dr. Thomas Shields	Catholic newspapers	training of Catholic Sisters	Georgetown University	Catholic news service
Lee de Forest	airplane	submarine warfare	radio	electric light
Victor Herbert	light opera	jazz	novelist	mural painting

II. COMPLETION TEST. Choose the word or phrase from the following list which correctly fills the blank in each of the sentences below.

Eighteenth Amendment
Atomic Energy Commission
Pure Food and Drug Act
Georgetown University
On the Christian Education of Youth
mural painting
Guglielmo Marconi
Thomas A. Edison
Charles Lindbergh
Air Commerce Act

celluloid industry
motion pictures
state
secularism
Dr. Thomas Shields
Catholic University
Social Security Act
propaganda
radio station
educational

Supreme Court
atomic energy
Pendleton Act
amendment
Joyce Kilmer
religion
Horace Mann
historical novel
radio
Father Finn

silk
taxation
nylon
fuel
medicine
book clubs
radar
rayon
jazz
airplane
bacteria

1. The only way of changing the Constitution is by adding an ....

2. It is the duty of the .... to interpret the Constitution.

3. Conveniences, which the public may enjoy, are provided by the government through ....

4. The .... did not improve social conditions in the United States because it led to a dangerous disregard of law.

5. The .... required applicants for government positions to take civil service examinations.

6. An important step made by Congress in protecting the health of the American people was the passage of the ....

7. Benefits were given to the unemployed and the aged by the ....

8. Education has been possible to all children since the time of ....

9. The oldest Catholic university in the United States is .... , founded by the Jesuits in 1789.

10. The main center for Catholic learning in the United States is .... in Washington, D. C.

11. To prevent .... , or lack of religion, from influencing Catholic children, Catholics now write their own textbooks.

12. State control of public schools has resulted in excluding .... from them.

13. The pioneer and leader in the movement towards better training of Catholic Sisters was ....

14. Public school education in the United States is controlled by the ....

15. The Church's stand on education is to be found in the encyclical ....

16. False news which is printed by individuals to accomplish selfish ends is called.................................

17. A poet who found inspiration for his work in the doctrines of the Catholic Church was the convert ....

18. A story which attempts to make past history live again in the minds of readers is a.......................... .

19. ....did much to make plain chant better known in America.

20. The organization of.......................... has been one reason why many twentieth-century Americans have become great readers.

21. ....beautifies the walls of many public buildings in the United States.

22. A typical form of American dance music begun in the early twentieth century was known as ....

23. Operettas have been made widely known among the people in the United States by being produced as.......................... .

24. The invention that has changed American transportation and communication in the twentieth century is the.......................... .

25. The United States did not become "air conscious" until after the flight of.......................... .

26. Systematic air travel began when Congress passed the.......... .

27. The first..........................was set up in East Pittsburgh in 1920.

28. The ends of the world have been brought into almost instant communication by means of the ....

29. Motion pictures have..............as well as entertaining value.

30. Modern "wonder drugs" which fight..............have reached large-scale production because of the excellence of American scientists.

31. The work of..............laid the foundation for the development of the radio.

32. Through the early efforts of ....electricity has come to play a very important part in the efficient running of a modern home.

33. The development of photography, motion pictures, and X-ray films has been made possible through the ....

34. Two substitutes for silk are ....and.......................... .

35. The greatest scientific achievement of the twentieth century in the United States was the development and use of.......................... .

36. One important duty of the.............. is to devise peacetime uses for atomic energy.

37. The discovery of..........................has enabled pilots to detect mountains or other obstacles, thereby making air travel safer.

38. Atomic energy has been used as ....and in ....

III. Answer as Briefly as Possible

1. Name three things mentioned in this Unit which influence public opinion.

2. Name one Catholic newspaper and one Catholic magazine mentioned in this Unit.

3. Mention two ways in which the airplane has changed living.

4. Name two ways in which the automobile has aided the farmer.

5. Why do many scientists tend to set up false standards of living?

Mary's Plenitude of Grace

HISTORY. When the Angel greeted Mary at the Annunciation, he said: "Hail, full of grace, the Lord is with thee." (Luke 1:28). It was at that time that God became Man, and Mary became His Mother. For this high honor it was fitting that God should give her a greater fullness of grace than was ever given to any other creature.

Feasts such as the Annunciation, March 25, and the Immaculate Conception, December 8, remind us of this dogma.

From the Bull of Pope Pius IX, in 1854, we learn that the Church always believed in Mary's Plenitude of Grace.

BELIEF. Catholics believe that, at the first moment of her existence, Our Lady received greater graces than any other creature, man or angel. For this reason she is the greatest of all merely human beings, and is superior to the Angels.

Prayer

VIRGIN most holy, Mother of the Word Incarnate, Treasurer of graces, and Refuge of us poor sinners; we fly to thy motherly affection with lively faith, and we beg of thee the grace ever to do the will of God. Into thy most holy hands we commit the keeping of our hearts, asking thee for health of soul and body, in the certain hope that thou, our most loving Mother, wilt hear our prayer. Wherefore with lively faith we say: Hail Mary three times.

An indulgence of 500 days (See "The Raccolta," the official book of indulgenced prayers, page 244).

TRUTH. Mary's Plenitude of Grace is a truth which, as can be learned from the Bull of Pope Pius IX in 1854, was always believed by the Church. It is one of the five great truths pertaining to Mary. The other four are: Her Immaculate Conception, her Assumption, her Divine Motherhood, and her Perpetual Virginity.

Courtesy of Rev. J. B. Carol, O. F. M.

UNIT FIVE

THE UNITED STATES AND THE STRUGGLE FOR WORLD SUPREMACY

PART ONE—THE FIRST WORLD WAR

CHAPTER I—ECONOMIC RIVALRY DRAWS EUROPEAN NATIONS INTO WAR

Causes of World War I

Progress of the War Before the United States Entered the Struggle

CHAPTER II—AMERICAN PARTICIPATION IN THE WAR

Reasons for Our Entrance into the War

The Home Front in the United States

Americans on European Battlefields

CHAPTER III—A PEACE THAT ENDED IN FAILURE

Peace Efforts During the War

The Treaty That Did Not Bring Peace

PART TWO—THE WORLD GOES TO WAR A SECOND TIME

CHAPTER IV—STEPPING STONES LEADING TO ANOTHER WORLD WAR

Restlessness Among European Nations Affects the World

The Spread of the Dictatorships in Europe and Asia

CHAPTER V—AMERICAN TEAMWORK AGAIN BRINGS AN ALLIED VICTORY

In Union There Is Strength

Main Battlegrounds of World War II:

The European War Picture

War in the Pacific Theater

United Efforts to Win the War and Establish World Peace

Returning to Peacetime Living at Home

Helping Other Nations to Return to Normal Living

UNIT FIVE

THE UNITED STATES AND THE STRUGGLE
FOR WORLD SUPREMACY

THE year 1914 found the United States content in her own achievements. Great advances had been made in agriculture, industry, and in scientific research. Can you mention some of these achievements? America had had a few struggles in the past, but none, with the exception of the Civil War, was particularly devastating.

The fact that the United States became engulfed in one of the greatest struggles in history came as a sudden blow to her. Although World War I actually was fought in Europe for three years before Uncle Sam was forced to send his armies overseas, Americans felt the effects of that conflict at home. However, true to the great American spirit of love of country, all of America's citizens rallied to "make the world safe for democracy."

Finally an armistice, signed in 1918, temporarily ended the hardships and sufferings caused by war.

The peace treaty which followed laid heavy and unjust penalties upon Germany, the aggressor.

People thought that World War I was the most vicious of all wars. So it was, until World War II made the first global war seem insignificant. A tricky kind of nationalism or love of country began spreading throughout many countries in the world. This fanned the fire of World War II which had been smoldering for several years.

Germany was determined that she would rise victorious from the unjust position in which the Treaty of Versailles had placed her in 1919. It was Germany who struck the first blow which began World War II just twenty years later, and one by one the nations of the world again found themselves at war. This time the Army and Navy of the United States went not only to Europe, but also to Asia and Africa.

223

CHAPTER I

ECONOMIC RIVALRY DRAWS EUROPEAN NATIONS INTO WAR

Getting ready for this chapter. On a summer day in 1914, the American people were surprised to read in their newspapers that a war had broken out in Europe. For several years, Americans had been aware that there was a great rivalry among some of the European nations, particularly between England and Germany.

The desire for increased trade led to a search for more possessions and the control of markets. Other nations on the continent had formed secret alliances, or agreements, to come to each other's assistance in case of attack. A growing spirit of national pride had been developing in the hearts of Europeans, especially those who lived in the more powerful countries. All of these desires burst into activity when the shot which killed Archduke Francis Ferdinand of Austria was fired. Immediately, the nations of Europe began to group themselves into two great camps, the Allies and the Central Powers.

Many injustices were committed during this war. Some neutral countries, that is countries not participating in the war, were invaded without warning. The Church disapproves of such conduct. There are times when warfare is justified, but the Church, speaking through her Popes, has always urged that disagreements between nations be settled peaceably. The Church has warned that wars only breed more wars.

In this chapter we shall study two points. The first point will deal with the causes of World War I, and the second point will tell about the progress of the war before the United States entered it.

1. The Causes of World War I

In the first decade of the twentieth century, there arose keen competition for world trade. This competition eventually was one of the greatest causes which led the entire world into war.

Trade rivals. Perhaps you have somewhere seen England referred to as the "Mistress of the Seas." Do you recall what that means? Because of her well-organized navy, England was able gradually to build up a vast empire, in fact, the largest in the world. From all points of this empire, she could secure many of the raw materials which were lacking in England itself. Besides the enormous trade she had built up within her possessions, it was only natural that England should also build a widespread trade with other nations in the world. This vast trade yielded England a profit which was the envy of other countries.

Germany, especially, was envious of this trade. Germany was located in the center of the continent of Europe, in good contact with outside nations by railroads and waterways. As her industrial strength increased, and eventually outstripped England's, Germany became the trade center of the continent. Steadily but surely, she began to extend her trade beyond the boundaries of the continent, reaching out to all parts of the world. This irritated England, who began to fear her rival. Although Germany entered the race for colonial possessions much later than England, she succeeded in getting some territories in Africa and the South Pacific.

Desire for military supremacy. The desire for trade, therefore, was one underlying reason why nations in Europe were becoming restless. England had always had the greatest navy in the world, but when other nations began acquiring colonies, they also began to expand their navies.

All of the greater European nations realized that, in case of war, the nation with the largest navy would be better able to protect its colonies. It could also cut off the supplies of its enemies. Therefore, by the end of the nineteenth century, the navies of industrial nations grew larger and larger. European armies also grew in proportion. Large amounts of money were spent for military training, defense equipment, and the strengthening of boundary lines. Each nation strove to take the lead in being the best prepared for war.

Secret alliances. In addition to the enlargement of armies and navies, and the military preparation for a possible attack, the nations of Europe formed military alliances with each other. In central Europe, Germany had made an alliance with Austria and Italy. This was known as the Triple Alliance. Encircling these nations were England, France, and Russia, who formed the Triple Entente (an-tant'). The word *entente* is the French word for "understanding." Both the Triple Alliance and the Triple Entente were organized with the understanding that member nations would support each other in case of attack.

The smaller nations of Europe watched these alliances with uneasiness. It was very evident that when one group increased its army and navy, the other did in like manner in order to keep a balance of power in Europe. What is meant by a balance of power?

Rise of a spirit of nationalism. While armies and navies were expanding, a strong spirit of *national-*

Assassination of Archduke Ferdinand.

ism was also growing. Nationalism is a strong love of country which unites a group of people who speak the same language and have the same customs. As long as nationalism results in bringing to these people freedom to live under the type of government which they desire, nationalism is good.

But there are dangers which result from too strong a spirit of nationalism. We shall discuss these dangers in the second part of this Unit. It is sufficient to know at this time that each larger European nation believed in its own supremacy.

While the conditions about which you have just read may not have led directly to war, they certainly helped to launch it on a big scale when war actually came. Europe was like a huge powderhouse waiting for somebody to strike the match which would cause an explosion.

The match is struck. On June 28, 1941, Archduke Francis Ferdinand of Austria was assassinated while driving through the streets of Sarajevo (sa-ra-ye'-voe) on an official visit. Sarajevo was a city in Bosnia, a province of Austria. The man held responsible for this crime was captured. When it was learned that he was a Serbian student, Austria held Serbia accountable for the assassination. From this moment, with lightning-like speed, one nation after another, because of secret alliances, became involved in the war. The only European countries which succeeded in remaining neutral were Holland, Spain, Switzerland, and the Scandinavian countries.

2. The Progress of the War Before the United States Entered the Struggle

How the first European nations became involved in war. At first, it seemed that only Austria and Serbia would be concerned in the war. The demands which Austria made upon Serbia were dangerous to Serbia's independence. Consequently, when she refused to comply with these demands, Austria declared war on Serbia. It was July, just about one month after the assassination. Russia, who had promised to help the Balkan states, of which Serbia was one, rushed to Serbia's assistance. The German government, which backed Austria, demanded that the Russian troops be disbanded. The Russian Czar (zahr) paid no attention to this de-

The German Army Marches into Belgium. A German column in Brussels, 1914.

mand, so Germany declared war on Russia. Because of her alliance with Russia, France was next drawn into the war. Then Germany declared war on France. Two vast armies now stood prepared in Europe, the Allies versus the Central Powers. Notice on the map where these countries are located.

Germany's plan violates Belgian neutrality. The German plan was to rush troops through France and strike a fatal blow at Paris before the Russian army could get into action. This move was made in order to avoid the necessity of fighting on two fronts at the same time. Germany and France had always had strong fortifications between their borders; therefore, Germany knew it would be difficult to strike anywhere along this boundary. But between these two powerful nations,

a little to the north, lay the peaceful little country of Belgium. This country had never fortified her boundaries because long before the war all the great powers, including Germany, had promised to respect Belgian neutrality. Do you remember what the word "neutrality" means? In spite of this agreement, the efficient and powerful German army swept across Belgium.

This action on the part of Germany was in direct violation of just principles. Any government which interrupts the peaceful life of a nation, especially of a smaller and weaker one, merely to suit its own selfish purposes, is guilty of injustice. Every Pope, from Pope Benedict XV, who was reigning during the First World War, down to the present day, has declared that world peace will be accomplished

King Albert of Belgium at the time he became King.

only when agreements between nations are based on standards of justice and are held sacred by the parties to the agreement.

Belgium's strength—a surprise to the Germans. The Germans expected little resistance on the part of the Belgians. But the Germans did not realize how firmly Belgium would uphold her right to neutrality. King Albert I declared that he relied fully upon his people to support him against the Germans. He did not intend that the Germans could use his country as a "highway" without offering them resistance. Cardinal Mercier, called the Voice of Belgium, also urged the people not to yield to this unjust advance of Germany.

There were two results of this delay in Belgium, both favorable to the Allies. The first result was that France had time to make better preparations to meet her enemy, and the second was that England, because of her agreement to assist Belgium, now entered the war on the side of the Allies. Later, other nations joined in the war, supporting one side or the other.

The armies press onward. By September, the German army had come within sight of the towers of Paris. The Germans hoped the English would not join forces with the French at this time. However, the German hopes were in vain, for an

Anglo-French army stopped them at the Marne River and they were forced to retreat to northern France. Here the Germans dug themselves into trenches, or ditches in the earth, protected by barbed wire. This type of warfare, introduced for the first time, continued throughout the war.

By 1915, the line of battle extended from the North Sea through Belgium and France to Switzerland. It was the job of the Allies to break through this line. They, too, had dug a system of trenches. For three years, the Allies and the Central Powers fought, but neither side was able to win a decisive victory. Do you remember what the word "decisive" means?

Can you explain these?

military supremacy   aggressor
Mistress of the Seas   nationalism
Triple Alliance   Triple Entente
balance of power   neutrality
decisive victory   resistance
trench warfare

Now answer these questions

1. What were the underlying reasons which plunged the European nations into war in 1914?
2. What nations formed the Central Powers? The Allies?
3. What two nations do you think were more responsible than any of the others for arousing the greed and jealousy which caused World War I? Explain your answer.
4. Why was Germany's entrance into Belgium a violation of justice?
5. What has been the opinion of the Church in regard to agreements between nations?

6. How did Germany's invasion of Belgium aid the Allies?

Another true-false test

Number a paper from 1 to 15. If a statement is true write X after the number representing it; if false, write 0.

1. England was the trade center of the continent of Europe before World War I.
2. In 1914, Germany had the best organized navy in the world.
3. The Triple Alliance and the Triple Entente were formed because of commercial rivalry.
4. Russia supported Germany in the First World War.
5. Both the Allies and the Central Powers used a system of trench warfare.
6. England, France, and Russia formed the Triple Alliance.
7. Before World War I, European nations began increasing their armies as well as their navies.
8. The Assassination of Archduke Francis Ferdinand of Austria was the incident which finally brought about World War I.
9. Albert I was the king of England during World War I.
10. England became involved in the war when the neutrality of Belgium was violated.
11. Cardinal Mercier was called the Voice of Belgium.
12. After three years of fighting, the Central Powers were gaining much territory.
13. Switzerland remained a neutral nation.
14. Pope Benedict XI was the reigning Pope during World War I.
15. The German army was successful in its attempt to capture Paris.

CHAPTER II

AMERICAN PARTICIPATION IN THE WAR

Getting acquainted with another chapter. In the last chapter we learned that for years there had been warnings of armed conflict in Europe. The struggle for power had finally involved the leading countries of Europe in war, and the spread of this war upon the seas soon made it a world conflict. President Wilson tried in vain to keep the United States out of the war. Until 1917, the United States succeeded in maintaining its neutrality. But as a result of Germany's submarine warfare our shipping became endangered. It was this menace which helped draw the United States into the conflict.

Immediately, the home front in the United States cooperated with Uncle Sam. Men and women came to the aid of their country. Money was raised, food was conserved, and industry was controlled by the government. Training camps were established. But in spite of all the splendid cooperation of the American people, it was some time before our country was really prepared for war.

When the American soldiers reached France to swell the ranks of the Allies, the world saw the value of teamwork. The fearlessness of our soldiers gave encouragement to weary allies who had been carrying on the struggle for three years. For over a year, American and European soldiers fought side by side in an attempt to conquer the forces which were spreading their power over Europe.

The main points we shall study in this chapter are: (1) Reasons for Our Entrance into the War, (2) The Home Front in the United States, and (3) Americans on European Battlefields.

1. Reasons for Our Entrance into the War

In the early days, the war seemed very far-distant to the people of the United States. Few thought that this country would become involved in the struggle.

The United States declares neutrality. Shortly after the war began, President Wilson, who had been elected in 1912, issued a proclamation stating that the United States was a neutral nation. However, it soon became evident that neutrality would be difficult to maintain. The great majority of the population of the United States was either foreign-born or descended from ancestors

President Woodrow Wilson in 1919.

German submarine fires at English freighter.

who had lived in the warring nations. It was this realization which prompted President Wilson to urge that the American people be "neutral in fact, as well as in name."

Another reason which made neutrality difficult was the fact that all of the warring nations demanded more and more supplies. As a result, the United States became the greatest neutral shipper in the world. Both sides in the conflict wanted American supplies, yet each tried to prevent the other from trading with America. This put the United States in an awkward position.

The British blockade. In order to stop war supplies from getting into Germany through trade with neutral countries, England blockaded German ports. According to international law, a blockade is lawful within three miles of a coastline.

England violated this principle by placing her blockade over two hundred miles from the ports of Germany. In this way, Germany was deprived of all help, even food supplies, coming from neutral countries. When England began searching American ships for *contraband,* or forbidden articles, President Wilson protested vigorously, but England would not alter her policy.

The submarine menace. England's violation of American neutrality threatened American property. Germany also violated our neutrality, but in a much more serious manner because her action threatened American lives. Since there seemed no way of keeping supplies from going to the Allies, Germany attempted to break the blockade by using *submarines.* A torpedo strikes

Brown Brothers

The sinking of the Lusitania. This great ship was torpedoed
and sank with a loss of many lives.

suddenly, giving a ship's passengers and crew very little opportunity of saving themselves.

Early in 1915, Germany warned all neutral vessels to keep away from the North Sea, which she declared a war zone. In spite of the warning, neutral vessels continued to enter this zone. Many of them were sunk, and Americans traveling or working on these ships lost their lives.

Lusitania torpedoed. On May 7, 1915, the entire world was horrified by the shocking news that the *Lusitania* (loos-i-tay'-nee-a) was torpedoed by a German submarine. The *Lusitania,* a ship of the British Cunard Line, was the first vessel to be called "a floating hotel" and was one of the swiftest vessels on the seas at that time. On the afternoon of the tragedy, she was about ten miles from the coast of Ireland on her way from New York. It took less than half an hour for this beautiful ship to sink, carrying to their death nearly 2,000 men, women, and children, of whom 124 were Americans.

Many Americans clamored for war. They felt that America had come "to the parting of the ways," and that we could no longer be neutral spectators.

President Wilson protested to the German government. The Germans promised to be more careful in the future, expressed sorrow for the loss of American lives, but would take no responsibility for the act. Did not the Americans who boarded the *Lusitania* know that she was a British ship, and, as such, liable to destruction? These people had been warned, and Germany felt that all passengers had entered this ship at their own risk.

Sabotage in the United States. While Uncle Sam was having trouble on the high seas, there were disturbances within the United States itself. During time of war, it usually happens that there are present within a country groups of people who wish to arouse sympathy for one or the other of the warring nations. These people sometimes try to stir up labor troubles in factories; they set fire to munitions plants, or cause "accidents" to happen to industrial machinery. This plan of action is called *sabotage,* and its purpose is to stop the production of war materials. Quite a few acts of sabotage were committed in the United States in order to prevent supplies from reaching the warring nations.

Moving closer to war. Meanwhile, the year 1916 brought another Presidential election. Woodrow Wilson was reelected on the Democratic Party's slogan, "He kept us out of war." But he was not to be able to live up to that slogan much longer. Early in 1917, Germany had ready a new fleet of submarines. Having been successfully starved out by England, Germany extended the war zone to all surrounding waters and declared that any ship entering these waters would be sunk without warning. All ships, neutral or enemy, would be treated alike. This was in direct violation of international law.

Wilson took this as a lawless disregard of the first promise Germany had made, and broke off diplomatic relations with that country. This meant that the German ambassador was dismissed from the United States and the American ambassador to Germany was ordered to return home immediately.

The Zimmerman Note. The situation between the United States and Germany grew more tense as the days passed. The final shock came when England turned over to the United States a note which came into its possession. The note was from the foreign minister of Germany, Alfred Zimmerman, to the German ambassador in Mexico. The note instructed the German ambassador to attempt to form a German-Mexican alliance in case of war between the United States and Germany. It promised Mexico a return of Texas, New Mexico, and Arizona in case of victory.

This incident, plus the continued sinking of American vessels by German submarines, hastened the entrance of the United States into the war. Besides, many Americans had come to believe that a victory for Germany in Europe would hurt the interests of the United States.

Congress declares war on Germany. On April 2, 1917, President

Brown Brothers

President Wilson delivers his war message to Congress, April, 1917.

Wilson addressed his war message to Congress, asking that war be declared on Germany. In this message he reviewed all of the reasons why the United States should enter the struggle. Part of this message read:

It is a fearful thing to lead this great peaceful people into war, into the most terrible and disastrous of all wars . . . But the right is more precious than peace, and we shall fight for the things which we have always carried nearest our hearts — for democracy, for the right of those who submit to authority to have a voice in their own government, for the rights and liberties of small nations.

War was formally declared by the Congress on April 6, 1917. The enthusiasm of the American people was shown in their wholehearted support of the President. The First World War was to unite the American people as they never had been united before.

The Church and war. Was the United States justified in participating in this war? Let us consider some things the Church teaches about war, and then we may be able to decide.

There are times when a country is permitted to go to war. A nation may declare war on another nation in order to defend itself from an unjust attack. A country may go to war in order to recover possessions which another nation has unjustly seized. Or it may enter a war to maintain rights which were violated. It also may be permissible for a nation to participate in a war when it is possible to help right a wrong that has been committed. Participation in war is an obligation

HELP YOUR COUNTRY

ENLIST IN THE NAVY

Signs like these appeared all over America to encourage the war effort.

of justice if an agreement has been made between nations to mutually assist one another in case of attack. A nation may go to war only as a last resort, when every peaceful means has been exhausted. Moreover, war can not be declared if greater evils would follow from the war than if peace were maintained by concessions.

It is very difficult for the ordinary citizen to decide whether a war is just or not because usually so many things are involved. More frequently than not, people follow the decisions of their leaders. But that is not always a safe road because too many leaders have been blinded by

power. If leaders would weigh carefully the causes of a war and be guided by just principles, many wars could be avoided. At least, we may be sure, they would be less frequent.

2. The Home Front in the United States

Now that the United States had declared war on Germany, the great task of preparing to take an effective part in that struggle began. Posters, appealing to the patriotism of the people, appeared everywhere — in cars, trains, and on billboards. Men, women, and children rallied to these appeals.

Increasing our navy. One of the first things which America did was

From Ewing Galloway, N. Y.

American Troops arriving in France.

to send a fleet of destroyers to help the Allies clear the seas of German submarines. Admiral William S. Sims was in command of this enterprise.

Besides having at our command our own ships, our government had taken over 87 ships of the German merchant marine which had been held in American ports. These vessels were now used to transport food, ammunition, and other supplies. New ships which were constructed brought our war fleet up to 2,000 by the end of the war. The entire cost of our Navy during the years 1917 and 1918 equaled the total cost of the United States Navy from the second administration of Washington to the First World War. **The first American soldiers go to Europe.** The United States had never believed in having a large

standing army as most European countries did. Our entrance into the war showed us that we really had no defense worth speaking about.

Wilson knew an army had to be organized but did not intend to send any American soldiers to Europe before the spring of 1918. He thought by sending our naval help, money, food supplies, and ammunition, the Allies would be satisfied. But European soldiers had been fighting in France for nearly three years and were war-weary. The Allies pleaded with Wilson to send troops. They said that the presence of even a few thousand men in the uniform of the United States would do more than anything else to bolster the courage of the Allies. Therefore, in June, 1917, a small force of American soldiers was trained and sent to France. This force, known as the American Expeditionary Force (the A.E.F.), was under the command of General John J. Pershing, who had a splendid record of service in leading large groups of fighting men in Cuba, the Philippines, and Mexico.

The Selective Service Act. To increase our army as quickly as possible, Congress authorized the passage of the Selective Service Act. This act provided for the draft of a certain proportion of men from each state, according to its population. There were two drafts taken. In the first draft, men between 21 and 31 years of age were enrolled in our army. They were sent to training fields in various parts of the United States. The second draft extended the age limits to between 18 and 45. By the time the war ended in 1918, our army numbered more than three and a half million men. Almost two million of these men actually reached France!

How the war was financed. Modern war is extremely costly. The transportation of troops, their medical care overseas, and the purchase of food and clothing for them drained the United States treasury. President Wilson believed that the war cost should be paid from current revenues, if possible. When it was learned that this source of money was insufficient, a drive for finances was made through the sale of Liberty Bonds. All Americans were proud to be able to say that they purchased at least one bond. In this way, they felt that they had a share in the winning of the war.

General Pershing,
Commander of the A. E. F.

There were five Liberty Bond drives, the fifth one being called the Victory Loan because it was launched after the war ended. Each of these drives went at least a billion dollars over the top. The generosity of the American people enabled the government to loan the Allies over nine billion dollars, some of which has never been repaid.

Meeting the emergency in other ways. In times of great crises, such as wars, the Congress gives the President great emergency power, which lasts only for the duration of the crisis. Such power has carried our country victoriously through some disastrous times. We have learned how the President used this power to organize an army and to finance the war. He also asked

A Liberty Bond rally in New York.

Sow the seeds of Victory!

plant & raise your own vegetables

WRITE TO THE NATIONAL WAR GARDEN COMMISSION— WASHINGTON, D.C. for free books on gardening, canning & drying.

A war garden Poster.

Americans to raise food and to save food. Many families responded to this plea by planting Victory Gardens. Herbert Hoover was made Food Administrator and took over the control of the entire food supply in the United States. The services he rendered to our country and to the starving people of Europe were outstanding.

Besides saving food, Americans saved fuel. During the summer of 1918, highways in the United States were very little traveled on Sundays because the government had asked the people not to drive cars for pleasure. This helped save gasoline for the front in France.

In order to transport troops with as little difficulty as possible, the government took over the control of the railroads. Industry, too, contributed to the war effort by speed-

ing up production and by agreeing not to strike during the war. A government may take control of such activities in case of emergency in order to help a country to protect itself. When danger is past, the government should restore control to rightful authority.

Helping to keep up the morale of the soldiers. Every effort was made by the government and other agencies to bring comfort and relief to our service men, both here in camp and overseas. The American Red Cross sent doctors and nurses to care for the sick and wounded.

Many organizations worked along with the Red Cross to assist in all types of welfare work. The Knights of Columbus, in cooperation with the National Catholic War Council, set up recreational "huts" where everybody was welcome, regardless of color or creed. The YMCA, the Salvation Army, and the Jewish Welfare Board performed similar services, and the American Library Association supplied the men with reading material. **American Catholics in World War I.** When war was declared in 1917, the archbishops, at their annual meeting at the Catholic University, adopted a resolution which pledged Catholic cooperation in the war effort. Cardinal Gibbons, who was the spokesman for the Catholic Church in the United States, sent the resolution to President Wilson. It was the first pledge received from any religious body in the country. In part, this resolution stated:

> Our people, as ever, will rise as one man to serve the nation. Our priests and consecrated women will once again, as in every former trial of their country, win by their bravery, their heroism, and their service, new admiration and approval. We are all true Americans, ready as our age, our ability, and our condition permits, to do whatever is in us to do for the preservation, the progress, and the triumph of our beloved country.

The response of Catholics was immediate. Bishop Hayes of New York, later made Cardinal, was selected as Chaplain-General of the armed forces. Under him were many priests who had enlisted to care for the spiritual needs of our men. By the time the war was over there were nearly 1,000 Catholic chaplains with the forces and about

Patrick Cardinal Hayes.

Marshal Foch

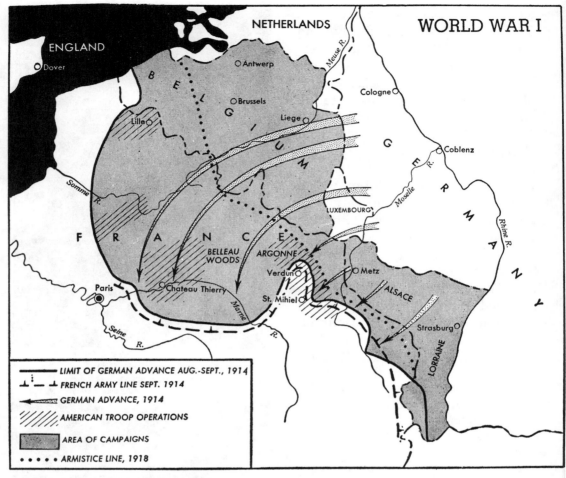

Map labels:

ENGLAND
Dover
NETHERLANDS
Antwerp
BELGIUM
Brussels
Lille
Liege
Cologne
Coblenz
Somme R.
GERMANY
LUXEMBOURG
Moselle
Rhine R.
FRANCE
BELLEAU WOODS
ARGONNE
Verdun
Metz
ALSACE
Paris
Chateau Thierry
St. Mihiel
Seine R.
Marne R.
Strasburg
LORRAINE

LIMIT OF GERMAN ADVANCE AUG.-SEPT., 1914
FRENCH ARMY LINE SEPT. 1914
GERMAN ADVANCE, 1914
AMERICAN TROOP OPERATIONS
AREA OF CAMPAIGNS
ARMISTICE LINE, 1918

500 more applications had been accepted. Their conduct and that of Catholic young men during the war proved beyond a doubt that Catholics are true Americans.

3. Americans on European Battlefields

By the time the Americans began arriving in Europe, the Allied cause was in great danger. The Germans had encouraged their people, civilians as well as soldiers, by declaring that the war would l e over before many American troops could land in France. The fact that Russia had dropped out of the war in 1917 be-

cause of a revolution in her own country enabled Germany to concentrate on the Western Front. We now follow the Americans and the Allies to the close of the war.

Germany makes a second attempt to capture Paris. The German army, under the direction of General Ludendorff, mustered all its strength for a last big push. Germany's plan was to split the Allied forces by driving the British back into England and the French back to Paris. In this way Germany hoped to make it easier for herself

In this French dining-car the armistice was signed November 11, 1918.

by fighting each army separately. At first the Germans were successful everywhere. Then, just at the right time, the long-awaited American troops came to the rescue!

In order to make a united front, all of the Allies were now placed under the supreme command of Marshal Foch (fosh), a great French Catholic general, who had displayed able leadership during the first Battle of the Marne.

American bravery in France. For the second time, the Germans were stopped at the Marne River where the American units helped to win a victory in the battle of Chateau-Thierry (sha-toe'-tee-ay'-ree). It was, however, in two other encounters, the one in Saint Mihiel (san me'-yel) and the other in the Argonne (ar-gon') Forest that American soldiers fought their bravest.

The French had declared that the Argonne Forest was impassable, yet our army never faltered. This battle was considered America's greatest battle in the First World War.

Germany had been strongly established in the Argonne Forest for four years. In spite of this, our men broke through and captured the supply line of the German army. Since the French and British were equally successful, there was nothing left for the enemy but to surrender or face disaster. This situation, together with the news that their home front was weakening, forced Germany to ask for an *armistice,* which meant that both armies agreed to stop fighting while the terms of peace were arranged.

The armistice was signed at eleven o'clock on November 11, 1918. While an armistice does not necessarily end a war, in this particular instance the fighting was not renewed, and, therefore, the war was over.

A new-type of mechanized warfare. The First World War was the most terrible war in history up to that time. Many scientists devoted their time to devising new weapons of destruction or improving old ones. The airplane, which had been invented in the first years of the twentieth century, was quickly improved. At first, its use was limited to watching the movements of the enemy. Later, planes dropped bombs upon railways, important crossroads, and ammunition dumps.

We have already learned about Germany's use of the submarine and its disastrous consequences. Another destructive weapon was the tank. This huge steel fortress helped the Allies to smash barbed wire entanglements and machine-gun nests, and aided them in crossing rugged territory.

Most of the world was terrorized when Germany began using poison gas against the Allies. Immediately, scientists began working on a gas mask which was perfected before the war was over.

As we mentioned in the preceding Unit, the development of science, which is a gift of God, often leads to more destruction.

Can you define these?

blockade   bolster
proclamation   current revenues
submarine   Liberty Bonds
neutral vessels   morale

sabotage   armistice
ambassador   tank
the "A.E.F."   war zone
barbed wire entanglements
mechanized warfare
diplomatic relations
contraband articles

How well have you read?

1. Why was it difficult for the United States to remain neutral even in the early days of the First World War?
2. In what ways did England and Germany violate the neutrality of the United States?
3. How did the English blockade of Germany violate the principles of international law?
4. Why did President Wilson sever diplomatic relations with Germany in 1917? What, then, would you say was the real reason for the United States' entry into the war?
5. In what European country did most of the war take place?
6. The Church allows participation in wars for just reasons. Can you give some of these reasons? Was the United States justified in joining the conflict?
7. What was the American Expeditionary Force?
8. How did the government of the United States meet the war emergency?
9. What part did Catholics play in proving their loyalty to the United States during World War I?
10. Why were the United States soldiers so warmly welcomed when they finally reached Europe?
11. What was the greatest battle in

which the Americans participated? Can you name any others in which Americans fought?

12. What type of warfare was introduced for the first time during World War I? Explain your answer.

Some blanks to fill

On a paper write the missing word or words which fill the blanks in the following sentences.

1. Before the United States entered World War I, both the Allies and the Central Powers wanted American ....

2. In order to keep Germany from getting supplies from neutral countries England .... German ports.

3. England searched American ships for .... articles.

4. Germany tried to keep neutral ships from getting to England by declaring the North Sea a............... .

5. The *Lusitania* was an .... ship.

6. Acts which attempt to stop war production are called acts of ....

7. An attempted German-Mexican alliance was checked by the discovery of the ....

8. The United States army was increased by the passage of the .... Act.

9. The World War was financed in the United States by the sale of ....

10. In order to conserve food for the armed forces, people planted ....

11. The great American clergyman, who was spokesman for the Catholic Church at this time, was ....

12. America's greatest battle in World War I was the battle in the ....

13. Three weapons used successfully for the first time during this war were .... , ... , and ....

Matching test

Match Column I with Column II by writing the letter of a phrase from Column II opposite the correct number from Column I.

Column I

1. Admiral Sims
2. Cardinal Mercier
3. Food Administrator
4. Bishop Hayes
5. Signing of the Armistice
6. Albert I
7. John J. Pershing
8. Marshal Foch
9. Russia
10. Submarine warfare

Column II

A. American war chaplains
B. United States Navy
C. withdrew from war in 1917
D. King of the Belgians
E. Herbert Hoover
F. the Voice of Belgium
G. American Expeditionary Force
H. cause of America's entrance into war
I. November 11, 1918
J. where most of the war was fought
K. April 6, 1917
L. Generalissimo of Allied Forces

CHAPTER III

A PEACE THAT ENDED IN FAILURE

Introducing the last chapter about World War I. We have learned that the First World War lasted four years. Perhaps you are wondering if nothing was done all that time to try to plan for peace. There were several plans suggested. Two of these plans were outstanding—that of Pope Benedict XV, and that of the President of the United States.

The Pope's peace proposals, like all suggestions made by any Pope to settle disputes, were based upon justice and charity. Both the Pope and the President realized the importance of forming some kind of organization of nations which would insure the peace of the world. The attempts toward a lasting peace were not successful, as we shall see.

In this chapter, we shall learn what the peace proposals of these two influential men were, whether or not the world accepted them, and why the treaty which was signed did not bring peace.

1. Peace Efforts During the War

The purpose of the peace plans suggested during the war was to bring to an end, if possible, the murderous activity in which the world was engaged. If this could not be accomplished, those who had

made the plans hoped that they would be included in the treaty written after the war.

Pope Benedict XV proposes plans for peace. Before the first World War was many months old, Pope Benedict XV became Christ's Vicar on earth. From the very beginning of hostilities, he had worked for peace, had aided the hungry and the homeless, and had spared no efforts to re-unite families which had been separated. His position as the Father of all Christendom was a delicate one because Catholics were involved in the war on both sides.

Pope Benedict's final peace move was made in the spring of 1917. He addressed his appeal for peace negotiations to Germany first. It made a great impression on the German people, and the majority of the Reichstag (the German Congress), led by the Catholic Center Party, passed a resolution in favor of negotiations for a just peace on July 19, 1917. Unfortunately, a new German Chancellor, named Michaelis (mee-kay'-lis) appeared just at this time. He was a tool of the army, and was not in favor of stopping the war. In fact, all his efforts were aimed at prolonging

244

From Ewing Galloway, N. Y.
Pope Benedict XV, the "Pope of Peace".

the struggle in the hope of a German victory.

The Pope appeals to the rest of the nations. Pope Benedict, anxious to see the end of the horrible war, now resolved to address all the warring nations on the subject of peace. In the peace note which he sent them on August 7, the Holy Father asked the nations to consider several important points as a basis for a just and lasting peace. He urged nations to reduce their armies and navies and to permit freedom of the seas. In place of armed force, he advised nations to have recourse to peaceful arbitration. Do you remember what "arbitration" means?

The Pope felt that when nations could be convinced that right and not might is supreme, then other obstacles would disappear. He also stated that any international orga-

nization which might be established should discuss peace terms on the basis of justice and charity.

Reaction of the great powers to the Pope's appeal. How did the belligerent, or warring, nations accept the Papal note? England stated that she was willing to enter peace negotiations with Germany if Germany would restore complete independence to Belgium. When France became acquainted with England's move, she also agreed. Austria, although a Catholic country, supported Germany in her rejection of the Pope's appeal. President Wilson's reply to the Papal peace note was that the United States would not talk of peace transactions so long as the Central Powers "remained under their present rulers."

While Michaelis has been blamed for the failure of Pope Benedict's peace proposals, the question arises: Would the Allies have accepted the plan if Michaelis had? Perhaps the answer to this question might be found in the Allies' treatment of the Pope when the peace treaty was to be written.

President Wilson's peace plan. Across thousands of miles of water, another peace plan was formulated. Several months before the armistice was signed, President Wilson presented his plan in the form of fourteen points to both houses of the United States Congress. This plan, too, was based upon just principles. Can you pick out any points which resemble Pope Benedict's plan? Below are the more important points of Wilson's plan:

Members of the Peace Conference at Versailles—Orlando, Lloyd George, Clemenceau, and Wilson

1. No formation of secret alliances
2. Freedom of the seas during peace and war
3. The restoration of the independence of Belgium
4. Equal trade rights between all nations
5. Reduction of armies and navies.
6. Formation of a League of Nations

The other points which the President suggested dealt with the readjustment of European boundaries.

President Wilson's entire peace plan called for world cooperation in order to prevent future wars. The League of Nations was to supervise and **control world affairs** to this end.

The formation of this league was the fourteenth point of the President's program and the one on which all his hopes for a lasting peace were based.

2. The Treaty That Did Not Bring Peace

President Wilson went to Europe as head of the American commission for peace. He intended to influence the writing of the peace treaty in such a way that his fourteen points would be included in it.

The peace conference begins. A few miles outside the city of Paris in France is a palace of the French kings at Versailles (ver-sy′).

In the beautiful Hall of Mirrors in this palace, delegates from the victorious nations of the world gathered in January, 1919, to write a treaty which, they hoped, would bring the long-awaited peace. The chief work of the conference was carried on by four men, spoken of in history as "the Big Four." These men were President Wilson of the United States, Lloyd George, the Prime Minister of Great Britain, Premier Clemenceau (kle-man-so´) of France, and Premier Orlando of Italy.

The conference dragged on for months. It seemed no agreement would ever be reached because European leaders still clung to their national ambitions. Eventually, it came to light that during the war secret agreements had been made between some nations by which they were to receive certain territory. Their delegates were unwilling to come to any settlement which would not bring a reward to their countries. Could such selfishness actually lead to peace?

An unjust treaty. After five months of disagreement, the Versailles Treaty was finally signed by delegates of all European nations, including Germany, on June 28, 1919.

The victors were determined to see Germany punished as the aggressor in the war. They stripped her of her colonies, which they divided among themselves. They required Germany to pay a huge sum of money to the Allies and left her very few means by which to raise this money. Not all of Wilson's fourteen points were accepted, but the League of Nations did become a part of the peace treaty.

The United States desired nothing for itself, except the peace of the world, which Wilson was certain could be accomplished through the League of Nations. President Wilson resented the excessive demands which the victorious European nations made upon Germany, but he hoped the League could eventually remedy this situation.

Could the treaty have been just? You have read about the interest which Pope Benedict XV had shown in bringing the war to a speedy conclusion. Did the Allies invite him to the peace conference? Unfortunately, the big nations of the world ignored the one man who could have influenced the victors to insert principles of justice into the treaty. He would have insisted that the victorious nations deal justly with Germany. Were the Allies just? Was it right to try to cripple Germany as a world power? Charity demands that a victorious nation does not rob a defeated people of its God-given rights.

Why did the Allies ignore Pope Benedict XV? During the war Italy had objected to what she called "Vatican interference" in international problems. Accordingly, a secret treaty was signed by the Allies in London in 1915. This treaty tied the Holy Father's hands as far as his participation in any peace conference was concerned. England, France, and Russia agreed

to support such opposition as Italy may wish to make to any proposal aimed at allowing a representative of the Holy See in any peace negotiations for the settlement of problems arising from the present war (World War I).

Later, in 1920, Pope Benedict wrote an encyclical about a just peace. He declared that the treaty which had been written filled his heart with anxieties for the future. He stated that even if some sort of peace were established,

> there can be no stable peace or lasting treaties, though made after long and difficult negotiations and duly signed, unless there be a return of mutual charity to appease hate and banish enmity.

Would this treaty accomplish the things which the Holy Father hoped for? As you read the story of the Second World War, try to answer this question.

President Wilson presents the treaty to the Senate. According to the Constitution of the United States, all treaties must be ratified or approved by two-thirds of the Senate before they become binding upon the government. When President Wilson returned from Paris, he asked the Senate to ratify the Versailles Treaty so the United States could become a member of the League of Nations. Imagine his disappointment when he met opposition in the Senate!

The failure to impress the Senate

Headquarters of the League of Nations at Geneva.

From Ewing Galloway, N. Y.

with the terms of the treaty aroused discussions all over the country. Those who were in favor of joining the League argued that there was only one way to keep the world from another war and that was by uniting to preserve the peace.

Those who opposed our becoming a member of the League did so because they feared that by joining it the United States would be obliged to participate in future European wars. They felt that it would be a violation of our original policy of not interfering with the affairs of other nations. In vain did Wilson argue that the policy of isolation had already become useless. **The United States rejects the League of Nations.** As a last resort, the President made a tour of the country. Everywhere he delivered speeches trying to convince the American people that the League of Nations was necessary for the preservation of world peace. Before the trip was completed, he was stricken with paralysis which made him an invalid for the rest of his life.

In the election of 1920, the dispute over the League of Nations became one of the leading issues of the campaign. When the votes were counted, Warren G. Harding, a Republican, was elected President. The Senate did not ratify the treaty and, therefore, the United States never became a member of the League of Nations. The new President finally signed separate treaties with Germany and Austria in 1921. **Why did the League fail?** After the first meeting of the League of Nations in Geneva, Switzerland, in 1920, delegates met year after year. In itself, the League was well built. It dealt successfully with a number of world problems but it failed in many other cases. The powerful nations of the world did not choose to use the League for the purposes for which it was established. When the League was founded it was hoped that all nations would cooperate to promote good will and to maintain peace. Throughout its history, events proved that nations were more interested in promoting their own selfish ends than in securing the welfare of the world as a whole. Consequently, in spite of the League of Nations, rivalries among nations persisted.

The United States cooperates to preserve world peace. Even though

Warren G. Harding.
Brown Brothers

the United States rejected the League of Nations, our government cooperated with the rest of the world after World War I in its attempt to establish peace. In 1921, as a result of a conference held in Washington, the leading nations of the world agreed to limit the strength of their navies and to take other measures which would lessen the possibilities of war. This was the first of a number of such conferences which endeavored to settle international quarrels. The years which followed World War I were filled with broken promises, distrust, and fear. Eventually, these evils plunged the world into a second world war.

Know the meaning of these
peace negotiations Papal peace note
belligerent nations to outlaw war

Think before you answer
1. What efforts did Pope Benedict XV make to hasten peace? Upon what did he base his plans for peace?
2. Compare the plans for peace suggested by Pope Benedict and President Wilson. Find points in which they were alike.
3. Do you think the Allies would have accepted Pope Benedict's peace plan if Germany had? Explain your answer.
4. Was the Treaty of Versailles an unjust treaty?
5. What was the attitude of the American people towards the Treaty of Versailles?
6. Do you think the United States should have signed this treaty? Why or why not?
7. Why did the Treaty of Versailles not bring the desired peace?

Another true-false test
Number a paper from 1 to 12. Write X after the number of each statement that is true, and 0 after the number of each statement that is false.
1. The best peace plan proposed during World War I was that suggested by President Wilson.
2. Pope Benedict XV wrote his Papal peace note to the Allies before consulting Germany about peace negotiations.
3. The Church has always urged that nations have recourse to peaceful arbitration.
4. Some of President Wilson's Fourteen Points were similar to the peace proposals of Pope Benedict.
5. President Wilson based his entire hopes for peace on the formation of the League of Nations.
6. European leaders cooperated with the plans suggested at the Peace Conference in 1919.
7. Unless charity and justice are the foundation of treaties, they will not accomplish desired goals.
8. A victorious nation has a right to ask the conquered nation to pay for damages it has caused, provided the victorious nation is just and charitable in its demands.
9. The Versailles Treaty was rejected by the United States because Americans did not want to belong to the League of Nations.
10. President Wilson made separate treaties with Germany and Austria in 1921.
11. Because the United States did not become a member of the League of Nations, it did not participate in measures to promote peace.
12. President Wilson was one of the principal figures at Versailles.

CHAPTER IV

STEPPING STONES LEADING TO ANOTHER WAR

Looking back and looking ahead. In the first part of this Unit we learned, first of all, that the war began in Europe, and then, after vain attempts on the part of the United States to remain neutral, we became involved in that war. Secondly, we learned that with the help of splendid American teamwork the war ended in a military victory for the Allies. The third point we learned about was that efforts were made to form a lasting peace.

The lasting peace, for which all men hoped, was not based upon justice and charity. The fine promises to promote peace and understanding were not kept because the Prince of Peace was ignored by the leaders of nations. Upon Him and upon Him alone can lasting peace be established. Without God's blessing, the hearts of leaders remained hard, and the peace failed.

The Second World War, which we shall begin to study in this chapter, runs along practically the same lines, namely, European beginnings, American preparedness, and attempts to make a lasting peace. In this first chapter about the war there will be two main points for you to keep in mind. These are (1) Restlessness Among European Nations Affects the World, and (2) the Spread of the Dictatorships in Europe and Asia.

1. Restlessness Among European Nations Affects the World

As you begin this chapter, try to recall a few facts which you have already learned. The greatest depression the United States ever experienced occurred in 1929. To bring the country out of that depression, President Franklin D. Roosevelt organized the New Deal. He also tried to build up the nation's economy by developing new trade markets through the Good Neighbor Policy. This policy was especially successful in promoting more friendly relations with Latin America. In November of 1933, the President recognized Soviet Russia, hoping perhaps to secure a good customer for American products.

The Results of War. A European city laid waste by bombing in World War II.

How this hope failed we shall learn in the following chapters.

Unhappy results of the depression in Europe. After World War I, all of the nations involved in the war were overburdened with staggering debts. They had lost thousands of ships. Towns, villages, and even industrial cities had been destroyed, and confusion was seen everywhere. People were roaming the streets searching for employment. The greatest suffering was experienced in defeated Germany.

The depression had two unfavorable results in Europe. Faced with starvation, European nations built around their countries high tariff walls which tended greatly to slow up trade. Do you understand now why President Roosevelt tried to improve our trade relations? Recall what act President Roosevelt passed in 1934 to improve American trade.

Another uphappy result of World War I was the collapse of democratic forms of government in some of the important European countries. During this time of unrest, ambitious men rose to power in both Italy and Germany and eventually established themselves as dictators. Their unwholesome love of power and their false nationalism brought even greater sufferings upon the people.

Italy loses democracy. Govern-

Mussolini reviewing a battalion of Italian boys. These boys were being trained to be Fascists.

ment by the people disappeared first in Italy. A man named Benito Mussolini organized a group of young men whom he called Fascists (fa'-shists). This group rapidly spread throughout Italy. Finally it became strong enough to seize the government.

Within a very short time, the Fascists party became the only political party in Italy. Anyone criticizing this party was seized, punished, and sometimes put to death. **Germany loses democracy.** After World War I, Emperor William II, who had ruled Germany for many years, was forced to flee into exile. A short-lived democratic form of government was organized in 1919, and an aged general, Paul von Hindenburg, became President of Germany in 1925. The new government tried hard to rebuild the nation. But when the depression came, German finances collapsed, and the people lost faith in democracy. Discontent spread rapidly throughout the country. Could this possibly have been the result of the Treaty of Versailles, which stripped Germany of her possibilities to regain her place as a nation?

One particularly discontended individual was a man named Adolf Hitler. The memory of the Versailles Treaty never left him, and he was determined that he would try to rebuild German national power.

Adolf Hitler, surrounded by high officials of the Nazi government.

Under his leadership a group of war veterans, ex-soldiers, attempted to overthrow the democratic government in 1923. The attempt met with failure and resulted in the imprisonment of Hitler and his followers. While in jail, Hitler perfected his plans for making Germany once more the great nation which it was before World War I.

Immediately after his release from jail, Hitler gathered his followers into a party known as the National Socialist German Workers. A more familiar name for this party was the Nazis (na'-tseez). By 1933, Hitler had secured enough power to force President von Hindenburg to appoint him Chancellor, a position of primary importance in Ger-

many. Just a year later, upon the death of Von Hindenburg, Hitler succeeded him as head of the German government which he had already turned into a dictatorship.

Soviet Communism. In Eastern Europe, another dictatorship existed. The people of Russia, likewise, were forced to live under the iron hand of a powerful leader, Joseph Stalin (sta'-len). The rise of this dictatorship began even earlier than the other two just mentioned. Do you recall what happened in 1917 that forced Russia out of World War I? This revolution marked the beginning of Communism as we know it now. Russia, Italy, and Germany were the first *totalitarian states,* that is, countries where the state has complete control over all things. As years passed, other totalitarian governments arose.

The Church and totalitarianism. God established both the Church and the state, each having its own special purpose. He gave the Church the authority to care for the spiritual needs of man. He charged the state with man's temporal welfare. God intended that the Church and the state should work in harmony, but never that one should try to rule the other. Modern totalitarianism attempts to submerge the Church in the state, and thus destroy it. In other words, this form of government aims at absolute control of all social and private activities of an individual or a country. It regards the state as supreme authority.

Such a doctrine is false. As Catholics, we know that God is the Supreme Authority. God created the state to protect the natural rights of man and, therefore, it may not usurp any right which God has given to man. In the next paragraphs we shall see how the dictatorships of Germany, Italy, and Russia violated these rights.

Dictators overstep their power. Some nations in Europe at first accepted the dictators because they made fine promises to lead the people out of the hard times and suffering which followed World War I. Many thousands of Germans, for example, learned too late that they had been fooled by Hitler. For merely disagreeing with Hitler,

hundreds of innocent people were imprisoned in concentration camps.

In a very short time spies overran Germany to track down anyone whose views did not agree with those of Hitler. Jews and Catholics were singled out for special persecution. There followed arrest, imprisonment, and frequently death. When a government acts in this manner, do you think it is protecting the individual or promoting the common welfare?

The people of Italy fared no better under Mussolini's iron hand. At first Mussolini ignored Hitler, then he feared him, and finally he formed a military alliance with him.

Comparison of the three dictatorships. All of the dictatorships mentioned were somewhat alike. Those of Russia and Germany were similar in three respects. They claimed:

Hitler and Mussolini.

Bettmann Archive

255

1. the power of the state was supreme
2. the state had all rights and the individual had none except those which the state permitted
3. religion was to be destroyed

Mussolini's dictatorship differed from Hitler's in only one respect; he did not outwardly persecute the Church. The two dictatorships were similar in that they both feared Communism as greatly as did the democracies of Great Britain and France. It was because Hitler and Mussolini both defied Communism that the democracies, unfortunately, permitted them to get as strong as they finally became.

It was not surprising, then, during the 1930's, to find Europe divided into three camps: the democratic powers, led by Great Britain and France; the Fascist States of Germany and Italy; and the powerful Soviet Union which planned to overthrow all other forms of government. This dangerous situation drew the entire world into war for the second time.

The dictators begin their aggression. In 1935, Mussolini ordered his soldiers to invade the independent African country of Ethiopia. In just a few months this country became part of the Italian empire, which Mussolini intended to make as great as the ancient Roman Empire. The failure of the League of Nations to stop this unjust invasion showed the League's inability to maintain the peace of the world.

Italian tanks lead the way for the conquest of Ethiopia.

Hitler's aim was to enlarge Germany as Mussolini was attempting to expand his empire. The German Fuhrer, as Hitler was called, had gradually built up a strong army and air force, with a view to making Germany the home of the "master race," regardless of the cost to other countries. His object was to "purge," or cleanse, the German people by waging a merciless campaign against German Jews, whom he considered an inferior race. Many unfortunate people lost their lives just because they were Jews.

Hatred of any class of people or of any individual is contrary to the law of charity which Christ made the cornerstone of His religion. Do you think Hitler's aim could have been successful since it was based on a direct violation of God's law? As we read on we shall find out.

Hitler invades Poland. By 1938, Hitler had taken possession of Austria and part of Czechoslovakia. The smaller nations surrounding Germany gradually were frightened into submission. President Franklin D. Roosevelt personally appealed to Hitler to settle his quarrels peacefully and stop interfering unjustly in the affairs of these smaller nations. At that time, Hitler promised that Germany would seek no more territory. That promise was not kept.

In the summer of 1939, the German government demanded that Poland give up a strip of its territory. When Poland refused to meet this demand, the Nazi armies advanced into the country. The other nations would have expected Russia to come to Poland's assistance. But just two weeks before the German move, Russia had signed a treaty with Germany by which they agreed not to make war upon each other for ten years, and to be of mutual assistance. This treaty left Germany free to attack Poland without any interference from Russia. As Germany marched into western Poland, Russian troops marched in from the east. Former enemies, these two countries now divided the conquered nation between them.

How did European nations accept these moves? Events had been happening so rapidly in Europe that Great Britain and France did not realize their danger at once. The invasion of Poland, however, made them see more clearly that their own safety was being threatened. Therefore, they came to the aid of Poland, and World War II began in Europe on September 3, 1939.

Mussolini, the dictator of Italy, not only approved of Germany's aggression against weaker nations, but entered into an alliance with Germany. This alliance was known as the Rome-Berlin Axis. From this time on, the countries which were fighting on the side of Germany were called the *Axis Powers*. What were these countries called during the First World War? The democracies were referred to as the Allies, just as they had been in World War I.

American attitudes towards another war. The people in the United

257

These heavy fortifications and the barbed wire of the Maginot Line
failed to hold back the Germans.

States watched with growing uneasiness the developments in Europe. They clung to the hope of keeping this country out of another war. However, when Americans realized that our democratic way of life was endangered by the spread of Nazi and Fascist propaganda in South America, something had to be done immediately.

The first step President Roosevelt took was to make a "good will" tour of the South American republics. By this tour he attempted to strengthen our relations with South America. Do you recall what President Roosevelt called his policy of strengthening our relations with these countries?

Between 1936 and 1939, at three separate conferences, the American republics pledged loyalty to the democratic way of life and agreed to defend it at any cost. What was this union of American republics called? Did you think of "Pan-American Union"? That was the organization's original name. What is its new name? See the last chapter of Unit One, if you have forgotten.

The second step which the President took towards safeguarding American interests was the repeal of the Neutrality Act which had been passed in 1937. This act stated, in part, that the United States could not export munitions to belligerent nations. The President replaced this part of the act by a "cash and carry" program. This program permitted the Allies to get munitions and other supplies from the United States provided they would pay cash for these materials and carry them away in their own ships. President Roosevelt hoped in this way to keep America from becoming mixed up in the European struggle. His intentions were well meant, but it was soon clear that this arrangement would not be effective in keeping us out of the war.

2. The Spread of the Dictatorships in Europe and Asia

Events in Europe moved with startling rapidity. The entire world was amazed at Germany's speed in conquering her neighbors. The story of World War II is so complicated that we shall learn only the very important points.

Nazi *Blitzkriegs.* We have seen how cleverly Hitler succeeded in subduing Austria, Czechoslovakia, and Poland. By May of 1940, Norway, Denmark, Holland, and Belgium were conquered. The Germans had their own name for their new type of sudden warfare. It was called *blitzkrieg* (blits'-kreeg), or "lightning war." Their armies, strengthened by air forces, would without warning mass themselves along the boundaries of helpless countries and attack them, meeting very little resistance from the surprised inhabitants. Was this just? According to Christian principles, no country may wage war merely to satisfy its desire to dominate or rule another country.

Hitler invades France. Hitler was becoming bolder with each victory. Early in June, 1940, the Nazi war machines began sweeping over France. Before the war, France had built, along her eastern boundary, a series of fortifications called the Maginot (ma-zhee-no') Line, but it was not strong enough to withstand the German blitzkrieg. It would have been a perfect defense against any infantry attacks, such as World War I had witnessed. But World War II was a different kind of war. Against the swarms of German airplanes which shot across the sky, France lay helpless. By the end of June, Germany had swept on to Paris and forced France to sign an armistice.

Two-thirds of France was then occupied by German troops. Many Frenchmen fell an easy prey to German power. They finally set up a Nazi-controlled capital at Vichy, France. The British army, which had been helping France, now was forced to retreat across the English Channel. With the surrender of France, England stood alone, without the protection of any Allied armies in northwestern Europe. Would her turn come next?

The battle for England. With the fall of France, practically all of the continent of Europe was in the hands of the Nazi power. The German air force then attempted to weaken England's morale by launching a series of large-scale air attacks. Wave after wave of bombers destroyed large cities and war production plants. Thousands of people were killed and wounded. But the Fighter Command of the Royal Air Force (R.A.F.), and the

London during the "Blitz".

Royal Navy succeeded in preventing the German army from ever entering England.

After months of actual war from the air, and the threat of the German army to strike on land, Hitler suddenly changed his mind about conquering England at this time and decided to invade Russia.

The invasion of Russia. Before moving into Russia, the German armies smashed through the Balkan Peninsula in southeastern Europe in the spring of 1941. Nazi Germany was then ready to attack Russia.

Let us recall the fact that Germany and Russia had entered into an agreement shortly before the invasion of Poland. Besides agreeing not to wage war on each other, these two countries planned an exchange of manufactured goods and raw materials. Imagine Russia's surprise when Germany suddenly decided to disregard the agreement she had made! Why did the Nazis decide to strike Russia so suddenly? They wished to secure for themselves the rich wheat lands of southern Russia and the oil fields near the Caucasus (kaw'-ka-sus) Mountains.

In a very short time, the Nazi armies had penetrated deep into Russian territory. But their measure of their enemy's strength was incorrect. The Russians had a vast army, and the people backed this army with every ounce of strength they had. Terrible battles were waged along the Russian front, but the German army was never able to capture Stalingrad (sta'-lingrad) or Moscow, the two most important objectives. The Russians burned crops and materials before the Nazis could seize them. For two years they repelled the Nazis with the help of American supplies.

Tenseness in the United States increases. The anxiety of the American people at the turn of affairs in Europe was ever increasing. Each of Hitler's victories made the Americans more determined than ever to embark upon a program to strengthen our own defenses and to aid the countries fighting Italy and Germany. President Roosevelt, who had been reelected for a third term in 1940, consulted Congress, and the necessary steps were taken to prepare the nation for what might lie ahead.

For the first time in our history, we had peacetime military conscrip-

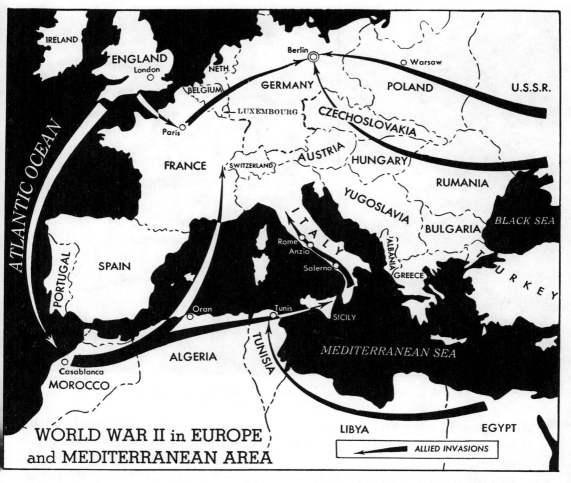

WORLD WAR II in EUROPE and MEDITERRANEAN AREA

ALLIED INVASIONS

tion. The Selective Training and Service Act of 1940 prescribed military training for men between the ages of twenty-one and thirty-six.

Then, in March, 1941, Congress passed the Lend-Lease Act. This act permitted the President to have war equipment sent to any country whose defense seemed vital to that of our own. Under this arrangement, the United States shipped raw materials, food, medicine, tanks, and planes to Britain, China, Russia, and those nations that were courageously resisting the Axis.

Japan's problem. As previously mentioned, World War II was a global war and, therefore, it is necessarry at this point to turn from Europe to Asia.

After the First World War, as you recall, the great nations of the world, including Japan, promised faithfully that they would not unjustly attack another nation. They promised, too, that they would not resort to war as a means of settling disputes. It was the duty of the League of Nations to see that these well-meant agreements were kept.

The Japanese invasion of Manchuria. These soldiers are shooting from the tops of box cars.

But Japan, like the European countries, did not intend to keep her bargain.

In 1930 there were over one hundred times as many people per square mile in Japan as there were in the United States. The care of this large population was a problem because Japan did not have the natural resources necessary to carry on her industries. Nor did she have sufficient food for these people. Therefore, Japan began to look around for both elbow-room and raw materials.

Japan violates her promises. Slowly but surely, the Japanese government became militaristic, just as did some of the European governments. Do you recall what "militaristic" means? Japanese generals and admirals looked longingly at neighboring lands and laid plans to build such a vast empire that one day Japan would control all of Asia.

Then, suddenly, in 1931 Japan dealt a surprise blow. She invaded a part of North China known as Manchuria. To try to justify her action, Japan stated she acted in self-defense. Immediately, the League of Nations reminded Japan of the international non-aggression agreement and scorned Japan's flimsy excuse of self-defense. Japan, however, refused to withdraw from Manchuria. She also changed that country's name to the Japanese word *Manchukuo* (man-choo'koe).

Unfortunately, the League of Nations and the rest of the world did nothing to stop Japanese aggression. As a result, Japan not only continued the warfare in China, but also fortified her island possessions in the Pacific. The United States either did not realize this danger at the time or else was careless in taking steps to strengthen our own possessions in the Far East.

It is not strange, then, that Italy, Germany, and Japan, countries with the same idea of enlarging their territories, should form an alliance. This alliance, formed in 1940, was known as the Rome-Berlin-Tokyo Pact. These powers promised each other military assistance if a new power should enter the war then in progress.

Japan enters World War II. After the passage of the Lend-Lease Act, American equipment was being shipped to Russia by way of the Pacific Ocean. Germany tried to prevent this aid from getting to Russia and urged Japan to help her. When Japan was not inclined to assist, Japanese nationalists overthrew the cabinet and set up a pro-Nazi one in its place.

All during the summer of 1941, then, Japanese troops began to spread over important points in the Pacific Ocean. It did not take the United States and Great Britain long this time to sense the danger, and in August they broke off trade relations with Japan.

The Atlantic Charter. Shortly after the break in our trade relations with

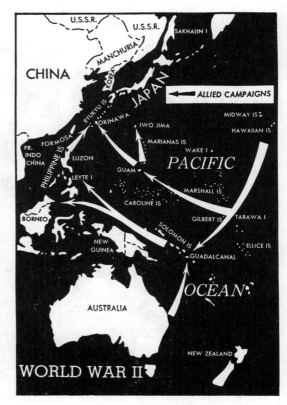

WORLD WAR II

Japan, an event of world importance took place. Somewhere in the North Atlantic, Prime Minister Winston Churchill of Great Britain met President Roosevelt aboard the American cruiser *Augusta* for the first of their many conferences. What was talked about at that meeting was, for a time, kept secret. These two men, who were destined to become great friends, finally proposed a program for peace known as the Atlantic Charter. This charter was released to the world on August 14, 1941, and upon it hopes for a better world were based.

The Atlantic Charter declared that Great Britain and the United States desired no additional territory after the war ended. It stated

President Roosevelt and Winston Churchill meet aboard ship on the Atlantic Ocean
to draw up the Atlantic Charter.

that no territorial changes would be made that would not please the people concerned. The people of all nations, great or small, were to have the right to choose their own form of government. All nations had a right to the world's resources and they could secure these resources through equal trade rights.

The Four Freedoms originally expressed by President Roosevelt to Congress on January 6, 1941, were also discussed at this time. These freedoms were:

1. Freedom of speech
2. Freedom of every person to worship God in his own way.
3. Freedom from want
4. Freedom from fear

Although the Atlantic Charter represented the personal views of Churchill and Roosevelt, most of the nations fighting against the Axis powers were in accord with them. Unfortunately, the terms of the charter were violated by the very men who wrote it when they permitted Russia to gain control of the small countries along her border.

Japan's treacherous attack on Pearl Harbor. As the year 1941 drew to a close, Japan's aggression increased. President Roosevelt appealed to the Emperor of Japan to cooperate with him in trying to secure peace in the Pacific. The Japanese government sent diplo-

President Roosevelt explains the Four Freedoms to Congress.
What were these freedoms?

mats to Washington who talked as if they desired peace.

But even while these conversations were in progress, the Japanese took the step which plunged the United States into the war. Before the surprised world could realize it, swarms of Japanese planes roared over our naval base at Pearl Harbor in Hawaii on December 7, 1941. American forces stationed there were not alert to defend themselves. They had not expected a "sneak" attack from a nation with whom we were supposedly at peace. Nearly five thousand Americans were killed, wounded, or missing, and much of our naval equipment was damaged. Needless to say, the at-

tack on Pearl Harbor was a terrible blow to our naval power in the Pacific.

On December 8, the United States and Japan declared war on each other, and three days later Germany and Italy joined Japan. Japan's attack broadened the war in Europe to a world conflict or a global war. When President Roosevelt addressed Congress to ask for a declaration of war he solemnly stated:

The forces endeavoring to enslave the entire world now are moving toward this hemisphere. Never before has there been a greater challenge to life, liberty and civilization. Rapid and unit-

From Ewing Galloway, N. Y.

The results of the Japanese attack on Pearl Harbor.
The U.S.S. West Virginia burns amidships.

ed effort by all peoples of the world who are determined to remain free will insure a world victory of the forces of justice and of righteousness over the forces of savagery and of barbarism.

Would the world unite to fight against this common enemy? In the remaining chapters of this book you will find the answer to the struggle of liberty-loving people of the world against the forces of tyranny.

With the attack of Japan on Pearl Harbor, a whole new era in world history was opened up. The battle lines were being drawn between the free world and the totalitarian states. It would not be long before Russia, who became our ally, would reveal that she was anxious for world conquest and would become hostile to those who had fought with her and had given her supplies.

Even though we were not too far from victory in the Second World War, we were later to be faced with the serious problem of Russia's desire for conquest after the peace treaties were signed. We shall read about this problem later.

What do these mean?

dictatorship	Axis Powers
Fascists	the Allies
Nazis	*blitzkrieg*
chancellor	Maginot Line

totalitarian state   Vichy France
militaristic   Lend-Lease Act
military alliance   global war
"cash and carry" program
good neighbor policy
Rome-Berlin-Tokyo Pact

How well can you talk about these?

1. How were the objectives of each of the three dictatorships mentioned in this chapter alike? Was there any difference in any of them?
2. Discuss the ways in which each dictator violated Christian social principles.
3. Why does the Church disapprove of totalitarianism?
4. What was the immediate cause of the beginning of World War II in Europe?
5. How did President Roosevelt attempt to safeguard the United States against the possibility of becoming involved in the Second World War?
6. Why did Japan become involved in World War II?
7. Discuss the main points of the Atlantic Charter. Do you think they follow Christian principles? Why?

Are you ready for this check-up?

Below are 15 groups of three words or phrases. One word does not belong to the other two. Find this word, and then on your paper write a sentence about the two words which are related.

depression of 1929	high tariff walls	good trade relations
Fascists	Mussolini	Russia
Nazis	Italy	Germany
totalitarian state	Germany	France
invasion of Poland	France	Germany
dictatorship	Great Britain	Hitler
Ethiopia	Stalin	Mussolini
"master race"	English	German
South America	Nazi propaganda	Maginot Line
Vichy France	Nazi-controlled	Fascist-controlled
Maginot Line	Germany	England
invasion of Russia	1939	1941
Manchukuo	France	Japan
Atlantic Charter	United States and France	United States and Great Britain
Pearl Harbor	Japanese	Chinese

Answer these questions as briefly as possible

1. When did World War II begin in Europe?
2. What caused the United States to enter World War II?
3. In what year did the United States enter the war?
4. Against what race was Hitler prejudiced?
5. What name was given to those countries which aided Germany in World War II?
6. Give two reasons why Germany invaded Russia.

CHAPTER V

AMERICAN TEAMWORK AGAIN BRINGS AN ALLIED VICTORY

What to look for in this chapter. The entrance of the United States into World War II brought welcome expressions of support from all parts of Latin America. The Good Neighbor Policy began to work. Every one of the Latin American countries eventually declared war upon the Axis powers or, at least, severed diplomatic relations with them.

How did Americans themselves react? The United States went on a full war footing immediately. Our main purpose was to bring this war to as speedy a close as possible. For a second time our resources were mobilized for all-out war effort. The nation cheerfully made whatever sacrifices were necessary to hasten an Allied victory. Our service men and women could be found on nearly every spot of the globe.

During the war and after its close, efforts were again made for a lasting peapce. Our Holy Father, Pope Pius XII, like his predecessor, Pope Benedict XV, appealed to the nations of the world for justice in the peace negotiations. Did the family of nations learn any lessons from World War I? Did they apply them

to the peace proposals made after World War II? We shall see that the United States endeavored to act justly towards the defeated nations even though our internal problems were great enough to make us concentrate on them.

In this chapter, you will learn how the United States organized for war at home, how the bravery of the Americans helped to hasten a military victory in Europe and Asia, and how the United Nations worked together to end the war and establish peace.

1. In Union There is Strength

Back in Civil War days, Americans learned that a country divided against itself would not stand. Labor, too, as we have seen, learned that, by uniting, its objectives would be more easily attained. World War I brought the people of America into even closer unity, but it remained for the Second World War to test the real unity of America.

Industry in the United States goes to war. The Axis powers believed that it would be impossible for the United States to get into production fast enough to furnish necessary war materials. But they did not know the determination of the American people.

Modern warfare requires an enormous number of guns, tanks, planes, ships, and ammunition of all kinds. In order to make these vital war materials, factories had to be converted from a peace-time production of such things as automobiles and radios. This turn-over completely changed the picture of American life. People were no longer able to purchase those articles which they could normally buy, but they willingly made these sacrifices for the greater objective of ending the war.

The government, which was the only power able to make this change in industry, organized the War Production Board, which took complete control of the nation's industry. Under government direction many new types of industries were established. Probably the most important of these new industries was the making of synthetic rubber, about which you have previously read. Turn to Unit Two if you have forgotten the story of the discovery of this vital substitute for natural rubber.

Uncle Sam regulates labor. From the beginning of the war it was very evident that the United States would have to send men, as well as supplies, to nearly all corners of the globe. However, if there were to be a sufficient number of men to meet the needs of industry at home, there had to be some way of controlling manpower. Therefore, the government set up a War Manpower Commission which decided that men who were in key industries, that is, industries which produced vital war materials, were exempt from military service. It also forbade these men to change their positions without the permission of the government.

Perhaps you may wonder whether or not such control over human lives should be tolerated in a democratic state like ours. This action is justified only when a country is fighting to preserve its life and the security of all its inhabitants.

Rationing. If civilians at home had not done their part in the war effort, the soldiers and sailors could not have won victories abroad. The war caused shortages in food, shoes, gasoline, and rubber. These com-

Ration book during World War II.
By Ewing Galloway, N. Y.

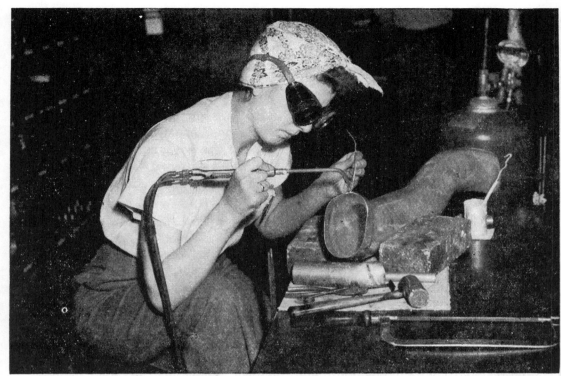

A woman war worker. Many women took the places of men in defense industries.

modities were rationed, that is, each person was permitted a specified amount, so that everyone would receive his fair share. Because so many of these articles were needed by our civilian population, prices began to rise quickly. In order to keep down the cost of living, the government established an emergency agency called the Office of Price Administration (OPA) which set limits, or ceilings, above which prices could not go.

Women come to Uncle Sam's assistance. A very active part in the war was taken by women. Wherever possible, women took the places of men in factory jobs in order to release them for service in the armed forces. This had many harmful effects, especially when the women were mothers of families. It is true that the men were needed to defend democracy, but some women never went back to their proper place in the home. The middle of the twentieth century found them still occupying positions which were previously always held by men.

Many young women volunteered as members of the Women's Army Corps (WACS), Women's Reserve of the United States Coast Guard (SPARS), and the Women's Reserve of the Navy (WAVES). Their self-sacrificing work at home and abroad will always be remembered.

Enlisted women of the Armed Forces.

American field commanders
in World War II.

2. Main Battlegrounds of World War II

We mentioned previously that this global war was so complicated that only the main points will be studied. In order to understand even the main points it will be necessary to divide this section into two subdivisions: (a) The European War Picture and (b) War in the Pacific.

a. The European War Picture

Planning a united attack. In December of 1941, Churchill and President Roosevelt decided at a meeting in Washington that they should combine their forces in an all-out offensive to defeat the Axis powers. They set up a military group known as the Combined Chiefs of Staff which was to direct the united efforts of Great Britain and the United States. One of their big problems was to make plans for conquering the enemy in all parts of the world. These plans had to fit into the Russian picture, since that country did not attend the meeting.

General Dwight D. Eisenhower was the first supreme commander of the joint British-American land, air, and naval forces in the Mediterranean Theater of Operations. Later, he was moved to the European Theater where he led the combined Allied forces to final victory. East of the Mediterranean Theater, Generalissimo Joseph Stalin commanded the vast Russian armies. Where would the Allies strike first? After some deliberation, the Combined Chiefs of Staff decided to begin with Germany.

Although we will not bring Asiatic affairs into this section, it is well for you to remember that all the while men were fighting in Europe, war was also being waged in Asia. **Hitler's empire begins to crumble.** Recall that Hitler decided to attack Russia in the summer of 1941. His victories had been so outstanding up until this time that he felt assured of the conquest of Russia. With the advent of a bitter Russian winter, however, Nazi plans were upset. Heavy snowfalls caught the German army unprepared to carry on a winter campaign. Without shelter and adequate clothing, the German army suffered terribly. Eventually, the Russian forces smashed through the entire front from Stalingrad to the Black Sea.

The failure to capture Stalingrad and Moscow, and the loss of many soldiers was Hitler's first serious defeat of the war. The Russians, on the other hand, gained confidence. Although they did pause from time to time, they kept advancing towards Germany until Soviet troops entered Berlin in 1945.

The Atlantic — a sea of danger. In 1942 the United States suffered great losses even before she got her armies into Europe. Men, munitions, and food had to be transported across the Atlantic Ocean. To prevent this aid from reaching Great Britain, Germany again had recourse to submarine warfare. Every effort was made to guard the

During the war, ships had to travel in convoys like this
as a protection against submarine attacks.

Official U. S. Navy Photo from Brown Brothers

American soldiers of the Fifth Army going to the front in the Italian campaign.

passage of men and materials but, in spite of this, losses steadily mounted. Germany had planted mines in the ocean, and for many months after the war was over, one could read in papers or magazines that a ship met with disaster in the Atlantic Ocean.

Another Axis defeat in North Africa. For some time, German and Italian forces had been occupying North Africa. British ships were finding it hard to get through the Mediterranean to Egypt. When it appeared that the Nazis were heading for the great seaport of Alexandria on the Suez Canal, General Sir Bernard Montgomery and the British Eighth Army fought against

them and, finally, pushed the Germans westward.

By the spring of 1943, General Eisenhower had landed American troops on the northwest coast of Africa. The German army was hemmed in on both the east and the west and, finally, General Eisenhower, in full command, defeated and captured the powerful Nazi army. In spite of the collapse of the German army in North Africa, Hitler still maintained that no one could capture his European Fortress.

The fall of Italy. In July, 1943, Eisenhower moved to his next target, the island of Sicily. British and American forces quickly conquered

Men and vehicles coming ashore on the beach in Southern France on D-Day.

the island against great resistance from German troops. The capture of Sicily led to a political crisis in Italy, and Mussolini resigned.

Eisenhower's troops now advanced into the mainland of Italy where they were held up for many months by Nazi armies which Hitler had sent into Italy. The new Italian government, tired of the domineering Nazis, surrendered to the Allies, and within a month declared war on her former Axis partner, Germany. Mussolini finally met a violent death at the hands of his own countrymen. The first victory had been won over an Axis country.

The dawn of D-Day. The Allied armies pressed onward, filled with determination to conquer Germany. The early months of 1944 saw great preparations for the invasion of western Europe. After liberating France from Nazi control, the British-American forces were ready for the last great stroke which would free Europe from Nazism.

As a last great preparation for D-Day, or Invasion Day, Allied air forces roared over German industrial centers, dropping thousands of tons of bombs. When D-Day finally dawned on June 6, 1944, allied troops swarmed on to the beaches of northern France. The D-Day invasion of Europe was the greatest invasion the world had ever seen. It cost many lives. The Nazi army also suffered heavy losses but it attempted to make a last bitter stand to defend Germany.

The end of the war in Europe. From D-Day to the close of the war, Russian troops moved steadily towards Berlin from the east until they captured the city on May 2, 1945. At this time Hitler was reported dead. The forces of General Eisenhower, advancing from the west, fought again on World War I battlefields. The battles surged back and forth against solid German defense lines.

Two of the hardest and bloodiest battles of World War II were fought in this last great push, the Battle of the Bulge and the Battle of Remagen (rem-a'-gen) Bridge. Both of these battles were victories for the British-American forces which shoved on until they met the Russian armies in the middle of Germany. On May 7, 1945, Germany surrendered unconditionally.

The following day was officially proclaimed V-E (victory in Europe) Day by Harry S. Truman, who became President at the death of Franklin D. Roosevelt in April 1945. A combined Allied victory had conquered the forces of tyranny in Europe, at least temporarily. The years following the war would be the test of the victory.

The end of the war in Europe.
The German General Jodl signs the terms of unconditional surrender.

Signal Corps Photo from Brown Brothers

Occupation of Germany. With the unconditional surrender of the German armed forces, the Allies took complete control of Germany. The country was divided into four zones of military occupation. An eastern zone went to Soviet Russia, the northwestern to Great Britain; a southwestern to the United States; and a western to France. All allied nations occupied Berlin. The occupying authorities then endeavored to remodel Germany along democratic lines. The problem which thus arose will be discussed in a later chapter.

b. War in the Pacific Theatre

The first year of American participation in the war was discouraging. The Japanese attack on Pearl Harbor had paralyzed our Pacific fleet, but the heroic courage of American and other allied forces finally ended in victory.

Japanese wave of conquest. The Americans passed grim and tragic days watching the Japanese extend their power in the Pacific. They captured many small but very important possessions of the United States. If you look on the map on page 263 you will find the names of these places, all of which we will not mention in the story of this conquest. The reason many of these possessions fell was because of a lack of planes, ships, and men to hold back the Japanese.

The Japanese, urged on by their successes, easily conquered the British naval base of Singapore. In a very short time they had control of all the rubber and oil of the Dutch East Indies. Then they extended their control over most of the islands north of Australia and later won successes in the Aleutian Islands, south of Alaska.

The fall of the Philippines. The Japanese army and navy rolled on and met with little resistance until they reached the Philippines. Here Japan's advance was checked by a people who were determined to save that freedom which had been promised by the Americans. Do you recall when that promise was made? Turn to Unit One to refresh your memory.

The Filipinos joined the American forces under the command of General Douglas MacArthur, but because they were greatly outnumbered by the Japanese, they were forced to surrender Manila, the capital of the Philippines, on January 2, 1942. The American-Filipino troops then retired to the Bataan Peninsula.

At this time President Roosevelt ordered General MacArthur to Australia, leaving General Jonathan Wainwright in charge of our forces. Before leaving, however, MacArthur made a pledge to come back and free the Philippines. Behind the Bataan Peninsula lay the great fortress of Corregidor (core-reg'-i-dore) where American and Filipino soldiers fought bravely for nearly four months, only to be compelled to surrender in May when food and ammunition failed.

Resistance to Japan stiffens. Until the second half of 1942, the Allies had been on the defensive, which means that they were merely able to hold back the enemy without gaining any victories. Towards the end of that year, Allied strength, which had been constantly growing, began to make itself felt.

Probably the biggest single reason why the tide of battle turned in 1942 was increased cooperation among the Allies. They realized that if they wished to continue to exist they must work together in a common cause. On January 2, 1942, the day Manila fell, twenty-six nations fighting the Axis signed a "Declaration by the United Nations." Three important pledges were taken by these nations: (1) they would fight with all their strength, (2) they would not make separate peace treaties with any nation, and (3) they would comply with the provisions of the Atlantic Charter. The keeping of these pledges would hasten final victory.

A New Order in Asia. The Japanese had intended to set up a "New Order" in Asia. This meant that Japan intended to dominate all Asiatic peoples and, thereby, keep Asia for the Asiatics. The Japanese tried to influence the people by telling them that people from the West had long been troublesome in Asia and it was time that the hands of the Westerners be tied.

Japan, as we have mentioned previously, desired elbow-room, and the cold lands of Russia did not suit her purpose. Therefore, she looked to the South Pacific where the climate was much more to her liking.

So far as China was concerned, Japan felt that it should belong to her.

Do you recall how at one time European nations were trying to grasp pieces of China? The United States took care of that difficulty in the last year of the nineteenth century when she proposed the open door policy. This leads us to the position of China at the time of World War II.

Across the Burma Road. China had been suffering from the effects of a war with Japan for four and a half years when Pearl Harbor was bombed. With the adoption of the Lend-Lease program, the United States began sending aid to China as an ally. In 1942, Japan invaded Burma and closed the Burma Road, the only remaining route to China and her life line for several years.

The winding Burma Road.
Brown Brothers

Bettman Archive

Generalissimo Chiang-Kai-Shek with his wife and General Stillwell.

The flag is raised on Iwo-Jima.

Brown Brothers

The Chinese had built this road when Japan began attacking them from the north.

The closing of the Burma Road cut off the supply of heavy army equipment, but medicine, food, and clothing, needed so badly to continue the war, were shipped in by American planes. Our planes also helped China by bombing Japanese bases. In 1945, the Japanese were driven out of Burma by the combined efforts of American, British, and Chinese forces.

At this time World War II came to an end in Europe, and the United Nations were now in a better position to end the war in Asia.

The Allies take the road back. The war in the Pacific was long and bloody. The American Marines fought desperately against such odds as tropical rains, marshy lands, and dense woods. One of the hardest and most bitter campaigns in American history was the Battle of the Solomons. Here on Guadalcanal (guad-al-can-al′), after six months of fierce fighting, the American fleet succeeded in clearing out the enemy.

Early in 1945, General MacArthur returned to the Philippines, as he had promised, and began to recover the islands from the Japanese. After slight resistance, the city of Manila was once more in American hands. At Iwo Jima (ee′wo jee′-ma), a tiny island in the Pacific, and at Okinawa (owe-kee-nah′-wah) the Marines raised the American flag in triumph. From Okinawa, which is only 325 miles from

General Mac Arthur returns to the Philippines as he promised.

Brown Brothers

Japan giant bombers directly attacked the Japanese homeland.

The success of the Allies in the Pacific was due in large measure to the outstanding work of the American fleet. From huge aircraft carriers, planes took off and struck at the Japanese fleet at every opportunity. While the Japanese fleet was being crippled, American soldiers were landed wherever possible. Back in the United States plans were being made for a final blow. **Japan is forced to yield to Allied**

attacks. Near the end of July, 1945, leaders of the United States, Great Britain, and China met in Potsdam, Germany. One important decision which they reached at this time was to issue an ultimatum of surrender to Japan. An ultimatum is a final warning. When Japan refused to heed this warning, the Allies decided to act immediately.

On August 6, 1945, an American B-29 flew high over Hiroshima (he-ro-she′-ma), Japan's seventh largest city. Before the citizens knew

279

Atom bomb exploding over Nagasaki.

On the same day that Russia joined the Allies, a second atomic bomb was dropped on the city of Nagasaki (na-ga-sa'-kee). Japan's position was hopeless, and the Tokyo radio appealed for peace. On August 14, 1945, President Truman officially announced Japan's surrender. This day has been called V-J Day — victory over Japan. On September 2, the formal surrender was signed on board the American warship *Missouri* in Tokyo Bay. So ended the most terrible war in the history of the world.

3. United Efforts to Win the War and Establish World Peace

Conferences between Churchill and Roosevelt. In a previous chapter, we learned that President Roosevelt and Prime Minister Churchill met somewhere in the North Atlantic for a conference. Do you recall the result of this conference? If you do not, turn to Chapter IV of this Unit to find out.

After this meeting, Roosevelt and Churchill had a number of other conferences. As already mentioned, the war had developed into a global one. The decisions to be made about such a large-scale war could not be made by the head of one government alone. Therefore, Roosevelt and Churchill met in a series of conferences at Washington, Casablanca, Quebec, and Teheran, a city in Iran. At these conferences they came to decisions about the manner of conducting the war. It was at Casablanca, in northwestern Africa, that the unconditional surrender terms to be imposed on the Axis

what had happened, there was a blinding flash of light, and a terrific explosion. A huge area of the city was destroyed and fire broke out. A dense cloud of white smoke leaped 40,000 feet into the air. What had caused this awful blast? A new type of weapon, an atomic bomb, had been used for the first time. The blast made by this bomb was felt 150 miles away and three-fifths of Hiroshima was leveled. Two days later, Russia finally joined the Allies against Japan.

Official U. S. Army Photo from Ewing Galloway, N. Y.

Roosevelt, Churchill, and Stalin pose for their pictures
in front of the Russian Embassy at Teheran.

Powers were finally decided upon.

A meeting in Moscow. In October, 1943, the representatives of the United States, Great Britain, Russia, and China held a meeting at Moscow at which they stated that these four nations, commonly called the Big Four, would cooperate more closely with each other. They also agreed to support a plan to establish some kind of permanent peace organization after the war.

The plan for a world security organization begins. Recommendations for a strong, definite world organization were made at Dumbarton Oaks, Washington, D. C., in 1944. The purposes set for this organization were: (1) to maintain the security of all nations, (2) to bring about peaceful settlements of disputes between nations, and (3) to work for the welfare of all people of the world. Questions such as the following were also discussed: Who shall be members? How often shall the organization meet? What topics shall it deal with?

Later, in Yalta, a city in the southern part of Russia, President Roosevelt, Prime Minister Churchill, and Premier Stalin continued their plans. It was decided at this meeting that the United Nations should hold a conference in the spring of 1945 to draft a charter for such an organization. The war had proved that it was possible

281

The Conference at Yalta. At left is Stalin. Center, Admiral Leahy, Secretary of State Stettinius, President Roosevelt, with Churchill in foreground.

for nations to work together. Could they not also cooperate during peace time? Cooperation should be possible in a world that is striving for justice for all men, but as you read on, watch the developments which proved that not all leaders of nations were interested in the welfare of the world.

The birth of the United Nations Organization. On April 25, 1945, delegates of the United Nations met in San Francisco to write the charter of this great world organization. Representatives of fifty nations arrived. President Roosevelt, probably the most interested of the planners of this convention, was des-

tined not to be present. He died suddenly at Warm Springs, Georgia, just two weeks before the conference began. Harry S. Truman, succeeded him as President.

The name given to the new international group was the United Nations Organization. Although there were some differences of opinion at the meeting, the final result was a written charter entrusting the organization with the task of keeping peace when it was once achieved. What other such organization have you already learned about? The story of the breaking up of the League of Nations and the formation of the United Nations Organization will be found in the next Unit.

Drafting the peace treaties. The making of peace after World War II proved to be a greater problem than winning the war. The task was begun in the historic Luxembourg Palace in Paris. Here, during the hot summer days of 1946, delegates from the twenty-one principal nations of the world attempted to draft peace treaties with five of the defeated countries. Peace terms with the two principal defeated powers, Germany and Japan, were to be discussed separately.

While these plans were going on, what was happening in the rest of the world? In China a civil war was raging. Palestine and India were scenes of bloody rioting. Russia was pouring her atheistic ideas into all of the neighboring countries, over which she began to tighten her control.

In the peace chamber itself there was little harmony. Sharp disagreements and bitter debate between Russia and the other great powers quickly developed. Some people were surprised at the attitude of Russia, which had come out of the conflict as one of the leading nations of the world. Communistic Russia's idea was not world peace, but on the contrary, world revolution!

A clash of ideas. Why did Russia not agree with other nations? Recall that Russia was one of the totalitarian states about which we have read. As such, Russia believed that the welfare of the state came before the welfare of her people. Her ideas

Brown Brothers

Stettinius signs UN charter at San Francisco.

of society and ways of living, therefore, clashed with the ideas of Christian democracy.

All during the war, Russia had enslaved the people in the countries which she had conquered and forced them to work for the Communistic state. Disagreement with the Russian tyrants meant persecution. Catholics, convinced in their belief in the supremacy of God, suffered untold trials.

This system of persecution was one of the greatest evils which grew out of Russia's increased power. Instead of using her power for good, Russia violated justice by depriving the people under her control of their right to worship God as they desired. Her action also violated the promise she had made to the United States when this country recog-

283

Pope Pius XII after Allies entered Rome.

nized Soviet Russia in 1933. The next paragraphs will tell you this story.

Russia violates her promise of religious freedom. Maxim Litvinoff (lit-vee'-noff) was the first Russian Ambassador to the United States after President Roosevelt recognized Soviet Russia in 1933. These two men began a series of discussions on what would be expected of each country in the way of cooperation "for their [the two nations concerned] mutual benefit and for the preservation of the peace of the world."

One of the things for which President Roosevelt specifically asked was the right of any Americans living in Russia to conduct, support, and practice any religious belief they desired. Mr. Litvinoff agreed to this request, referring to the following quotations taken from laws and regulations which existed in the various republics of the Soviet Union at that time:

Every person may profess any religion or none . . . Within the confines of the Soviet Union it is prohibited to issue any local laws or regulations restricting or limiting freedom of conscience, or establishing privileges . . . of any kind based upon the religious profession of any person.

In regard to the religious education of American children living in Russia, Litvinoff wrote that Russia would grant the right to Americans to

impart religious instruction to their children either singly or in groups or to have such instruction imparted by persons whom they employ for such purpose.

This right was also supported by Russian law.

From what you have read regarding the enslavement of people in countries dominated by Communist Russia and the persecution of religion in these countries, you can see how little regard the Communists have even for their own laws. It is true that the promise made concerned Americans living in Russia, but the law was written for any inhabitant of Russia.

The Papal Peace Plan. The treaties made during the years after World War II satisfied no one. Jealousies and dissatisfaction continued. Although Pope Pius XII did not attend the peace conferences, his words did influence those countries which sincerely desired to see justice done. The United States was one of these countries. The letters between President Roosevelt and, later, President Truman and the Holy Father proved that.

With the outbreak of the war, Pope Pius XII was determined, since he could no longer prevent the struggle, at least to try to shorten it. Beginning with his first Christmas as Christ's representative on earth in 1939, Pius XII delivered at least once a year a discourse on the type of peace which the world must seek. His ideas, taken together, form what has been called the Papal Peace Plan. Some of the main points in this plan are:

1. Religious freedom is a basic condition for peace in the world.
2. Nations have a right to freedom because without freedom there is no responsibility.
3. Whether a nation is large or small, it has a right to life and independence.
4. The natural resources of the world should be available to all peoples.
5. International agreements should be respected and carried out.
6. Nations should reduce armaments.
7. Justice and charity, rather than hatred and revenge, should be the basis of international relations.
8. The mutual rights of the employer and the employee must be understood.
9. Some kind of international organization should be estab-

lished to insure the peace of the world.
10. Family life is the foundation of every government and, therefore, should be held sacred.

As you grow older you should study the Papal Peace Plan more fully because there are other important points included in it not mentioned in this text. Christian citizens know and live up to their responsibility to God and their country. Citizens of this kind will help the world to secure the peace for which it has been groping for the past thirty years.

Remember these words or phrases

on the defensive	D-DAY
aircraft carrier	V-E Day
officially proclaimed	ultimatum
Papal Peace Plan	V-J Day
military zones of occupation	
unconditional surrender	

More questions about the Second World War

1. Discuss the way in which the United States met the war situation at home.
2. What was the purpose of the Combined Chiefs of Staff? Who were members?
3. Compare the points of the Atlantic Charter with Wilson's Fourteen Points.
4. Japan hoped to set up a "New Order" in the Far East. Explain what this means and tell how Japan went about trying to accomplish this.
5. Discuss the main events which led to the downfall of the Nazi empire.

6. What two battles led immediately to the surrender of Germany?

7. Why did the tide of battle turn in favor of the Allies in 1942?

8. Why were the Allies better able to concentrate on conquering Japan after 1945?

9. In which theater of the war did most of the fighting take place on water?

10. What promise to the United States did Russia fail to keep?

How did Communist Russia violate Christian principles?

Are you ready for another test?

I. Arrange the following events in the order in which they happened.
a. D-Day
b. Japanese attack on Pearl Harbor
c. Hitler became Chancellor of Germany
d. V-E Day
e. Outbreak of World War II
f. First use of the atomic bomb

II. From the list of words below choose the one which correctly fills the blanks in the statements which follow.

Philippine Islands
rationed
Hiroshima
1945
Papal Peace Plan
Axis
Russia

War Production Board
Dumbarton Oaks
key industries
General Sir Bernard Montgomery
Maxim Litvinoff
mutual agreement
Europe

Asia
Italy
September 2, 1945
Guadalcanal
Germany

1. Industry in the United States during World War II was controlled by the ....

2. Men in .... were exempt from military service.

3. In order to give every American a fair share of food and clothing, certain articles were ....

4. World War II was fought in ...., ..., and ....

5. In the first part of the war, Italy was on the side of the ....

6. Russia did not aid Poland when Germany invaded her because of a .... previously made.

7. Hitler first experienced defeat in ....

8. The British army in North Africa was commanded by ....

9. .... was the first Axis nation to surrender.

10. The war in Europe ended with the surrender of ....

11. The first resistance which Japan met was on the ....

12. The most bitter fighting of World War II was waged on ....

13. The first atomic bomb was dropped on ....

14. The surrender of Japan was signed on .... , 19........ .

15. The first plans for the UN were made at ....

16. The United Nations Charter was written in the year ....

17. The first ambassador of Communist Russia to the United States was ....

18. Our Holy Father's suggestions for a return to normal world relations were expressed in the ....

CHAPTER VI

PROBLEMS RESULTING FROM WORLD WAR II

What this chapter tells us. World War II was not merely a war of conquest but a struggle between two ways of living—that of freedom and that of enslavement. The end of the war did not bring an end to the struggle. Communism merely replaced totalitarian Germany and Italy as our opponent. Our entire way of life was still challenged. Would the United States, now the leading nation of the Western World, be able to meet this challenge? How was she to go about this?

In this chapter you will learn that the United States had to face problems not only at home but also abroad. The two main points we shall study, then, are: (1) Returning to Peacetime Living at Home, and (2) Helping Other Nations Return to Normal Living.

1. Returning to Peacetime Living at Home

The return to peacetime living in the United States was not a simple matter. We shall see that changes were to be made which would affect American life for many future years.

Dropping controls. Probably the first change which the government made in the United States was an economic one. The people were tired of the controls which came with war. The government tried to eliminate controls on such articles as gasoline, fuel oil, and shoes, and rationing was gradually lifted. This caused an added problem because, as the price controls were withdrawn, the cost of goods rose higher than during the war.

Labor troubles. During the war, American labor had cooperated with the government by making "no-strike" pledges. With the end of hostilities, labor considered itself free of this pledge. In order to meet the high cost living, labor demanded higher wages, many of which had dropped because extra overtime pay was ended. Industry at first refused these wage increases and, consequently, serious strikes immediately developed. These strikes paralyzed production of some of the articles which Americans could not obtain during the war and to which they felt entitled when the war was over.

Labor, on the other hand, got what it desired, but the government tried to restrict some of the unfair

Brown Brothers
Roosevelt signs GI Bill of Rights.

practices of labor unions by the passage of the Taft-Hartley Act about which you have read. Do you recall what this act provided. If not, this is a good time to review. Turn to Unit Two.

The GI Bill of Rights. Another problem before the government was the placement of soldiers and sailors in civilian life.

In so many instances in this book, we have mentioned the word "rights." Do you know what a *right* is? A right entitles an individual to something which is definitely his own. Your life is your own; you have a right to it—a God-given one. Recall from Unit Two some rights of labor. You should also recall what rights are stated in our Constitution. This brings us to a new bill of rights called the GI Bill of

Rights, which was passed in 1944.

The men of the armed service were called GI's. This was a joking reference to the word "Government Issue," used to describe the supplies issued to our troops. After having devoted their services to the welfare and safety of their fellow citizens, the men and women of the armed forces were, in justice, entitled to certain rights. The government realized this and gave special benefits to GI's through this new bill. They were given the opportunity to go to a college of their choice. Those who were disabled were given pensions; those who could not get jobs were given unemployment compensation. All federal and private employers were asked, if possible, to reinstate veterans in their former positions.

The government also loaned money to veterans to purchase homes. There had been very little building of homes during the war, and, as a result, a great housing shortage existed.

Taking everything into consideration, the GI Bill of Rights was a greater help to returning soldiers than has ever been given by any other government in history.

Compulsory military training. The United States was perhaps the only nation in the world at the end of World War II which had never had compulsory military training. Compulsory military training means that one is obliged to enter for a time some branch of the armed service. When the idea was first introduced in the United States, no

By Ewing Galloway, N. Y.

Living quarters for married GI students on the campus of an American college.

one took it seriously. Nor was it popular. Questions arose. Could a democratic government compel anyone to take any action which he did not desire? Was this not what the dictators had done?

In spite of this questioning attitude on the part of the people, in 1947 President Truman formed a special committee which began a study to decide whether or not compulsory training during peacetime should be enforced. This commission was composed of nine men from various fields — education, the clergy, and industry. For six months this group worked intently. Then they made the unanimous statement that universal military training was a matter of "urgent military necessity" for the United States. This decision resulted in the passage of the Third Selective Service Act in June, 1948, for the duration of two years.

A new UMT law. At the end of this period, universal military training, commonly called UMT, again came before Congress. Unrest in Europe and Asia demanded that the United States continue to have a standing army for its own safety. After months of discussion, the new law was passed in June, 1951. The change was merely a temporary arrangement.

According to this arrangement, the draft age was lowered from 19

James V. Forrestal.

tary of Defense was James V. Forrestal, who formerly served as Secretary of the Navy. Under him were three assistant secretaries, one for each of the three chief divisions of our armed forces, the Army, the Navy, and the Air Force. Each separate service was to be an aid to the others whenever the need arose. It was hoped that such coordination would provide better for our country's safety in an atomic age.

Presidential succession. Under the Presidential Succession Act of 1886, members of the President's Cabinet succeeded to the presidency if both President and Vice-President either died or were unable for some reason to accept the office.

President Truman gave two reasons why this arrangement should be changed. First, in a democracy a person who has been elected by the people should hold the office of President. Cabinet members are not chosen by the people but appointed by the President. And second, a President should not have the power to name his successor.

In 1947 Congress passed a new Presidential Succession Act. Now Presidential succession is:

1. The Vice-President (who is also the presiding officer of the Senate.
2. The Speaker of the House of Representatives.
3. The President of the Senate (that is, the one who is filling a deceased Vice-President's place).
4. The members of the Cabinet beginning with the Secretary of State.

to 18½ years but the term of service was lengthened from 21 to 24 months. There were other provisions, but they were subject to change with the end of hostilities in Korea, where Americans were at that time fighting.

Americans were ready to accept this proposal, realizing that the law was necessary in our effort to keep world peace. This brings up again the principle that men should be willing to make personal sacrifices for the welfare of the group.

The Armed Forces Unification Act. World War II showed the advisability of a change in the armed forces.

Originally, we had a Secretary of the Navy and a Secretary of War. By the Armed Forces Unification Act these two offices were combined to form the office of the Secretary of Defense. The first Secre-

Ewing Galloway, N. Y.

President Harry S. Truman.

This would insure a more democratic succession because it would rarely happen that all three of the first officers mentioned would be unable to accept the office.

This brings us to the interesting 1948 election.

A predicted defeat ends in victory. This election was one of the most surprising in the history of the United States. It swept President Truman back into the Presidency for his first elected term. Do you understand what "first elected term" means?

The campaign was not too exciting. The major points at issue were price controls, labor relations, civil rights, and housing. In 1948 President Truman had asked Congress to pass a law against lynching and poll-taxes in the South. This was part of his Civil Rights Program. The Southern Democrats, who called themselves "Dixiecrats" protested against this program. Would this division among the Democrats mean defeat for the President? Defeat was certainly predicted, but the nation was surprised. Truman was re-elected.

2. Helping Other Nations to Return to Normal Living

The United States had come out of the second world conflict in a key position, and the rest of the world now looked to her for all kinds of assistance. Our nation was untouched by the ravages of war, and hence our responsibility to join the other nations in an effort to maintain peace was even greater. One growing doubt filled the minds of Americans. How far could we go in agreeing with Communist Russia without endangering our own welfare? The remainder of this book will attempt to answer that question.

An occupying army. At the end of the war, some of the defeated nations like Austria, Rumania, Italy, and Hungary had existing governments. As soon as they had made peace treaties with the Allies, there was no longer any need for an Allied occupation of these countries.

Germany, on the other hand, was left without a government of any kind. No peace treaty could be made with her until a new government was created for her. The Allies wanted to make very sure that any new German government would not resemble that of Hitler. Consequently, they took every measure possible to keep high Nazi officials from government positions and to encourage the formation of a democratic state. They also deprived Germany for the second time of her power to make war. Her munitions factories, therefore, were dismantled.

As we have seen, Germany was divided into four zones of military occupation. It was evident that Germany could not become self-supporting unless it should be unified. Immediately, a problem arose. Were the Allies willing to come to a decision about the type of government Germany should have? Communist Russia opposed a democratic government, and Great Britain and the United States did not want Germany to become communistic. Finally, the British, French and American occupation zones were united, but no contact between this new zone and the Russian zone was permitted by Russia. There existed then East Germany and West Germany. The former was communistic, another country "behind the iron curtain," and what happened behind that curtain no one knew. West Germany very slowly began to rebuild itself along democratic lines.

Russia's reaction. Russia did everything she could to block peace. Other elements also combined to cause tension between Russia and the United States. First, Russia was angered because the zones of occupation in Western Germany had been unified. She showed her opposition by blockading supplies which had to go through Russian occupied Germany to the American zone in Berlin. These supplies reached Berlin in spite of the blockade by means of an air-lift, that is, they were brought in by planes.

This situation lasted for about a year, when Russia finally lifted the blockade. Second, the United States, not trusting Russia, proposed that the democracies of western Europe form a mutual agreement of military assistance if they were invaded. Third, the United States was discovering Soviet spy activities in this country and bringing them to light. Lastly, the United States was also supplying aid to any country of Europe which promised to keep a democratic form of government. The next few paragraphs will explain in more detail some of these points.

The United Nations Relief Program. As early as 1943, the nations which had pledged themselves to work for the preservation of democracy had organized a program of relief for the stricken people of Europe. This program has often been called UNRRA, United Nations Relief and Rehabilitation Administration. It supplied food, clothing, and medicine to the people in the months following the war. When the United Nations Organization was formed officially in 1945, UNRRA ceased to exist, but its activities were carried out by other groups.

CARE. Another agency for relief of people in stricken lands was the Cooperative for American Remittances to Europe. That was a very long name for most people to remember, so it was more conveniently called CARE.

CARE had its beginning in November, 1945, when twenty-two of America's great welfare agencies grouped together. All creeds and nationalities were represented in this organization, including the War Relief Services of the National Catholic Welfare Conference. During the following three years, CARE had delivered more than 156,-000,000 pounds of food and great quan-

Brown Brothers
CARE package from America.

tities of clothing materials to the cold and the hungry.

The Truman Doctrine. President Truman realized that if the war-stricken nations could not rebuild their devastated lands, restock their farms, and clothe their people, Communism would continue to spread. Eventually, this would affect the interests of the United States as well as those of other countries and endanger the peace of the world. Therefore, on March 12, 1947, the President gave to Congress his Truman Doctrine in which he asked for authority to stop the march of Communism through the giving of aid. This doctrine was at the time considered by many people as important as the Monroe Doctrine.

Many questions arose in the

George C. Marshall.

minds of our lawmakers. Where would this new policy lead us? Would it cause war with Russia? Why not refer the entire matter to the United Nations? The policy was a new foreign policy, to be sure, one that we had not held before.

The European recovery program. Secretary of State George Marshall then suggested a plan known as the Marshall Plan. He proposed that a committee of the foreign ministers of Great Britain, the United States, France, and the Soviet Union meet in Paris. Each nation desiring aid was to prepare a report of its needs and submit it to the committee. These reports were studied and American relief was given.

It soon became quite clear that Russia was definitely not in favor of this aid. While she could not openly forbid the aid, she decided upon another move. She and her satellites behind the iron curtain immediately announced that they, too, would form an organization. No one except the Communist nations ever knew what the organization accomplished. Its real purpose eventually came to light, namely, to fight American influence in Europe.

From this time on, the nations supporting Russian ideas were called the Soviet Bloc. This meant that whenever an American proposal was made, Russia and her Communist neighbors would resist its passage.

American influence in Japan. After the war, General Douglas MacArthur was appointed Supreme Military Commander of the Allied forces in occupied Japan. Under his direction, a complete transformation of that country was effected. A democracy replaced the ancient monarchy, and within two years Japan was entirely disarmed. The first free election in Japanese history was then held under American supervision, and Japan was on the road to peaceful reconstruction.

Sore spots in the Far East. After the defeat of Japan in World War II, Chiang Kai-shek, leader of the Chinese Nationalist Government, tried to reestablish that government over all of China. But the northern part of that country for some time had been influenced by Communists. These consistently resisted Chiang Kai-shek, and no agreement could be reached between them.

General George Marshall was

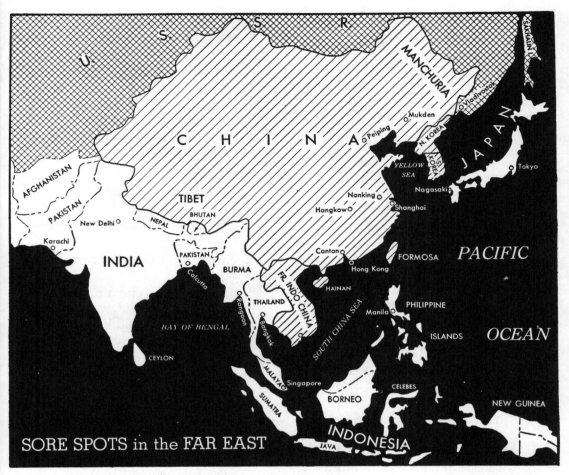

SORE SPOTS in the FAR EAST

sent to China by the United States in 1946 to try to convince Chiang to admit Communists into his government. Chiang naturally refused. American aid was temporarily withdrawn. By 1949, the Chinese Communist armies had won a number of victories over Chiang Kai-shek and forced him to withdraw to the island of Formosa.

Another sore spot was the peninsula of Korea. After the war, the United States occupied South Korea and the Russians took control of North Korea. The thirty-eighth parallel was the dividing line be-

tween these two sections. In 1947, the United Nations attempted a unification of these nations and tried to hold a joint election. What was the result? Russia refused to permit the United Nations commission to enter North Korea, South Korea held its own election, and the country remained divided.

The important point to notice about these post-war conditions in the Far East is that the friction was caused by communistic influence. Was this the initial step for another war? Keep these ideas in mind as you read the last Unit in this text.

New and review words

compulsory military training
an "elected" term

lynching	airlift
poll tax	devastated lands
Dixiecrats	Soviet Bloc
Iron Curtain	monarchy

How well have you read?

1. How did the end of World War II bring about labor difficulties in the United States?
2. What provisions did Uncle Sam make for returning soldiers?
3. What law passed after the war greatly affected the lives of the people?
4. How would the Armed Forces Unification Act result in better protection for America?
5. What problems faced our occupying armies in Germany?
6. Explain briefly the causes of friction between the United States and Russia.
7. Through what means did the hungry people of Europe and Asia receive aid from the United States?
8. Discuss the success or failure of the occupying forces in the Far East.

Choosing the correct ending

Number lines on a paper from 1 to 12. After each number write the letter of the ending which best completes the statement.

1. The first change which the government made in returning to peacetime living after World War II was
   a. caring for returning GI's
   b. passing the Armed Forces Unification Act
   c. dropping the rationing of foods and price controls
   d. decreasing the size of the army

2. After the war, labor
   a. revolted against high prices and went on strike
   b. received the same high salaries as during the war
   c. continued to make unjust demands upon capitalists
   d. continued to cooperate well with the government

3. The GI Bill of Rights
   a. was an added burden to the returning soldiers
   b. gave special benefits to returning soldiers
   c. encouraged boys to remain in the service
   d. did not give returning soldiers as many benefits as they received after World War I

4. A committee which studied the problem of compulsory military training after World War II
   a. felt that compulsory peacetime training was undemocratic
   b. rejected the problem as unnecessary
   c. thought that an army could be raised fast enough without compulsory peacetime training
   d. decided that compulsory peacetime training during peacetime was necessary for the preservation of the United States

5. The Armed Forces Unification Act
   a. proved successful during World War II
   b. benefited only the military forces in Europe
   c. insured greater efficiency among our armed forces because of better coordination
   d. saved money for the country because it reduced the President's Cabinet to nine members

6. President Truman changed the Presidential Succession Act in 1947 because
   a. it was not sufficiently democratic
   b. he thought he could gain the respect of officers elected by the people
   c. all Cabinet officers are elected directly by the people
   d. he wanted to make sure that a President's friends could succeed him

7. The Civil Rights Program of President Truman
   a. concerned labor practices in the southern part of our country
   b. defeated Truman in the 1948 election
   c. was considered impossible to be carried out by Congress
   d. caused Southern Democrats to protest against him, thereby dividing the party

8. By 1948 the British and American occupying army in Germany
   a. worked well with the Russian occupying army in East Germany
   b. united to form West Germany
   c. accepted a few high Nazi officials into government positions
   d. cooperated fully with Russia

9. Russia showed her attitude towards the unification of West Germany by
   a. cooperating with British and Americans
   b. withdrawing her army of occupation from Berlin
   c. blockading supplies going to the American zone in Berlin
   d. welcoming British and American forces to West Germany

10. The Truman Doctrine
    a. attempted to stop the spread of Communism by aiding war-stricken nations
    b. did not succeed because of the Marshall Plan
    c. surpassed the Monroe Doctrine in importance
    d. gave aid only to European countries

11. After the war General Douglas MacArthur
    a. cooperated with Russian plans to rebuild Japan
    b. was appointed Supreme Military Commander of the Allied Forces in occupied Japan
    c. failed to make Japan a democracy
    d. maintained an active interest in political affairs

12. Sore spots in the Far East after World War II were caused primarily by
    a. the poverty of the people living there
    b. the terrible destruction resulting from the atomic bombs
    c. the conduct of the soldiers towards the natives of the Far East
    d. friction caused by Communistic influence

Highlights of the Unit

Catholic Principles to Remember:
1. All authority comes from God.
2. Nations should work for a lasting peace rather than their own growth in power or politics.
3. The state gets its power and authority from God.
4. The purpose of the state is to promote the welfare of the people.
5. It is contrary to justice and charity for a victorious nation to com-

pletely deprive a defeated nation of its God-given right to continue its existence.

6. No country may wage war upon another for the sake of vengeance or to satisfy its desire to dominate or rule over another nation.

7. A nation may wage war only for just reasons. Some of those reasons are:

   a. to defend itself from an unjust attack

   b. to recover some of its possessions which another country has unjustly seized

   c. to help right a wrong that has been committed

   d. to maintain rights which were violated

8. Nationalism is dangerous when it makes people intolerant of others.

9. A promise made by a nation to help another in case of attack is an obligation of strict justice, providing the welfare of the people is at stake.

10. A country should not remain neutral if it can right the unjust treatment of a weaker nation by a stronger one.

11. Broken promises, distrust, and jealousy between nations only breed more wars.

12. Totalitarianism is contrary to Catholic teaching because it makes the state supreme and does not recognize the dignity of man nor his God-given rights.

13. A government which prohibits its people from worshipping God as they desire seldom abides by international law or lives up to its just agreements.

The first World War

MAIN POINTS about World War I:

Why Europe Went to War:

1. Hidden Reasons:

   a. rivalry for trade, especially between England and Germany

   b. increase of European armies and navies

   c. formation of secret alliances

   d. a growing but unhealthy love of country

2. The incident which actually caused the war: the assassination of Archduke Francis Ferdinand of Austria on June 28, 1914.

Why the United States Joined the War:

1. Main reason: submarine warfare used by Germans

2. Incidents which hastened our entrance into war:

   a. violation of our neutrality by England and Germany

   b. sabotage in the United States

   c. sinking of the *Lusitania*

   d. Zimmerman note

How the United States Prepared for War at Home:

1. Government took control of railroads and industry

2. Army and navy was increased

3. Food and fuel were conserved for the army

4. Recreation centers were established for the boys

European Armies Begin the War:

1. Two great forces in Europe: The Central Powers and the Allies

2. Most of the war was fought in France

3. No decisive victory was won by either side for three years.

Americans in the War:

1. England blockaded German ports to prevent supplies from reaching her.

2. Germany used submarines to prevent help from going to England.

3. Germany bombed neutral vessels without warning

4. United States declared war on Germany on April 6, 1917

5. Russia withdrew from war in 1917 because of revolution at home

6. Americans fought in Chateau-Thierry, Saint Mihiel, and the Argonne Forest.

7. America's greatest battle in World War I was the battle of Argonne Forest.

8. Armistice was signed on November 11, 1918

New Weapons Used in World War I:

1. tanks
2. improved airplanes
3. poison gas
4. barbed wire entanglements

Peace Efforts:

1. Nations would not accept peace proposals of Benedict XV because they did not want Vatican intervention in their plans.

2. President Wilson proposed Fourteen Points for a possible peace treaty.

3. The formation of the League of Nations, Wilson's fourteenth point was accepted.

4. The peace treaty was signed in Versailles on June 28, 1918.

5. This treaty was unjust because it stripped Germany of any possibility to continue its life as a nation.

6. Allies ignored Pope Benedict because of a secret treaty made in 1915.

7. The United States did not sign the peace treaty because it did not want to join the League of Nations.

8. The United States refused to join the League of Nations because it did not want to become involved in another European war.

9. The United States cooperated with the rest of the world in trying to establish a just peace.

10. Jealousies and suspicions continued among the big powers of the world in spite of the Treaty of Versailles.

The second World War

MAIN POINTS about World War II:

1. Rivalry between nations persisted.

2. High tariffs slowed up trade relations.

3. Democracies began to collapse under unprincipled leaders.

4. Small nations were oppressed by large ones.

5. World War II began when Hitler attacked Poland on September 3, 1939.

6. England entered the war to save the democratic way of life.

Beginnings of European Aggression:

1. Mussolini ordered the Italian army to invade Ethiopia in Africa in 1935.

2. Mussolini's plan was to form another great empire like the ancient Roman Empire.

3. Germany endeavored to become supreme in Europe:

   a. By means of "blitzkriegs" the Nazis successfully invaded and captured Austria, Czechoslovakia, the Low Countries, and Poland.

   b. In June, 1940, France fell under Nazi attack. A Nazi capital was set up at Vichy.

   c. Germany then tried to weaken England by large-scale bombings.

   d. Resistance from the R.A.F. caused Hitler to discontinue attacking England and invade Russia in 1941.

   e. After two years of terrible battles the Nazi army was forced to withdraw from Russia without having gained anything.

4. Mussolini and Hitler finally formed an alliance known as the Rome-Berlin Axis. All nations fighting on their side were called the Axis Powers.

5. Russia fell under the sway of Joseph Stalin and atheistic Communism began to spread rapidly.

What the Totalitarian Dictators Believed:

Totalitarianism means complete control of the lives of individuals by the state. Totalitarianism claims that:

   a. the power of the state is supreme.

   b. individuals have no rights except those the state gives them.

   c. religion should be destroyed.

Three Great Forces in Europe before the United States Entered the War:

1. The democracies led by Great Britain and France.

2. The Fascist states of Germany and Italy.

3. The Soviet Union, which was determined to destroy all government.

American Attitude Towards World War II:

1. People wanted to stay out of war.

2. President Roosevelt tried to strengthen our Latin American relations.

3. The "cash and carry" program was inaugurated to safeguard American interests.

4. In 1941 the Lend-Lease Act was passed. This permitted us to send supplies to any nation whose safety would be vital to our own.

5. President Roosevelt and Prime Minister Churchill formed the Atlantic Charter.

6. President Roosevelt said all nations should be entitled to Four Freedoms:

   freedom of speech
   freedom of religion
   freedom from want
   freedom from fear

War in the Far East:

1. Japan invaded Manchuria, part of North China, in 1931.

2. The League of Nations was not able to stop Japan's aggression.

3. Japan joined Italy and Germany in the Rome-Berlin-Tokyo Pact in 1940.

4. The United States' trade relations with Japan were broken when Japanese troops spread throughout Pacific Islands.

5. On December 7, 1941, Japan bombed Pearl Harbor, Hawaii. This act drew the United States into the war.

American Home Front Goes to War:

1. Government took control of industry.

2. Food and certain types of clothing were rationed.

3. Labor was controlled by the government to insure that men in key industries would not be drafted for war.

4. Women joined the armed services as WACS, WAVES, and SPARS.

Main Battlefields of World War II:

1. *In Europe:*

a. A Combined Chiefs of Staff was formed to direct the war.

b. First strike was to be made in Europe.

c. Americans and British saved North Africa from the Nazis.

d. Allies pushed through Sicily to Italy.

e. Italians joined the Allies against the Nazis, and after Italy's surrender Mussolini was assassinated by his own countrymen.

f. The D-Day Invasion — Began June 6, 1944.

Large scale bombings of German industrial cities

Thousands of allied troops landed on beaches in northern France

Greatest invasion the world had ever seen

British-American forces met Russian forces in central Germany

Berlin captured — Hitler reported dead

Greatest battles of D-Day: The battle of the Bulge and the Battle of Remagen Bridge

Unconditional surrender of Germany on May 8, 1945.

g. V-E Day was officially proclaimed on May 8, 1945.

h. Germany was divided into four zones of military occupation.

2. *In the Pacific Area:*

a. The Japanese captured many small but important American possessions.

b. Manila, the capital of the Philippines, fell to Japanese on January 2, 1942. The same day 26 nations, fighting the Axis, agreed to cooperate more closely. They called themselves the United Nations.

c. Japan invaded China and closed the Burma Road. American planes brought supplies to China and also bombed Japanese bases.

d. Japanese were driven out of Burma in 1945.

e. Manila was recaptured by Americans in 1945.

f. Americans fought bravely at Iwo Jima and Okinawa.

g. Japanese refused to comply with surrender ultimatum so the United States dropped its first atomic bomb on Hiroshima on August 6, 1945.

h. Russia joined the war ten days later, and a second atomic bomb was dropped on the city of Nagasaki.

i. Japan surrendered on August 14, 1945—V-J Day.

j. Terms of Surrender were signed on board the *Missouri* on September 2, 1945.

Allied Efforts to Win the War and Establish Peace:

1. Conferences were held at: Washington, Casablanca, Quebec, Teheran, and Moscow.

2. Plan for a United Nations Organization was begun at Dumbarton Oaks, Washington, D. C., in 1944.

3. The Charter for the United Nations was drawn up at San Francisco on April 25, 1945.

4. Peace treaties with five of the defeated nations were drawn up at Paris in 1946.

5. Discord mounted in spite of peace efforts.

6. Communist Russia disagreed with everything the Allies suggested.

7. Russia violated her promise of religious freedom by a systematic persecution of religion.

8. All during World War II Pope Pius XII urged nations to seek peace. His ideas for a just peace are called the Papal Peace Plan.

Nations Try to Return to Normal Living:

1. The United States:

   a. Controls and rationing of food were dropped.

   b. Strikes and discontent spread in industry.

   c. Government passed the GI Bill of Rights to re-establish returning soldiers in civilian life.

   d. Compulsory military training during peacetime was established for the first time in American history.

   e. American Army, Navy, and Air Forces were united in the Armed Forces Unification Act to insure better protection.

   f. The Presidential Succession Act was changed to make it more democratic.

2. Other Countries:

   a. Allied armies left all defeated nations as soon as they were able to care for themselves on a democratic basis.

   b. Germany had no government; therefore, occupation armies remained.

   c. Russia opposed a democratic government for Germany so the Allies unified their part of Germany into West Germany and held a democratic election.

   d. Russia blocked supplies going to West Germany through the Russian zone.

   e. President Truman ordered aid for war-stricken countries in order to stop the spread of Communism. This was the Truman Doctrine. Aid was given as provided in the Marshall Plan.

   f. Douglas MacArthur set up a democratic form of government in Japan and was made Supreme Military Commander of the Allied Forces after World War II.

   g. Communistic influence divided China into Nationalist China, governed by Chiang Kai-shek, and Red China.

   h. Korea was divided at the thirty-eighth parallel. Russia occupied the north and the United States, the south. Russia blocked the idea of a unified Korea, but a democracy was set up in South Korea.

Clinching the highlights

1. Prepare oral reports on the activities of the following groups in the United States during World War I and World War II:

   a. school children
   b. government
   c. women in the service
   d. the Catholic Church
   e. Red Cross
   f. scientific research

2. Make a scrap book about each war studied in this Unit. Include in the book pictures of soldiers' uniforms, women's uniforms, types of ammunition or weapons in each war. Draw maps of important regions mentioned. Cartoons would make it interesting, too. Can you think of any other things to include in your scrap book?

3. Have a living time-line. Pick out the important dates mentioned in the Unit. Write the date and the statement about each date on separate papers and distribute them about the class. Hold a conversation similar to this:

   FIRST SPEAKER: The date is 1914.

   SECOND SPEAKER: The First World War began in Europe.

4. Prepare a report on the relief work done by the United States to help European nations return to peacetime living. Include in your report the contributions of the National Catholic Welfare Conference.

5. Make a collection of titles of popular wartime songs sung during both wars. Learn several of them.

6. You are a war correspondent. Report on one of the following:

   D-Day Invasion
   The Sinking of the *Lusitania*

Violation of American Neutrality in World War I
The United States Rejects the Versailles Treaty
German *Blitzkrieg*
The Bombing of Pearl Harbor
Russia's Lack of Cooperation After World War II

7. Have a debate: *Resolved:* World War II was a greater threat to American democracy than World War I.

8. Have an identification contest. Appoint a committee of three to arrange clues (at least two for each person) for twenty-five persons mentioned in World War I and World War II. Divide the class into two groups and give one point for each correct answer. Example:

   President Franklin Roosevelt—

   held conferences with Prime Minister Churchill; died before the United Nations' Charter was written

A final check-up

I. ARRANGING EVENTS AND PEOPLE. Below is a list of names and events connected with either World War I or World War II. Arrange those which are connected with the First World War in a column on your paper headed WORLD WAR I and those connected with the Second World War in a column headed WORLD WAR II.

Nazism	Pope Benedict XV
Pope Pius XII	United Nations
League of Nations	Organization
Papal Peace Plan	"purge" of Jewish
rationing	race
Argonne Forest	Woodrow Wilson
Nazi *blitzkrieg*	Central Powers
Benito Mussolini	Sinking of
Lend-Lease Act	*Lusitania*
D-Day Invasion	Marshal Foch
Atlantic Charter	Maginot Line

Axis Powers
Ethiopia
"cash and carry" program
Hiroshima
totalitarian states
American Expeditionary Force
bombing of Pearl Harbor
General Douglas MacArthur
Beginning of trench warfare
British blockade of Germany
Archduke Francis Ferdinand
Zimmerman Note
Treaty of Versailles
atheistic Communism
WACS, WAVES, SPARS
Battle of the Philippines
first use of submarines
Prime Minister Churchill
oppression of small countries
Franklin D. Roosevelt
General J. Pershing

General Dwight Eisenhower
Maxim Litvinoff
Joint Chiefs of Staff
Iwo Jima

II. FILL THESE BLANKS. Number your paper from 1 to 26. If a statement has more than one blank in it, write all the words which fill these blanks after the same number.

Example: *Statement*—1. American neutrality was violated during World War I by both.................... and.....................

Answer—1. England, Germany

1. The immediate cause of World War I in Europe was..................... in 1914.

2. The United States became involved in the First World War when Germany refused to stop using..................warfare.

3. In the years previous to World War I, the European countries of .... and .... were trade rivals.

4. Most of the fighting during World War I was carried on in the country of ....

5. Activities which aim at crippling industries in a country to prevent it from aiding belligerents are called acts of.....................

6. An armistice, ending World War I, was signed on..................... in the year.....................

7. President Wilson's hopes for world peace were based on the last point of his peace program, namely, the formation of a................... ....

8. The "Big Four" of World War I were.....................of the United States, ...of Great Britain,..................... of France, and.....................of Italy.

9. The treaty that ended World War I, was known as the..................... Treaty. It was signed on..................... in the year.....................

10. The only country at the Peace Conference in Paris which did not desire anything for itself after World War I was.....................

11. Pope Benedict XV was kept from the Peace Conference because the Allies had formed a ....in 1915.

12. The Versailles Treaty was a great injustice to the country of.....................

13. The collapse of democracies in Europe after World War I led to the formation of a new kind of government known as.....................

14. The first totalitarian states in Europe were..................., ..., and..................... .

15. World War II began when Hitler invaded Poland in the year.....................

16. The United States entered World War II when the Japanese bombed our naval base at..................... in the year.....................

17. The first major set-back which the Nazi armies experienced in World War II was in the country of..............................

18. The combined Allied forces in Europe during World War II were led to victory by General ....of the United States.

19. The greatest invasion which the world had ever seen was that known as.............................

20. V-E Day was proclaimed by President Truman on......................, 19.............

21. World War II was officially over when ....surrendered to the United States on August 14, 1945.

22. After World War II the country of.................... constantly blocked peace proposals by refusing to accept decisions of the majority of nations.

23. The ideas which Pope Pius XII proposed to solve world difficulties are known as the..........................Plan.

24. Better cooperation between the branches of the American armed forces was brought about by the passage of the.............................Act.

25. The........................Doctrine was an attempt to check the spread of Communism by aiding war-stricken countries in Europe after World War II.

26. During World War I the enemies of the Allies were called the ....; during World War II our enemies were referred to as the........................

III. CHOOSE THE BEST ANSWER.

1. The United Nations Charter was drawn up at (London, Paris, San Francisco).

2. The aggressor which the Allies had to fight during World War II in the Pacific was (China, Japan, India).

3. The campaign in (North Africa, France, England) was the beginning of the British-American conquest of Nazism in Europe.

4. The first atomic bomb ever to be dropped destroyed the city of (Hiroshima, Nagasaki, Tokyo).

5. The greatest battle of World War I, in which Americans participated, was the battle of (Argonne Forest, San Mihiel, Chateau-Thierry).

6. The supreme commander of the Allied forces during World War I was (General Pershing, Marshall Foch, General Ludendorff).

7. The country which withdrew from World War I in 1917 because of a revolution within her boundaries was (France, Italy, Russia).

8. The United States entered World War I in (1914, 1917, 1918).

9. The first Axis power to be defeated in World War II was (Italy, Germany, Japan).

10. The first free election in the history of Japan was held under the supervision of (General MacArthur, General Eisenhower, General Wainwright).

IV. ANSWER THESE QUESTIONS BRIEFLY

1. Why was the Treaty of Versailles an unjust treaty?

2. Mention three instances when a country is allowed to participate in a just war.

3. Explain the difference between an ultimatum and an armistice.

4. Give two reasons why Russia and the United States clashed after World War II.

UNIT SIX

THE PRESERVATION OF OUR AMERICAN HERITAGE

CHAPTER I—THE AMERICAN IDEAL OF DEMOCRACY AND THE DANGERS WHICH WEAKEN ITS FOUNDATIONS

The American Ideal of Democracy:
    Our Inheritance from Europe
    American Democracy
    A Country Established on a Religious Foundation
Dangers Which Threaten to Weaken Our Democracy:
    Communism
    Divorce
    Intolerance
    Anti-Catholic Bigotry in Politics
    Anti-Catholic Sentiment Strikes at the Schools
    The Question of Federal Aid to Education

CHAPTER II—SAVING AMERICAN DEMOCRACY

The United Nations Organization Struggles to Save Democracy:
    The United Nations Charter
    Important Divisions of the United Nations Organization
    Special Agencies Which Help the United Nations
    Accomplishments of the United Nations
    Problems Facing the United Nations
    Universal Declaration of Human Rights
    UNESCO
    Lack of Religion in the United Nations Organization
Saving Democracy Through Catholic Action:
    Growth of the Church in the Twentieth Century
    Defining Catholic Action
    The National Catholic Welfare Conference
    Catholic Youth Organization
    Boy and Girl Scouts
    Newman Clubs
    Confraternity of Christian Doctrine
    Legion of Decency
    Our Lady—The Hope of the World

UNIT SIX

THE PRESERVATION OF OUR AMERICAN HERITAGE

EACH day throughout this beautiful Land of Our Lady, American children raise proud voices to recite the Pledge of Allegiance to America's flag. Have you ever thought very seriously about the words of this pledge? One phrase in particular should have some meaning for you, now that you have reached the last Unit in your study of American history. "With liberty and justice for all" should recall many Christian principles about which you have read during the past months in school.

As true Americans, you should be aware of the principles upon which our great country was established. If you thoughtfully read the Declaration of Independence and the Bill of Rights you will find that these same principles of liberty, justice, and equality are definitely stated in both of these precious documents. Since the United States was founded on principles of justice and charity, all freedom-loving citizens of this great country should wish to preserve our cherished heritage.

There have been dangers threatening to destroy the democracy which Americans have always cherished, but the people of the United States and their government have acted wisely in order to preserve our ideals. You have already learned about the official formation of the United Nations Organization at the end of World War II. In this Unit we shall attempt to show you how this organization has endeavored to preserve the democratic way of life throughout the world by striving to maintain peace among nations. Our own welfare depends upon the welfare of the rest of the world; the United States, therefore, has taken a leading role in the activities of the United Nations Organization.

America must have citizens who are ever alert to recognize and be willing to fight any undemocratic forces in the United States.

THE AMERICAN IDEAL OF DEMOCRACY AND THE DANGERS
WHICH WEAKEN ITS FOUNDATIONS

A short story of the chapter. The unsettled state of world conditions which followed World War II made Americans aware of the greater blessings of liberty which they enjoy in the United States. They had often read the word "democracy" in books and newspapers, but it did not always mean much to them. The old saying, that we never appreciate a thing until it is taken from us, began to penetrate the minds of liberty-loving Americans. The majority of them became more conscious of the blessings of our democratic way of life.

Unfortunately, not all Americans were loyal to our ideals. The first half of the twentieth century saw an increase of the forces which tended to weaken democracy.

In this chapter you will study two points. First, you will review the meaning of our democratic heritage and, secondly, you will learn about some of the dangers which threaten to undermine that heritage in the United States.

1. The American Ideal of Democracy

When an individual inherits property from another, we say that he has received an inheritance. An-

other word for inheritance is *heritage* — something handed down from one descendant to another. In the following paragraphs, we shall learn that a very valuable heritage has been left to us in the United States, and is one to be guarded zealously.

What we inherited from Europe. Various elements of the culture of our country were brought here from other sections of the world. Europeans introduced into this Land of Our Lady their ideas about religion, education, government, and happiness. These ideas differed from those of the natives living here. However, a combination of what the explorers brought and what was found here, together with the ideas added by later immigrants, formed our cultural heritage. Let us see what some of these contributions were.

First of all, our ideas of the family came from Catholic Europe. The Church denounced the possession of more than one wife or husband at the same time, and this teaching has been accepted by all good citizens in the United States. The roots of education in this country were first planted in Europe where they too were nourished by the Catholic Church. Our system of measuring time is European. The factory system, which has contributed to the economic development of the United States, was imported from England. The tools first used in American industry were developed by skillful Europeans, and labor organizations were set up in European nations even before Columbus discovered America.

The idea of personal liberty, of the right of the individual to develop the kind of life he desired, also came from Europe. Democracy itself, the way of life which Americans prize, had its beginnings in Greece, and was preserved and grew in Christian Europe.

American democracy. You have learned that American democracy is "government of the people, by the people, and for the people." But it is more than a form of government. It is a way of life. In the United States every individual is free to live and work as he wishes, so long as he violates no rights of God or man. He is not obliged to follow the demands of a dictator as many twentieth-century European people must do. An American is free to worship God as he desires. Our government was formed to protect and promote the right and the well-being of its citizens.

We know that American citizens have the right to elect government officials, and they expect these officials to use their power for the good of the nation. Freedom of speech grants Americans the right to express their ideas as to what action the government should take on matters that concern the public welfare.

The totalitarian governments of Europe grant no such rights. There the government is the supreme authority, and all citizens are considered to exist only for the sake of the state, deprived of all rights except those which the government grants them.

A country established on a religious foundation. American democracy was born on two principles: the first was the desire for personal liberty, and the second was the desire for religious liberty. There were times when these two principles met stormy weather, but the storms cleared and the ideals still remained. When Thomas Jefferson wrote the Declaration of Independence, he stated that

all men are created equal, that they are endowed by their Creator with certain inalienable rights, that among these rights are life, liberty, and the pursuit of happiness. That to secure these rights, governments are instituted among men, deriving their just powers from the consent of the governed. That whenever any form of government becomes destructive of these ends, it is the right of the people to alter or to abolish it, and to institute a new government, laying its foundation on such principles . . . as shall seem most likely to effect their safety and happiness.

This document publicly declares

to the world that American democracy is devoted to the task of safeguarding the dignity of the individual as a creature of God. When the Founding Fathers signed this document, they recognized God as the Source of all our rights and duties, our freedom and responsibilities, and our equality in His sight. In this sense, American democracy is a Christian democracy. Although the United States has not yet achieved perfectly the democratic ideals of equality and justice, her development has always aimed towards that goal.

2. Dangers Which Threaten to Weaken Our Democarcy

Americans have always cherished the ideals which we mentioned in previous paragraphs. However, in the past twenty-five years, especially, forces which have tended to weaken American ideals have slowly edged their way into this country. The remainder of this chapter will tell you briefly what some of these evil forces are.

Communism. One of the greatest dangers to democracy is Communism, which some unprincipled individuals have tried to spread in the United States. Communism, as we know it today, began after the Russian Revolution of 1917. At this time, the entire Russian nation was organized into Soviet republics. The group of republics was known as the Union of Socialist Soviet Republics, commonly called the U.S.S.R. The plan which was worked out for organizing society in the U.S.S.R. was called Communism.

Communism falsely promised the people of Russia an ideal life, but it taught that only material things are real. Therefore, God does not exist. Because of this belief, Communism is atheistic. Do you know what the word "atheistic" means?

In Russia the all-powerful state takes the place of God, and man exists only to serve that state. The government controls all means of production, housing, food supply, and even tells people where they may work. Communism also aims to overthrow all governments and create a world revolution. In other words, the purpose of Communism is to make the whole world communist.

Why the Church opposes Communism. Communism is opposed to Catholic teaching and also to democratic ideals. All Christians know that there is a God and that man belongs to Him — not to the state. They know, too, that the state exists to render service to the people and that it must recognize the God-given rights of man as well as his dignity as a human being. The state must, therefore, grant freedom to worship God, freedom of speech, and the right to own property. Communism denies men these rights and, therefore, Christianity as well as democracy is opposed to it. Can you see how dangerous it would be then if such an evil influence were permitted to spread in the United States?

Our Holy Father, Pope Pius XI,

in 1937 wrote an encyclical on *Atheistic Communism* in which he expressed the dangers of Communism. He stated that: "Communism is intrinsically (basically) wrong and no one who would save Christian civilization may collaborate (cooperate) with it in any undertaking whatsoever."

Pope Pius XI also enumerated some ways by which Communism may be overcome. We shall read about them in the next chapter.

The Bogota affair. Communists have tried to penetrate into the affairs of democratic nations by causing disturbances and riots. One striking example of such a demonstration was the affair at Bogota, Colombia, in South America. In April, 1949, twenty-one American republics held their Pan-American meeting in this city. It was believed to have been the first time in modern history that an important international conference had been opened officially with a Mass attended by all the delegates. At this conference, it was definitely declared that international cooperation must be built upon Christian principles and that Communism must be systematically repulsed in the Americas.

Suddenly, this peaceful conference was broken by the shots and yells of a wild mob. The purpose of this outburst was to try to wreck the meeting and the unity of the American democracies, thereby making it easier to spread communist ideas. Secretary of State Marshall, who was present at the meet-

ing, stated: "It is the same definite pattern as occurrences which provoked strikes in France and Italy."

This occurrence was surely evidence of the fact that the Red tide was sweeping dangerously near to American shores.

Threats of Communism in the United States. The disturbances in Latin America, together with the spread of communist propaganda in the United States through the newspaper, *The Daily Worker,* and by many other means, brought the danger closer to us. In fact, there was proof of Communists high up in government office. Accordingly, President Truman began an investigation designed to remove from federal jobs all disloyal persons. Reds were also to be barred from future government employment.

Many favored this action, but some said that it would merely tend to create sympathy for the Communists and force them into hiding. But still others said this was sly communist propaganda to protect Communists in government jobs. Two groups which have done outstanding work in bringing Red sympathizers to light are the House of Representatives Committee on Un-American Activities and the Federal Bureau of Investigation.

Traitors in high places. Were there individuals in the United States who were willing to sell our country into Red slavery? It is hard to believe, but in 1949 a group of America's top Communists was discovered. What was their crime? Conspiracy to overthrow the government of the United States by violence and to deliver the American people into slavery under communist dictators.

The trial of these men took place in New York City and lasted for 169 days, the longest criminal trial in American history. Sentences were passed by Judge Harold Medina of the Federal Circuit Court of New York. As a loyal American and a true Christian, he realized that his obligation was to pass judgment on these traitors without endangering the cause of democracy by any unjust accusations. For this reason, he did not hesitate to state publicly that each night he went home and prayed for heavenly guidance.

This investigation led to the discovery of communist sympathizers in the motion picture industry, radio, television and, as we have indicated, even in some departments of our government.

What God hath joined together. From your study of religion you know that the rest of this quotation reads: "Let no man put asunder," and that it pertains to the Sacrament of Matrimony. This quotation expresses the Catholic belief in regard to one of the greatest safeguards of our American heritage, sound family life, and condemns divorce.

Divorce has been considered by the American hierarchy a greater danger to democracy than the atom bomb. Pope Pius XI considered the problem of the breaking up of the family so vital to a nation and to the Church that in 1930 he wrote an encyclical on *Christian Marriage*. In this encyclical he brings out the value of sound married life to the welfare of a country. The Church is against divorce not only for religious reasons, but because it is an enemy of human happiness and a danger to the human race. The next paragraph will tell you why divorce weakens the foundation of our American heritage.

Evils of divorce. Divorce is the breaking of a solemn pledge which a man and woman make to each other when they are married. The violation of this pledge is wrong. A nation whose citizens can not make a success of marriage and the management of a home can not reasonably be expected to manage the more complicated business of running a government wisely.

The family is the social cell of the nation. It is the family that produces the citizen. No nation can be greater than the strength of its families. Since divorce weakens and breaks up family life, it consequently weakens national life.

Children suffer from insecure family life. If parental love is absent, they seek entertainment outside the home. Children, neglected because of divorce, sometimes become juvenile delinquents—young people who violate lawful authority, citizens without loyalty for our democratic ideals.

Pope Leo XIII, the great friend of the workingman, also condemned divorce, stating that since the destruction of family life and the loss of national wealth is brought about more by the corruption of morals than by anything else, it is easily seen that divorce, which is born of the perverted (irregular) morals of a people . . . is particularly opposed to the well-being of the family and of the state.

The fact that one out of every four marriages between 1940 and 1950 in the United States ended in a divorce court is sufficient ground for Catholics to remember that marriage is sacred and upon its success will depend in great measure the strength or weakness of America.

"With liberty and justice for all." Let us refer again to this meaningful phrase of the Pledge of Allegiance. The word "all" refers to every human being in the United States, regardless of race, color, or creed. But let us ask this question: Is the "liberty and justice for all" ever violated in America by boys or girls or adults? If it is, then there exists *intolerance,* or unwillingness to accept a particular group or individual because of race, color, or creed. In the next few paragraphs we shall see that intolerance does exist in America and that it also is a force which tends to weaken the foundation of our democracy.

Intolerance towards Negroes. You have learned about the early attitude of American citizens towards the Negro. All too frequently, Americans forgot that all of us, regardless of color, were created "to the image and likeness of God."

There were Jim Crow laws which separated Negroes and whites. The Ku Klux Klan was organized to frighten Negroes out of politics. The Southern states found means of making the Fourteenth and Fifteenth Amendments to the Constitution ineffective. While the attitude towards Negroes has improved, the fact still remains that many Southern whites and some Northerners have opposed changes which would improve the economic and the social position of the Negro.

Organized labor has not always been particularly sympathetic towards the Negro. Intolerance has sometimes excluded him from unions. It is true that the Communists have made efforts to entice the Negro to accept their ideas, but that is not the real reason he has been kept out of labor organizations. Have we not seen that some white people are communist sympathizers?

In some states Negroes' salaries were as much as fifty per cent less than those given to white men for the same type of work. At times, during a shortage of manpower, because of war, for instance, industry hired colored men. When the emergency was over, the Negro help was the first to be fired.

To deprive a person of the means of livelihood to which he is naturally entitled, merely because of his race or color, is unjust and contrary to charity.

Drawing the color line. Although the more violent forms of discrimination are getting rarer, Southerners still hold to *segregation,* which means separation of the whites from the Negroes. In many places, the Negro is barred from white restaurants, schools, and hospitals and must sit in the galleries in theaters. He must ride either in separate street cars or else go to the back section of the car.

While more Negroes voted between 1940 and 1950 than ever before, their educational opportunities were still inferior. The number of schools for Negroes in the South was far short of those for whites. This condition was the result of segregation. The South was not wealthy enough to afford two separate but equally good school systems. The schools for Negroes were the ones to suffer. Jews, Catholics, and others also suffer from discrimination in the United States, but to a less degree than the Negro.

Among other victims of intolerance have been Orientals, people from the eastern part of the world. There were riots against the Chinese in the 1870's. In 1880 California passed a law forbidding corporations to hire Chinese help, and denying the latter employment in public works. The federal government severely restricted Chinese immigration. In 1906, Japanese were excluded from the San Francisco public schools, and

Educational opportunities for Negro boys and girls are growing throughout the South, as shown by this modern Catholic School.   *By Ewing Galloway, N. Y.*

By Ewing Galloway, N. Y.

Dilapidated and overcrowded tenements make bad living conditions
for Negroes and Puerto Ricans in a big city.

a bigoted feeling prevailed against them for several years. It revived on the West Coast during World War II when many loyal Americans of Japanese descent were driven from their homes.

The only way in which these terrible conditions can be improved is to banish forever that un-Christian attitude of intolerance and discrimination.

Anti-Catholic bigotry in the United States. Catholics also have had to fight a long warfare against bigotry or intolerance. This struggle has dated from colonial days. In the nineteenth century, the Nativist Movement, together with the "Know-Nothing Party," continued to rouse feeling against Catholics. The Civil War and the question of slavery for a time pushed anti-Catholic movements into the background. Then, in the 1880's, came the American Protective Association, commonly called the APA. This society was organized to "protect" the United States from Catholics! It went so far as to forge a document which the APA called an "encyclical letter." This forgery purported to free all Catholics from allegiance to the United States. The APA was scorned by true Americans, and soon ceased to exist, for the majority of Americans have always rejected such intolerance.

Revival of the Ku Klux Klan. Perhaps you can remember from last year's history the origin of the Ku Klux Klan. It was a secret society, whose purpose was to frighten the Negro in the South, often using violence to maintain white supremacy. In 1915, the Ku Klux Klan was revived. This time it conducted a bitter campaign against Negroes, Jews, aliens, and Catholics. The activities of the Klan were contrary to just principles, for no group may deprive others of the right to live according to the dictates of conscience.

The influence of the Klan in politics. In 1924, the Klan exerted a very powerful influence on the Democratic national convention and attempted to split the party. Do you know what is meant by "a split" in a political party? The following paragraph will help you to understand this expression.

At this convention two men sought the Democratic nomination for President. One was the Catholic governor of New York, Alfred E. Smith. The other was William McAdoo, of California. The Ku Klux Klan, through spreading anti-Catholic propaganda, succeeded in dividing the Democrats, urging those from the South and West not to nominate Alfred Smith. The re-

A meeting of the Ku Klux Klan. The men without uniforms are being initiated into this secret society.

From Ewing Galloway, N. Y.

sult was that neither of these two men received the nomination, and the Democratic party was split. When this occurs, usually the Republicans win the election. This is what happened in 1924, and as a result Calvin Coolidge began his first elected term as President of the United States. What does "elected term" mean?

The "whispering" campaign against Al Smith. As the next campaign drew near in 1928, it became clear that Alfred Smith would be the Democratic candidate. This roused the zeal of all those anxious to "protect" America from a "Roman" invasion. Even certain Senators, influenced by the Klan, toured the country lecturing on the peril to America from the Catholic Church. Many Americans became convinced that a Catholic in the White House would mean that the Pope would shortly take over America. The campaign was so successful against Catholics that some states in the South, usually referred to as the "Solid South," that is, solidly Democratic, voted Republican. Herbert Hoover, a Republican who had done successful work as Food Administrator during World War I, won the election.

The influence of the Klan declined rapidly soon afterwards, and little was heard of it until after World War II when a new attempt to revive it was made in Georgia during 1946. In spite of vicious attacks from without, the Catholic Church still remains in America the greatest single force which

From Ewing Galloway, N. Y.
Alfred E. Smith.

challenges any form of evil threatening to weaken our democracy.

Anti-Catholic sentiment strikes at the schools. We have seen how the Ku Klux Klan tried to influence politics in the United States. The Klan also attempted to use state politics to destroy the Catholic school system in this country.

As we mentioned in a previous Unit, the American school system is controlled by the states and not by the federal government. Therefore, each state has the right to make its own school laws. In the early twentieth century, several states, urged by the Ku Klux Klan, tried to abolish parochial schools by changing their state constitutions. Remember that a parochial school is one connected with a parish. It may be Protestant as well as Catholic.

317

The Oregon school case. The dispute in the state of Oregon in 1925 is one example of an attempt to abolish parochial schools. This state passed a law which compelled all children to attend public schools. Many Catholics protested against such a law and the case was carried to the Supreme Court of the United States. The highest court of our land declared that parents had the right to send their children to any school they desired. The Supreme Court declared that Oregon's law was unconstitutional because it would have prohibited people from sending their children to parochial schools, thereby depriving them of freely exercising their parental rights.

Embarrassed because of religion classes? We have seen that the highest judicial body in the land decided in favor of religious schools in 1925. Not twenty-five years later, that body decided against religious instruction. Here is the story.

Between 1940 and 1950, in many schools in the United States provision was made for released-time teaching of religion. Sometimes boys and girls were dismissed from public schools to attend religion classes elsewhere. At other schools, priests, ministers, and rabbis came into the public school building to teach religion. In Illinois, the latter custom prevailed. One of the children in a particular school in that state was the son of a non-religious mother, Mrs. Vashti McCollum, who did not want her child to have any religious instruction. This mother claimed her child was embarrassed because he had to remain alone while the rest of his classmates went to their respective religion classes. She therefore appealed to the courts to stop such classes. For three years her suit climbed from one court to another until it reached the Supreme Court of the United States. In 1948, this Court ruled that the use of the public school for the teaching of religion was "an aid to religion" and violated the First Amendment.

This decision was criticized by both Catholics and non-Catholics.

Some important terms

heritage	segregation
democracy	bigotry
Communism	A.P.A.
Anti-Catholic	Federal Bureau of
propaganda	Investigation
intolerance	Solid South
discrimination	parochial school

Atheistic Communism
Committee on
   Un-American Activities
Communist sympathizer
Christian Marriage
juvenile delinquents

Think well before you answer

1. In what ways is America's ideal of democracy a Christian ideal?
2. Explain how each of the following endangers or weakens our democratic heritage: Communism, divorce, intolerance, anti-Catholic sentiment.
3. Prove that the anti-Catholic feeling shown towards religion in schools is unjust and contrary to the principles of our Founding Fathers.
4. What part did the Ku Klux Klan have in attempting to abolish

parochial schools? Can you name any other group which carried on anti-Catholic activities?

5. What evidences of anti-Catholic feeling have been shown in politics?

6. Why is the Catholic Church opposed to Communism?

7. Do you know of any other kind of parochial schools besides Catholic schools?

Test your knowledge

I. ARE YOU A REAL THINKER? Below is a list of ten phrases. On your paper, opposite the number, write the idea it suggests to you.

Example: government of the people, by the people, and for the people—suggests "*Democracy*".

1. life, liberty, and the pursuit of happiness
2. only material things are real
3. Judge Medina
4. destroys family life
5. Negroes banned from schools, theaters, hotels
6. "protected" America from Catholics
7. split in the "Solid South"
8. First Amendment
9. forbade religious dress
10. school aid question

II. ANSWER "YES" OR "NO" (*On your paper*)

1. Democracy and Christianity are two different ideals.
2. Communism is a danger to our democratic heritage because it deprives man of his dignity and rights as a human being.
3. Pope Pius XII wrote an encyclical entitled *Atheistic Communism*.
4. The American ideal of democracy had its beginnings in the United States.

5. American democracy was established on religion.
6. The purpose of the affair at Bogota in South America was to weaken American cooperation.
7. *The Daily Worker* is a paper which attempts to discover Communist sympathizers in industry.
8. Judge Medina solved the Oregon Case in 1925.
9. The Catholic Church opposes divorce because it is contrary to the law of God and is a danger to the human race.
10. Because divorce breaks up family life, it also weakens national life.
11. Racial intolerance is the only kind of intolerance found in the United States today.
12. The American attitude towards the Negro has improved.
13. After World War I the Ku Klux Klan conducted a bitter campaign against Negroes, Catholics, Jews, and aliens.
14. The McCollum Case was an attempt to prevent public schools from assisting religious education.
15. Alfred Smith was defeated in the Presidential election of 1928 mainly because he was a Catholic.
16. The Catholic Church in America is the greatest single force which opposes the evils which threaten to weaken democracy.
17. Parochial schools have no right to ask for any federal aid because they are not controlled by the state.
18. Catholics want aid for the support of their schools because Catholic children are American citizens and, as such, are entitled to aid.

CHAPTER II

SAVING AMERICAN DEMOCRACY

IN THE first part of this Unit, we briefly reviewed the meaning of American democracy and learned about some of the dangers threatening to shake its foundation. Hopefully, America's citizens have struggled against these dangers.

One institution which was established in an effort to guard democratic ideals is the United Nations Organization. After World War II the United Nations Organization, which replaced the unsuccessful League of Nations, did valiant work to save democracy, not only for the United States but also for the world. The United States has played a leading role in that work —in fact, she has earned the name "Guardian of Freedom." The Catholic Church, true to her principles of justice, has also had an active part in saving true democracy.

The last chapter in our textbook, then, will deal with two important points. The first point discusses the work of the United Nations Organization and its struggle to save democracy, and the second point tells the story of the Church's part in saving American democracy through Catholic Action.

1. The United Nations Organization Struggles to Save Democracy

Recall that the nations fighting against Fascism during World War II had pledged themselves to mutual assistance on January 1, 1942, and from that time on they were called the United Nations. However, no official organization could be formed until after the fighting ceased. This world organization has been dedicated to the keeping of international peace through general cooperation.

The chapter of the United Nations. We have already learned that the United Nations was officially born at San Francisco. Edward R. Stettinius, Secretary of State, was chairman of the conference at San Francisco and directed its work. There were numerous meetings of small committees, which talked over plans and then wrote draft after draft of the Charter. The work continued for about nine weeks. Then came success. Fifty nations agreed, and the final draft of the Charter was completed.

The Charter is the constitution of the United Nations. Like our own Constitution, it explains the make-up of the different bodies which do the work of the United Nations. The Preamble, or the opening words of the Charter, reads as follows:

We, The Peoples of the United Nations, Determined ....

... to save succeeding generations from the scourge of war, which twice in our lifetime has brought untold sorrow to mankind, and

... to reaffirm faith in fundamental human rights, in the dignity and worth of the human person, in the equal rights of men and women, and of nations large and small, and

... to establish conditions under which justice and respect for the obligations arising from treaties and other sources of international law can be maintained, and

... to promote social progress and better standards of life in larger freedom

And For These Ends ....

... to practice tolerance and live together in peace with one another, as good neighbors, and

... to unite our strength to maintain international peace and security, and

... to insure, by the acceptance of principles and the institution of methods, that armed force shall not be used, save in the common interest, and

... to employ international machinery for the promotion of the economic and social advancement of all peoples, *Have Resolved to Combine Our Efforts to Accomplish These Aims.* ....

Accordingly, our respective governments, through representatives assembled in the City of San Francisco, who have exhibited their full powers found to be in good and due form, have agreed to the present Charter of the United Nations and do hereby establish an international organization to be known as the United Nations.

Who belongs to the United Nations? Any peace-loving nation in the world may apply for membership in the United Nations. Whether or not a nation is accepted depends upon the decision of the two most important bodies of the organization, the Security Council and the General Assembly. There were fifty original members in the UN. By 1951 it totaled sixty members.

The United States was one of the original members of this new world organization. Recall that we did not join the League of Nations. Many believed this fact might have been one of the reasons the other big powers deserted it. The League had no real leader. By joining the new organization, the United States took a leading role and assured her world neighbors of her intention to put forth every effort to promote peace, and thereby save the democratic way of life.

Where the UN meets. The United States is the permanent home of the UN. It has beautiful headquarters in New York City. The Secretariat with its many workers always stays in the United States, but the General Assembly can meet anywhere. In the next few

The Security Council of the UN debates the Korean question. At this session it was decided to open military operations against North Korea.

paragraphs we shall try to give a picture of what some of the more important committees of the UN attempt to do.

The Security Council. The Security Council is often called the "police force" of the UN. It is composed of eleven member nations, each nation having one representative. Five nations are permanent members: the United States, Great Britain, France, Russia, and China. You may have heard them spoken of as the "Big Five." The other six members are elected by the General Assembly for a term of two years each. In order that there may always be some members familiar with the problems under discus-

sion, only three of these six members are changed each year.

The Security Council has the important job of trying to settle peacefully disagreements between nations. If a war has already begun, the Council can order the belligerent nations to stop fighting. Another step it can take is to send a committee to investigate the causes of a dispute. The Council also has the right to declare a nation guilty of violating international law or of being an aggressor in a war.

A weakness in the Security Council. When the Security Council was set up, it was decided that if one of the permanent members disagreed with a measure being discussed, he had the power to "veto" it. The word "veto" means "I forbid." By using the veto, any action to preserve peace could be blocked because the vote of seven members, including the "Big Five," is necessary for a decision. It was thought that the five permanent member nations would use good judgment concerning the veto power, but, unfortunately, one of those members was not honest in trying to save the peace of the world. That nation was Russia. Up to September, 1952, Russia had used the veto 51 times. This resulted in a complete deadlock on some vital world problems.

What could be done about this situation? United States Secretary of State, Dean Acheson, suggested that when no action could be taken by the Security Council because of a veto, the Assembly should meet within 24 hours and take over the Council's obligations. The success or failure of this new arrangement is yet to be seen.

The Secretariat. The Secretariat of the UN employs about 3,000 workers who do all the things necessary to keep the organization running smoothly. Their work includes letter writing, filing of important documents, looking up information for speeches, translating speeches,

The General Assembly of the UN in session when it met at Flushing Meadows, New York.

Trygve Lie.

printing of pamphlets, and any work which a secretary might be expected to do. Mr. Trygve Lie (trig'-vay lee) of Norway was the first Secretary-General of the UN; he served his term of five years, and was reappointed in 1950.

The town meeting of the world. The General Assembly is the only part of the UN in which *all* member nations are represented. Each member nation sends five delegates, five alternates, and several advisers to the Assembly. The total number of members in the Assembly, therefore, reaches over 500 persons. All nations, however, are equal, and regardless of size are permitted only one vote. Meetings are scheduled for once a year, but extra ones may be called.

World problems may be discussed publicly in the Assembly.

While the Assembly cannot *force* any nation to comply with its decisions, it *can* arouse the world to back its decisions. It may refer any problem to the Security Council where force can be invoked to bring an offending nation to justice.

Other agencies in the UN. The men who wrote the UN Charter at San Francisco realized that economic problems often cause war. Therefore, they planned for a Social and Economic Council which would work to raise the standards of living in various parts of the world. This council believes that as nations become more prosperous, there will be a greater possibility of realizing that social justice to which all people have a God-given right.

The Charter of the United Nations also provides for an International Court of Justice which meets at The Hague in the Netherlands. This court judges disputes over treaties or legal disputes between nations. Its decisions are final — something like an international Supreme Court.

There is also a Trusteeship Council which promotes the welfare of peoples who do not govern themselves.

Agencies which help the UN. A number of special UN agencies, not actually part of the United Nations, but cooperating with it, also work for the betterment of world conditions. One such agency was set up to help nations to keep the value of their money from changing, another to help to rebuild and reestablish industries in countries which may have been ravaged by war. Still another strives to improve agricultural conditions in the world that all may be properly fed. The International Labor Organization attempts to better conditions of working people throughout the world, and another agency seeks to improve air travel between nations.

One of the most important of these special agencies is the United Nations Educational, Scientific, and Cultural Organization, more popularly spoken of as UNESCO (younes'-co). A more detailed explanation of the work of UNESCO will be found later in this chapter.

What has the UN accomplished? The UN has succeeded in "putting out several fires," one in Iran, one in Indonesia, and another in Palestine, but as a whole it has not proved equal to its task of preventing war, as we shall see. There are several things, however, which it has brought into the open. The United States, which has taken the lead in sponsoring the UN has repeatedly stated that our foreign policy was based in faithfully adhering to the principles of the UN Charter. In our strict adherence to it, America has, through the UN, disclosed Russia's unscrupulous methods of dealing with world problems. These actions have discredited Russia in the eyes of the democratic nations of the West.

Secondly, the UN has probably accomplished more through its social and economic agencies than through its security functions, or attempts to secure the peace of the world. In its social undertakings it has promoted a better understanding of the problems which confront people in different regions of the world. It has also created a deeper appreciation of their cultural and scientific achievements.

Thirdly, the UN has kept the democracies more closely allied than they would have been without it. If the democracies have the courage to fight for Christian principles and to protect themselves from aggression, the UN will have been successful. Thus far, the democracies have not given full proof of being able to achieve these ends.

Programs remaining to be solved. Five years after the end of World War II there were still weighty problems to be solved by the United Nations Organization. Three major issues which control the destiny of the world faced the United Nations in 1951. First, how can atomic energy be controlled for the safety of the world? Second, what can be done about investigating communistic activities behind the "Iron Curtain?" Third—this question became a real crisis—can the United Nations settle the difficult Korean problem? We shall consider each of these issues separately.

Controlling atomic energy. When the United States used the first atomic bomb on Hiroshima in 1945, it was the only country in the world possessing the bomb. Then, through disloyal Americans, the secret of producing it was learned by Red Russia

An Atomic Energy Commission was organized in the United States in 1946, as you have already learned. Do you remember the purpose of the AEC? Turn to Unit Four. in case you have forgotten. In 1946, the United Nations also established an International Atomic Energy Commission. The United Nations Commission was to investigate international problems relating to atomic energy and to devise some plan for controlling the production or possibly outlawing the use of the atomic bomb.

In 1948, the United States and Soviet Russia tried but failed to reach any agreement on international control of atomic energy. The result was a race for the making of atomic bombs.

The world went about its business, when suddenly one day in September, 1949, news of an atomic explosion in Russia struck the world like a thunderbolt. This incident caused the United Nations to strive more ardently to achieve international control of atomic energy, which Russia had blocked for several years. Russia had demanded that the United States destroy its stock of atomic bombs before any kind of international control should be established. No agreement could be reached because the other great powers insisted just as strongly that the creation of international controls and the outlawing of the A-bomb should go hand in hand.

For three years the Soviet delegation to the UN, by means of a skilful filibuster, prevented the adoption of any plan for international control. What is meant by a "filibuster"? Will the United Nations win this vital point or not? World safety is at stake.

Trying to pierce the "Iron Curtain." Another unsolved problem before the United Nations is that of trying to get through the "Iron Curtain." The "Iron Curtain" refers to the Communist practice of strictly controlling travel and of censoring all matters in the nations under Soviet domination.

Behind the Iron Curtain exist slavery and such infamous "treason" trials as that of Cardinal Mindszenty, the Catholic Primate of Hungary, and of many other Catholic and Protestant clergymen. At these trials, "confessions" of guilt were extorted by medical and mental torture. But the world was not blind to the terrorism which surrounded the trials from which foreign observers were excluded.

And what has the United Nations accomplished in trying to prevent such injustice? In 1949, the suggestion was made that a commission be formed to visit any member nation and then disclose possible findings of injustice of slave or forced labor before the United Nations. Some member nations of the Soviet Bloc were not willing to accept this proposal. Why? Could it be that the commission might find one of them guilty of violating human liberty?

Korea—the first major crisis in the UN. The real test of the strength or weakness of the United Nations lay in its decision on a war in Korea. As we have previously learned, when World War II was over, Korea was divided into two zones. The Russians occupied the North and the Americans the South. The division between these sections lay at the thirty-eighth parallel of latitude.

On June 25, 1950, the North Koreans unjustly invaded South Korea. Immediately, the United Nations termed North Korea an aggressor, and under United States leadership, with mostly American forces, the United Nations got together its first army. General Douglas MacArthur was named Supreme Commander of the United Nations forces in the Far East. This new international army also received its own flag, a white symbol of the United Nations on a field of blue.

Faced with a big aggressor. Branded an aggressor, the North Korean army was finally pushed back across the thirty-eighth parallel. Everyone breathed a sigh of relief, and hope ran high that the United Nations had achieved another victory. Then came aggression on a big scale. Early in November, 1950, Chinese troops attacked the United Nations forces in Korea. The United States asked that the United Nations declare Chinese Communists, as it had North Korean Communists, aggressors. The United Nations hesitated, though its troops continued to fight the Chinese. Was it afraid of a big aggressor? Was it leaving business

From Ewing Galloway, N. Y.
UN troops in Korea.

and trade betray it into winking at injustice?

Is the United Nations breaking under its first big test? We have learned that when the Security Council was unable to stop aggression, Secretary of State Dean Acheson had proposed that the Assembly take over obligations to stop the war. The Korean war offered the first opportunity. Fifty-two nations had voted for the Acheson Plan, but in the six-week period that followed Russia's veto on branding China an aggressor, none of these fifty-two nations succeeded in getting the Assembly to act.

Some of the big powers in the United Nations had recognized Communist China and wanted to pay either part or all of the price China asked. Communist China asked nothing less than the seat in

General Mac Arthur says the Lord's Prayer in the Capital Building at Seoul, Korea, when the city was restored to the Korean Republic.

the Security Council which was occupied by Chiang Kai-shek's Nationalist China. If this price were paid to Red China, then another Communist nation would have the right to veto in the Security Council of the UN. Finally, Communist China was condemned as an aggressor in Korea.

In an effort to end the war, representatives of the United Nations have been meeting with the Communists to discuss truce terms. Repeatedly, the UN offers have been rejected. Meanwhile, the enemy has gained a great deal of time to build up his forces. It remains to be seen whether or not the UN approach to the settlement of the war will bring peace desired by the world.

The Korean war. Although no war with Korea was formally declared, the United States and its allies in the United Nations were definitely fighting hard battles. Thousands of soldiers, as well as innocent women and children in Korea, lost their lives. The war passed like a shadow up and down the tiny Korean peninsula, some cities changing hands as many as four times.

For almost a year, General Douglas MacArthur directed the UN armies in Korea. Then, suddenly, one day in April, 1951, the stunning news of MacArthur's dismissal rocked the nation. President Truman relieved the general of all his military commands. The President said he did so because of the general's open disagreement with United States and UN policies in conducting the war.

What is ahead for the UN? Even the League of Nations kept going, at least as a debating society, right up to World War II. But more is expected of the UN than that. Will the United Nations continue to have the courage required to challenge big aggressors, even Russia if necessary? President Truman's message at the opening session of the Eighty-second Congress in January, 1951, can appropriately be applied to the world situation:

> We and the other free nations must build up strength to defeat Russia should she attack us. We are willing to negotiate with Russia, but we will fight for our freedom and for justice if fight we must.

The President stated that free nations would fight for the dignity of man and the right of peoples to independence. He recognized the Korean situation as crucial and said: "Let us stand together as Americans . . . asking divine guidance that in all we do we may follow God's will."

Will the United Nations stand together with us?

Universal declaration of human rights. Man's struggle to gain and protect his rights and freedoms reached a high point when the United Nations approved a Declaration of Human Rights program in December, 1948. This document set forth a standard of achievement for all peoples and nations. It was not a legally binding document, but it has strong moral force. It can rightfully be called a World Bill of Rights.

Here are some statements in this World Bill of Rights. The Preamble declares that the recognition of the inalienable rights of man is the foundation of justice, freedom, and peace. Everyone has the right to life, liberty, and the security of person, regardless of race, color, or religion. Everyone has the right to freedom of thought and expression; this right entitles men to express their opinions freely and to assemble peacefully for such purposes. It also gives men the right to teach or practice their religion or any belief that does not impair the welfare of the group.

Everyone has the right to work, to choose the kind of work he desires, to work under wholesome conditions, to be protected against unemployment, to receive a just wage, and to join trade unions.

Everyone has the right to receive an education. This education should strengthen respect for human rights and promote understanding, tolerance, and friendship among all nations, races, and religious groups. Parents have the first right to choose the kind of education that shall be given to their children.

The family is the foundation of society and is entitled to protection by society and the state.

Everyone has the right to own property and no one may unjustly deprive another individual of it. **God's name omitted.** Many of the principles mentioned above are found in our Bill of Rights and are based on Christian teachings. However, the World Bill of Rights does not mention that these basic rights to which all men are entitled come from God. In fact, His name does not appear anywhere in it. Why was the name of the Author of all rights omitted? God's name was voted out in order not to offend certain Godless countries, Russia in particular. This was a great disappointment to men of Christian nations.

While the principles expressed in this Universal Declaration of Human Rights represent a great advance towards human freedom, there are still some Godless nations whose leaders glorify the state above human dignity.

The genocide treaty. The General Assembly, at this time, also approved a treaty known as the *genocide* (jen'-o-side) *treaty*. Genocide is formed from two Latin words which mean race destroyer. Recall that Hitler committed a crime of genocide by trying to destroy the Jewish race.

In order to prevent such crimes in the future, the United Nations approved the genocide treaty. This treaty condemned the destruction in whole or in part of a national, racial, or religious group. By October, 1950, the required twenty nations had ratified the treaty.

Will *all* nations of the world live according to these principles? That is yet to be seen. Dr. Charles Malik, a UN delegate from Lebanon, a tiny country in the Near East, said that man has blinded himself "to God's constant hold on him. He is seeking for his rights elsewhere in vain."

UNESCO—A help to world understanding. We have learned that one special agency of the United Nations is UNESCO. Do you recall what that abbreviated name means?

The purpose of UNESCO is to preserve the democratic way of life and to obtain international peace through a program of mutual understanding. UNESCO was officially born in London in 1945, where representatives of 44 nations met to discuss the rebuilding of their educational and cultural centers destroyed by the war.

The first general conference of UNESCO was held at Paris in 1946, and since that time a conference has been held yearly in various parts of the world. The United States has organized its own National Commission for UNESCO which cooperates with the international organization.

The Preamble of UNESCO's Charter says: "Since wars begin in the minds of men, it is in the minds of men that the defenses of peace must be constructed."

In accordance with this statement, UNESCO has striven to banish war from the minds of men through developing an appreciation and understanding of the educational, scientific, and cultural contributions of peoples of other nations. Such interchange of information has been made by means of radio programs, films, literature, and an exchange of students and teachers. Again religion is neglected.

UNESCO needs religion. The UN, through UNESCO, has tried to bring people to have a friendly feeling for one another. Only nations with this understanding can live together in peace; only by a free exchange of information can barriers between nations be broken down. There is one big danger which UNESCO must avoid and that is indifference to God and religion.

As Catholics, every boy and girl should make use of every opportunity to develop a conscience that is tolerant to those in error but intolerant to evil and error as such.

A United Europe to fight Communism. We have seen how the big and the little nations of the world have organized to preserve peace. The free countries of Western Europe were closest to the danger of Communism and felt the need of some kind of union. Accordingly, in April, 1949, twelve nations, including the United States and Canada, met in Washington, D. C., and signed the North Atlantic Pact. While this pact is not part of the United Nations Oragnization, it has been approved by the UN. To what did these nations bind themselves? They declared that should one or more of them be attacked by an aggressor, it would be considered an attack against all. To preserve peace in the North Atlantic area, all would take any action necessary, "including armed force."

Russia and her satellite countries loudly denounced this pact as a means of beginning a war against them. That did not stop the United States from taking further action. In 1951, President Truman named General Dwight D. Eisenhower Supreme Commander of the Atlantic Defense Forces. In order to find out whether or not European countries would be willing and able to contribute men and material to an international army for Europe, General Eisenhower made a tour of European nations. Immediately a question arose. What part would Germany play in this international army? Some German munitions factories had been dismantled after World War II. Would Germany be

Signing of the Atlantic Pact.

From Ewing Galloway, N. Y.

permitted to rearm? These and similar questions must be answered in the future. An international armed force in Europe is intended to make Communist Russia think seriously before taking up arms against Western Europe.

A new President. General Eisenhower gave up his duties as Supreme Commander of the Atlantic Defense Forces to run for President on the Republican ticket in the 1952 election. When the votes were counted he won over his Democratic opponent, Adlai E. Stevenson, by a large majority.

2. Saving Democracy through Catholic Action

We have seen how governments have striven to preserve the peace of the world. We have also learned that in most of their undertakings to save that peace they have forgotten or been indifferent to the fact that unless peace is based upon a religious foundation it will crumble. The Catholic Church in the United States has not forgotten this fact and, as we shall see, has made some outstanding, though not always recognized, contributions to the preservation of American democracy.

Spread of the Church in United States. Before going into the study of Catholic Action, we should get a picture of the size of the Catholic Church in our country. We have learned that Bishop Carroll was consecrated the first bishop of the United States in 1789. A bishop, as you know, is the head of a diocese, such as the one in which you live.

Can you imagine a diocese as large as the thirteen original states? That was the size of Bishop Carroll's diocese. You will understand, however, that in 1789 this territory was sparsely populated. At that time, there were less than fifty thousand Catholics in the United States, but they were widely scattered.

As the country expanded, more priests were ordained or came to the United States from other lands, and more dioceses were created. Immigration made a very definite contribution to the growth of the Catholic Church in the United States because many immigrants were Catholic.

The largest religious denomination in the country. Bishop Carroll would be justly proud of the growth and spread of the Church in the past one hundred fifty years. At mid-century, the Church in the United States claimed 157 bishops, 21 archbishops, and 4 cardinals. Nearly 43,000 priests, about half of whom are diocesan, cared for the religious needs of the people. There were 15,000 parish churches which dotted the country from coast to coast. There were 388 seminaries and houses of study for training priests.

There are six dioceses, each with a Catholic population of more than a million. The largest diocese in the country is the Archdiocese of Chicago, with 1,691,000 Catholics. This is followed in succession by Boston, New York, Brooklyn, Philadelphia, and Newark. The latter is the last diocese to reach the million mark with 1,028,000 Catholics. **What is Catholic Action.** It is the wonderful work of Catholic Action which has partly contributed to this unusual growth of the Church. Our Holy Father, Pope Pius XI, has defined Catholic Action as "the participation by the lay people in the apostolate of the hierarchy." Do you know the meaning of these words? *Apostolate* means a mission for the salvation of souls, and *hierarchy* is the governing body of the Church, namely, the Pope and the bishops.

Catholic Action is not concerned solely with the spread and defense of the Catholic Church, although that is its main purpose. Its interests extend to the fields of morals, social movements, and economics. The Church, with her divine life and action, can accomplish what men have often vainly sought to achieve through peace treaties, social reforms, and economic measures.

Why the Church speaks. Perhaps you wonder why the Catholic Church is better able to realize these aims than any other organization. There are a number of reasons. First, since the Catholic Church is a divine institution, her social principles and moral code are right. Second, since the Church is the oldest organization in the world, she has had the widest experience in dealing with the problems of mankind. Third, she is the only truly international organization — and only international cooperation can materially improve

world conditions. Catholics respect and abide by her decisions. Even non-Catholics are aware that the Catholic Church has the best program for improving the social conditions of the world.

How can Catholics participate? In order that the Catholic laity participate in Catholic Action, they must work under the bishop of their diocese. Unless work is directed by the bishop, it cannot strictly be termed Catholic Action.

Among the lay people strong leaders are necessary, and throughout the United States many of them have rallied fearlessly to the cause of Christ and His Church. They have contributed to the progress of our country by defending religious and moral principles. They have developed a strong social crusade for living, independent of politics or business.

Catholic Action has been promoted in the United States, as well as in other countries, through the "cell movement." Each cell has its leader and a small group of followers. Cells have been formed in factories, on farms, in studios, and in offices. Under the direction of their bishops, and priests, zealous lay people contact fellow workers. They often meet with better success than a priest who sometimes is hindered when confronted with the sign at the gate of a place of business, "Employees Only."

Spread of Catholic Action through NCWC. The central agency for the coordination of Catholic activity in the United States is the National

Catholic Welfare Conference, usually called the NCWC. This organization was formed in 1919, when the country was still feeling the effects of the first World War. The bishops of the country met in Washington to discuss the social ills resulting from the war and to offer some practical solutions. The outstanding achievement of this first meeting was a document known as the *Bishops' Program of Social Reconstruction.*

Each year since 1919 the American hierarchy has met to explain and reassert the Christian principles which can serve as a guide to sound Catholic living. If Americans accept these principles and let them influence their lives, then our democracy will be safe.

In the next few paragraphs we shall learn about various Catholic activities which the Church has promoted in order to train citizens for the kind of living which will preserve our democratic ideals.

The National Catholic Youth Council. Our Holy Father, Pope Pius XII, along with his predecessors, believes that Catholic social principles can best be saved and spread through the youth of the world. Consequently, in 1937, the bishops of the United States launched a project which resulted in the formation of the National Catholic Youth Council. Its purpose is to help Catholic youth groups to better understand problems of national importance, and to train leaders in Catholic Action. Through this council, youth conferences have

been encouraged in every diocese, and a special attempt has been made to reach Catholic youth in secular schools.

Perhaps you belong to a Catholic Youth group. If you do not, you should enroll in one of them. Here are a few to which young boys and girls can belong: the Catholic Order of Foresters, the Columbian Squires, which prepares boys for entrance into the Knights of Columbus, the Junior Catholic Daughters of America, and the like.

Catholic Scouts. Thousands of American boys and girls belong to the Boy Scouts of America. Are you aware that there is a Catholic Committee on Scouting? A bishop is at the head of the Catholic national committee. Other bishops appoint the Scout chaplains and committees of laymen, who together direct activities in accordance with Catholic principles and in cooperation with the Boy Scouts of America. There are about 450,000 boys enrolled in Catholic scouting.

The Girl Scouts also have a number of troops under Catholic auspices. Membership has passed 240,000. The purpose of the Catholic Girl Scouts is to help girls realize the ideals of womanhood, in preparation for their responsibilities as future Catholic homemakers in the United States.

Newman Clubs. If you have an older brother or sister in college you have probably heard of the Newman Clubs. These clubs play an important role in safeguarding the faith of students in secular institu-

Boy Scouts.

Girl Scouts.

tions, where frequently so many pagan ideas are circulated.

The first Newman Club was established in 1893 by five Catholic medical students attending the University of Pennsylvania. The idea grew rapidly and, by 1902, the bishops of the United States approved the clubs and appointed regular chaplains for those which had already been formed. Through the influence of these chaplains, many colleges have even provided campus chapels, where the spiritual needs of Catholic students can be cared for.

There are 553 Newman Clubs in non-Catholic institutions of higher learning, with a membership of about 80,000 students. The idea has also spread into about six foreign countries.

If you have sufficient reason to receive permission to attend a non-Catholic college, you should enroll in a Newman Club. Perhaps you may even become the leader in organizing one, if the college of your choice does not have a Newman Club.

Boys Town—"City of little men." All of the activities mentioned previously have aided social progress in the United States. One other which can not be overlooked is the development of Boys Town in Nebraska.

Boys Town has been the means of saving many American youths from the possibility of developing into individuals capable of endangering our democracy. It was begun by Monsignor Edward J. Flanagan, who has often been called the "world's best friend of boys." He devoted his life to helping boys

Boys Town, Nebraska, consisting of these handsome buildings, grown from humble beginnings under the leadership of Father Flanagan.

who had no other friend, determined to save them from the influence of a friendless world.

In this "town," no exception has ever been made because of race, creed, or color. All boys in need have been welcomed. Some were even young criminals. But Father Flanagan treated them all like proud young Americans and sent them out into the world as good citizens.

Boys Town is an incorporated village with its own government. It has its own mayor and city officials, elected by the boys from among their own number. The first permanent building was erected in 1921,

and at that time about 450 boys could be cared for. The desire to enlarge the village was never to be realized by Father Flanagan because he died in 1948. Since that time, new buildings have been erected, and 1,000 boys can be accommodated in wholesome surroundings where they will receive training in Christian living and citizenship.

Confraternity of Christian Doctrine. Another activity in the Catholic Church which aims to produce not only good Catholics but good citizens is the *Confraternity of Christian Doctrine*. All Catholic children are not so fortunate as to be able to attend a Catholic school. Many of them, for one or another reason, are forced to attend public schools where no religion is taught. One of the purposes of the Confraternity is to care for these children.

This was not a new idea because, in 1905, Pope Pius X issued an encyclical called *The Teaching of Christian Doctrine,* in which he directed that each parish was to establish a Confraternity of Christian Doctrine.

The work of this organization has been noteworthy. Instruction classes in religion have been held in nearly every parish, both after school and during vacation, for children in public elementary schools. Study clubs for high school students have kept Catholic teenagers in closer contact with the Church and have furnished wholesome social and athletic programs. Even adults have shared in the work of the Confraternity through discussion clubs which are open to both Catholic and non-Catholic laity.

The Legion of Decency. Most Catholic boys and girls are well acquainted with the Legion of Decency because it concerns a favorite pastime — movie-going. The drive for clean movies was originated by the NCWC. Since 1934, bishops throughout the United States have asked people each year to pledge that they will not attend indecent movies or read indecent literature.

When this movement began, Americans doubted that the motion

Brown Brothers

Pope Pius X.

picture producers would be guided by the principles decided upon in the Legion. Yet, the good example of Catholics who refuse to attend movies which are offensive to truth, Catholic thought, or decency has been the cause of the widespread movement to produce better movies. However, there are many still being produced which no good Christian should see. You should consult the Legion of Decency list of motion pictures before going to the movies. It can be found in your local Catholic paper.

Tributes to Our Lady—the hope of the world. We have learned how the Communists have tried consistently to destroy democracy throughout the world. About sixty years ago, the first of May was chosen by the Communists as a day for the demonstration of their

Part of the crowd at the Family Rosary Crusade Rally in New York, in October, 1952. Does your family say the rosary?

power. It is often marked by riots and violence.

Recently, religious groups have set aside this same day for activities to answer the communist challenge. Special devotions to Our Lady, Queen of the World, have been held in all parts of the United States.

Two other devotions honoring Our Lady which have attracted public notice are the World Sodality Movement and the Family Rosary Movement. Our Holy Father, Pope Pius XII, approved of World Sodality Day, which has been observed each year since May, 1940.

The Family Rosary Movement began in the United States in 1947, from which country it has spread throughout the world. Originated by Father Patrick Peyton, C.S.C., it has for its object the conversion of Russia and the peace of the world. The Family Rosary Movement has even penetrated countries behind the Iron Curtain.

The Vatican—a reliable source of information. Except for a few decades in the nineteenth century, and the early part of the twentieth, the United States government has been continuously, though not always officially, represented at the Vatican. In December, 1939, President Franklin Roosevelt sent Myron C. Taylor to the Vatican as his personal representative, with the title of ambassador, but without salary. At this time the President told Pope Pius XII that he was sending Mr. Taylor in order to strengthen the endeavors of the United States and the Vatican for the peace of the world.

Since World War II, the Vatican has been recognized as one of the few accurate sources of information, especially about Russian-controlled countries. President Truman reappointed Mr. Taylor, expressing his feelings in these words:

> I feel that he [Myron Taylor] can continue to render helpful service to the cause of Christian civilization . . . I feel the necessity of having for my guidance the counsel and cooperation of all men of good will . . . that the voice of conscience may be heard in the councils of the nation as they seek a solution to the age-old problem: the government of man.

On January 18, 1950, Mr. Taylor resigned his office as American representative at the Vatican. Should a successor be appointed? Dissenting voices arose immediately to answer that question. Some Protestants "protested" that in the name of the "separation of Church and state," there should be no appointment. They urged that those "who value American liberty" and "think democracy worth keeping" should demand that there be no United States Ambassador to the Pope. What will finally be done remains to be seen.

America — the hope of a better world. All through human history efforts have been made to achieve a unity of mankind. This unity can be secured in only one way— through Christ, the One who came that we might have peace and life in abundance. He has promised both of these gifts to anyone who would follow Him. Men follow Him when they do His will; when they look upon their neighbors as brothers.

The United States has gradually unified itself as a nation built of men of all races and nationalities. It is not a perfect state by any means, because there are still in it some forms of injustice and discrimination. But we have given evidence to the world that, regardless of historical background, we have learned to live with one another.

But while America has grown more united, the religious condition of our land is not completely healthy. Formerly, we claimed certain rights because God had created us and had given them to us; we claimed also that we all were free and equal in His sight. The Declaration of Independence puts it that way. Recently, some Americans have turned away from religion. This is a handicap to Americans whose mission it is to bring about universal peace.

Our role of leader in preserving the democratic way of life will not be achieved apart from belief in and dependence upon God. Brotherhood of man—the aim of all nations that have not lost the ideal of human dignity—cannot be accomplished except under the Fatherhood of God. Therefore, Americans must find again the great country which our Founding Fathers established—the America that believed in God, the America that worshipped Him in churches, the America of men, women, and children who prayed. Lasting peace and unity can come about only under the banner of the Prince of Peace, and America can help in uniting the world only in the degree that she accepts Christ's leadership.

You and Democracy. How can you, personally, help to strengthen this heaven-blessed land of ours? No one can teach you better than the Holy Father himself. Let us see what he says. Pope Pius XII declares that there must be a sincere renewal of Christian living in every individual.

Besides renewing our own lives in Christ, we must affect the lives of those around us. There must be a practical application of all the Christian social principles which you have learned. Let us recall a few of the important ones: Recognize God as Supreme Authority. Realize that any rights you have come from Him, and that you have obligations to fulfill as a consequence of possessing these rights. Be fair and just to people of other races, nationalities, and religions. Be honest in your work. Think of the welfare of others rather than your own good. Fulfill your ob-

ligations to the state. Stay close to the Catholic Church and be interested in all its activities. Have no part with any communistic movements. And, above all, pray that God will enlighten this land of Our Lady and continue to bless it, that it may yet, through her, lead our world back to Christ and peace.

Define these words and phrases

economic problems	preamble
military significance	veto power
security functions	alternates
Soviet domination	ravaged
Catholic Action	discredited
hierarchy	filibuster
cell movement	genocide
apostolate	satellites
campus chapels	laity
religious denomination	

Some things to talk about

1. Discuss the work of the six main bodies which form the United Nations Organization.
2. Think of some Catholic principles which you have learned in the course of this year. Read over the Preamble of the United Nations Charter and discuss the ways in which it follows these principles.
3. What three major unsolved problems faced the United Nations in 1951? Explain why no decision on them could be reached in the U.N. How do you think they may be solved in the future?
4. What was the purpose of the Universal Declaration of Human Rights? How can we put the principles of this declaration into practice in our daily lives?
5. How has UNESCO furthered the ideas expressed in this Declara-

tion? What weakness is to be found in both the Declaration and UNESCO?

6. What was the purpose of the Genocide Treaty?

7. Explain the purpose of the North Atlantic Pact. Is this the same as the North Atlantic Charter? Distinguish between them. First, review briefly the North Atlantic Charter.

8. In what ways have the following contributed to American progress?
   Boys Town
   The Legion of Decency
   Catholic Girl Scouts
   Confraternity of Christian Doctrine

9. Explain the work of Catholic Action.

10. Discuss American representation at the Vatican. Do you think it is valuable as a means of preserving democracy? Why?

11. How can you personally help to further the cause of democratic living?

Answer in as few words as possible

1. What important document was written in San Francisco, California, in 1945?

2. Who may belong to the United Nations Organization?

3. What body of the UN is called the "Town Meeting of the World"?

4. What body of the UN has the use of the veto power?

5. Which part of the UN organization takes care of the filing of important documents?

6. Why is the Security Council often called the "police force" of the UN?

7. In what part of the UN can all world problems be discussed publicly?

8. Is UNESCO one of the six important parts of the UN?

9. What country has blocked the international control of atomic energy?

10. What was the first major crisis to be solved by the United Nations?

11. Why was God's name omitted from the Universal Declaration of Human Rights?

12. What document attempted to prevent the destruction of a national, racial, or religious group?

13. What special agency of the UN hopes to preserve peace and the democratic way of life through a program of exchange of ideas?

14. What did western Europe do in 1949 to prevent the spread of Communism?

15. What general name is given to the participation of lay people in the work of the priests and bishops of a diocese?

16. What is the central agency for the spread of Catholic information in the United States?

17. What organization has been established in non-Catholic colleges for the purpose of spreading Catholic principles?

18. What two devotions to Our Blessed Lady have been outward demonstrations of the Church's opposition to Communism?

19. What must the United States do if it wants to continue to lead the world in preserving democracy?

Highlights of the unit

I. Catholic Principles to Remember

1. God is the source of all our rights

and duties and we are all equal in His sight.

2. Governments have no authority to take away from man the natural rights which God has given him.

3. Christianity is opposed to atheistic Communism because Communism denies the existence of God and deprives man of his dignity as a human being.

4. Divorce weakens the life of a nation because it destroys the family which is the foundation of society.

5. No person, group of persons, or government has a right to persecute another person or group of persons because of race, color, or religion.

6. Parents have a right to educate their children as they desire, and the state may not deprive them of this right.

7. Every human being is responsible for helping to spread the Kingdom of God at home and abroad.

II. WHO'S WHO in Unit Six

Pope Pius XI—
wrote an encyclical called *Atheistic Communism;* wrote an encyclical called *On Christian Marriage*

Judge Harold Medina—
passed sentence on American Communists in 1949

Alfred E. Smith—
Catholic, who was defeated in the election of 1928

Trygve Lie—
First Secretary-General of the UN

Chiang Kai-shek—
Leader of Nationalist China

General Dwight D. Eisenhower—
Supreme Commander of the Atlantic Defense Forces in 1951

Monsignor Edward Flanagan—
Founder of Boys Town, Nebraska

Myron C. Taylor—
Personal representative of Presidents Roosevelt and Truman at the Vatican

III. Important Terms to be Remembered

heritage—
something received from our ancestors

Communism—
atheistic plan for organizing society

intolerance—
unwillingness to accept a person because of race, color, or religion

segregation—
separation of the white race from the Negroes

bigotry—
intolerance

the "veto" power—
the power used by any one of the Big Five in the Security Council to block decisions

the "Big Five" of the UN—
the United States; Great Britain; France; Russia; China

filibuster—
the practice of making long speeches to prevent a bill from being passed

Iron Curtain—
the communistic practice of preventing other countries from finding out what goes on in Russia and her satellites

genocide—
race destruction

Catholic Action—
participation of the laity in the work of the hierarchy

"Solid South"—
the term applied to the South,

which is usually solidly Democratic in voting

IV. IMPORTANT FACTS to Be
Remembered

1. American democracy is a way
of life in which every individual
is free to live and work as he
pleases as long as he violates no
rights of God or man.
2. American democracy was
founded on religious principles
by our forefathers.
3. Communism is directly opposed
to democracy because it deprives
individuals of their dignity as
human beings, takes from them
freedom to worship God, freedom of speech, and the right to
own property.
4. Catholics are forbidden to cooperate with Communism in any
way whatever.
5. Threats of Communism have
penetrated the United States:
a. Communists have tried to
weaken democracy by stirring
up economic and social discontent.
b. Communist propaganda has
been spread through *The Daily
Worker,* a Communist newspaper.
c. Communists have been discovered in the motion picture
industry, radio, television, and
even in government positions.
d. Eleven top Communists were
convicted by Judge Harold
Medina of New York, in 1949,
in the longest criminal trial in
our history.
e. Communists have been discovered through the House Committee on Un-American Activities and the F.B.I.

f. The strongest single force
fighting Communism is the Catholic Church.
6. Divorce weakens American democracy because it destroys
family life, which is the foundation of all society.
7. Intolerance is sometimes practiced in the United States against
Catholics, Negroes, foreigners,
and Jews.
8. Anti-Catholic bigotry has existed in the United States for
many years.
a. The American Protective Association (the APA) was organized in the late nineteenth
century to "protect" the United
States from Catholics.
b. The Ku Klux Klan, revived
in 1915, attempted to influence
politics against Catholics and to
destroy the Catholic school system in the United States.
c. The Ku Klux Klan was responsible for spreading anti-Catholic
propaganda in 1924, and 1928,
when Alfred E. Smith ran for
President.
d. The Oregon School Case of
1925 was an attempt by the state
of Oregon to compel all children
to attend public schools. The
Supreme Court ruled in favor of
the right of parents to send children to any school.
e. Twenty-five years later, the
Supreme Court upheld a mother
(the McCollum Case of 1948)
who tried to force schools to
abolish the teaching of religion.
9. The United Nations Organization
was formed to keep international
peace through general cooperation.
10. Divisions of the United Nations

Organization are:

a. Security Council—the "police force" of the UN

b. General Assembly—The Town Meeting of the World

c. Secretariat

d. Social and Economic Council

e. International Court of Justice

f. Trusteeship Council

11. The permanent home of the United Nations is in New York City.

12. The General Assembly may meet anywhere in the world.

13. A weakness in the Security Council is the power of the veto which may be used by any member of the Big Five, thereby possibly blocking peace efforts.

14. UNESCO is a special agency of the UN which attempts to bring about understanding between nations through an appreciation of their educational, scientific, and cultural contributions.

15. The United Nations has its own flag, a white symbol of the world on a blue background.

16. In order to protect man's rights and freedoms, the United Nations approved a Universal Declaration of Human Rights in 1948.

17. The nations of western Europe and the United States formed the North Atlantic Pact in 1949 to protect themselves against the danger of Communism.

18. The Atlantic Defense Forces were commanded by General Eisenhower, who returned to military service in 1951.

19. The preservation of American democracy has been aided greatly by the spread of Catholic Action.

20. Catholics can participate in Catholic Action by making con-

tacts in factories, studios, or offices.

21. The central agency for coordinating Catholic activity in the United States is the National Catholic Welfare Conference.

22. The Vatican has cooperated with the United States in searching for a just peace. Mr. Myron C. Taylor, who retired from his position as personal representative of the President in 1950, has not been replaced.

Clinching the highlights through activity

1. Have a pictorial display which shows how the Universal Declaration of Human Rights links with daily life. Mount newspaper clippings which illustrate this point. Mount pictures or cartoons showing the exercise of a human right, such as a town meeting, voting, trial by jury, public housing; or the lack of certain rights, as slums, mob violence, signs in public places which show discrimination.

2. Hold a debate. *Resolved:* The United Nations Organization has a better solution for securing and maintaining a just world peace than the Catholic Church.

3. Divide the class into several groups. Let each group make a study of the educational, scientific, and cultural contributions of some country in the United Nations Organization. Put their findings into a scrapbook in the form of reports, drawings, costumes, etc.

4. Make a movie entitled "Catholics in Action." Some pictures which you may like to include are:
Meeting of a Bishop with the laity to illustrate Catholic Action

The NCWC (the building, pictures of various departments of NCWC)

Various Catholic Youth Activities

Newman Club Activities (Campus Chapel will be a lead for the talk on the Newman Club)

Can you think of any other Catholic Activities not mentioned in this text?

5. Draw posters illustrating the meaning of the Pledge of Decency.

6. Write reports on the following to show their contributions to democracy:

George Washington Carver, the Negro Scientist

Marian Anderson

Xavier University in New Orleans

Catholic Radio and Television Programs

7. Use your imagination. Write a brief address such as George Washington might give before the United Nations Assembly. What would he praise that the UN has accomplished? What would he criticize? What would he suggest for the solution of important problems?

A final check-up

I. CHOOSING THE BEST ANSWER. Copy the number before each statement. To the right of the number write the letter of the word or group of words which best completes the statement.

1. The Charter of the United Nations was written at
   a. Dumbarton Oaks
   b. San Francisco
   c. Lake Success
   d. Paris

2. All members of the United Nations are represented in the
   a. Security Council
   b. North Atlantic Pact
   c. General Assembly
   d. League of Nations

3. The first United Nations Army was organized to fight in
   a. Germany
   b. Russia
   c. China
   d. Korea

4. The permanent home of the United Nations is in
   a. United States
   b. Great Britain
   c. Russia
   d. France

5. The part of the United Nations which has the important job of trying to settle disagreements between nations without war is the
   a. General Assembly
   b. Secretariat
   c. North Atlantic Pact
   d. Security Council

6. The first Supreme Commander of the North Atlantic Defense Forces was
   a. General Dwight Eisenhower
   b. Generalissimo Chiang Kai-shek
   c. General Douglas MacArthur
   d. General Patton

7. The veto power of the Big Five nations is a weakness in the
   a. Court of International Justice
   b. Security Council
   c. General Assembly
   d. Secretariat

8. Threats of Communism in the United States have been discovered by
   a. the *Daily Worker*
   b. the American Protective Association
   c. United Nations Assembly
   d. Federal Bureau of Investigation

9. The flag of the United Nations is
   a. red, white, and blue
   b. blue and white
   c. green and white
   d. yellow and white
10. When action in the Security Council is blocked because of the use of the veto, an important issue may be carried to
   a. General Assembly
   b. Court of International Justice
   c. UNESCO
   d. Congress of the United States

II. A MATCHING TEST. Match Column I with Column II by writing the letter of a phrase from Column II opposite the correct number in Column I.

Column I
1. Trygve Lie
2. Genocide Treaty
3. cell movement
4. Monsignor Edward Flanagan
5. college students
6. Legion of Decency
7. Confraternity of Christian Doctrine
8. Myron C. Taylor
9. Pope Pius XI
10. segregation

Column II
a. Catholic Action in factories
b. Newman Clubs
c. drive for clean movies
d. Catholic children in public schools
e. race destruction
f. *Atheistic Communism*
g. Secretary-General of the UN
h. *Bishops' Program of Social Reconstruction*
i. Boys Town
j. discrimination because of color
k. Former U.S. presidential representative at the Vatican
l. Security Council

III. FILL THESE BLANKS. (Be sure to use a paper; do not write in this book.)

1. The life of a nation is weakened by .... because it destroys the family.
2. The Big Five nations of the Security Council are ...., ..., ..., ..., and ....
3. The way of life in which individuals are free to live as they please, provided they violate no laws, is ....
4. The Catholic who was defeated in the 1928 presidential election was ....
5. The organization which attempted to influence politics against Catholics and to destroy the Catholic school system in this country was the ....
6. The agency which coordinates all Catholic Action in the United States is the ....

IV. ANSWER AS BRIEFLY AS POSSIBLE.
1. Mention three dangers which threaten American democracy.
2. Name three instances mentioned in this Unit which show that anti-Catholic feeling existed in the United States in the twentieth century.
3. What is UNESCO?
4. What has been the main weakness in all the efforts made to secure universal peace?
5. Why should we pray to Our Lady in order to secure peace for the world?

THE DECLARATION OF INDEPENDENCE

Reasons for Declaration.

When, in the course of human events, it becomes necessary for one people to dissolve the political bonds which have connected them with another, and to assume among the powers of the earth the separate and equal station to which the laws of nature and of nature's God entitle them, a decent respect to the opinions of mankind requires that they should declare the causes which impell them to the separation.

Rights given by the Creator.

We hold these truths to be self-evident: That all men are created equal; that they are endowed by their Creator with certain inalienable rights; that among these are life, liberty, and the pursuit of happiness. That to secure these rights, governments are instituted among men, deriving their just powers from the consent of the governed; that, whenever any form of government becomes destructive of these ends, it is the right of the people to alter or to abolish it, and to institute a new government, laying its foundation on such principles, and organizing its powers in such form, as to them shall seem most likely to effect their safety and happiness. Prudence, indeed, will dictate that governments long established should not be changed for light and transient causes; and accordingly all experience hath shown that mankind are more disposed to suffer, while evils are sufferable, than to right themselves by abolishing the forms to which they are accustomed. But when a long train of abuses and usurpations, pursuing invariably the same object, evinces a design to reduce them under absolute despotism, it is their right, it is their duty, to throw off such government and to provide new guards for their future security. Such has been the patient suffering of these colonies, and such is now the necessity which constrains them to alter their former systems of government.

The tyranny of the British King.

The history of the present king of Great Britain is a history of repeated injuries, and usurpations, all having in direct object the establishment of an absolute tyranny over these states. To prove this, let facts be submitted to a candid world.

1. He has refused his assent to laws the most wholesome and necessary for the public good.

2. He has forbidden his governors to pass laws of immediate and pressing importance, unless suspended in their operation till his assent should be obtained, and, when so suspended

he has utterly neglected to attend to them.

3. He has refused to pass other laws for the accommodation of large districts of people, unless those people would relinquish the right of representation in the legislature— a right inestimable to them and formidable to tyrants only.

4. He has called together legislative bodies, at places unusual, uncomfortable, and distant from the repository of their public records, for the sole purpose of fatiguing them into compliance with his measures.

5. He has dissolved representative houses repeatedly for opposing with manly firmness his invasions on the rights of the people.

6. He has refused for a long time after such dissolutions to cause others to be elected; whereby the legislative powers, incapable of annihilation, have returned to the people at large for their exercise: the state remaining, in the meantime, exposed to all the dangers of invasion from without and convulsions within.

7. He has endeavored to prevent the population of these states; for that purpose obstructing the laws for naturalization of foreigners; refusing to pass others to encourage their migration hither, and raising the conditions of new appropriations of lands.

8. He has obstructed the administration of justice by refusing his assent to laws for establishing his judiciary powers.

9. He has made judges dependent on his will alone for the tenure of their offices and the amount and payment of their salaries.

10. He has erected a multitude of new offices and sent hither swarms of officers to harass our people and eat out their substance.

11. He has kept among us, in times of peace, standing armies without the consent of our legislature.

12. He has affected to render the military independent of and superior to the civil power.

13. He has combined with others to subject us to a jurisdiction foreign to our constitutions and unacknowledged by our laws, giving his assent to their acts of pretended legislation.

14. For quartering large bodies of armed troops among us;

15. For protecting them by a mock trial from punishment for any murders which they should commit on the inhabitants of these states;

16. For cutting off our trade with all parts of the world;

17. For imposing taxes on us without our consent;

18. For depriving us in many cases of the benefits of trial by jury;

19. For transporting us beyond seas to be tried for pretended offenses;

20. For abolishing the free system of English laws in a neighboring province, establishing therein an ar-

bitrary government, and enlarging its boundaries so as to render it at once an example and fit instrument for introducing the same absolute rule into these colonies;

21. For taking away our charters, abolishing our most valuable laws, and altering fundamentally the forms of our government;

22. For suspending our own legislatures and declaring themselves invested with power to legislate for us in all cases whatsoever.

23. He has abdicated government here by declaring us out of his protection and waging war against us.

24. He has plundered our seas, ravaged our coasts, burnt our towns and destroyed the lives of our people.

25. He is at this time transporting large armies of foreign mercenaries to complete the work of death, desolation, and tyranny already begun, with circumstances of cruelty and perfidy scarcely paralleled in the most barbarous ages and totally unworthy of the head of a civilized nation.

26. He has constrained our fellow citizens taken captive upon the high seas to bear arms against their country, to become the executioners of their friends and brethren, or to fall themselves by their hands.

27. He has excited domestic insurrection amongst us, and has endeavored to bring on the inhabitants of our frontiers the merciless Indian savages, whose known rule of warfare is an undistinguished destruction of all ages, sexes, and conditions.

In every stage of these oppressions we have petitioned for redress, in the most humble terms; our repeated petitions have been answered only by repeated injury. A prince whose character is thus marked by every act which may define a tyrant is unfit to be ruler of a free people.

Attempts to avoid separation from Britain.

Nor have we been wanting in attentions to our British brethren. We have warned them, from time to time, of attempts by their legislature to extend an unwarrantable jurisdiction over us. We have reminded them of the circumstances of our emigration and settlement here. We have appealed to their native justice and magnanimity; and we have conjured them by the ties of our common kindred to disavow these usurpations, which would inevitably interrupt our connection and correspondence. They, too, have been deaf to the voice of justice and sanguinity. We must, therefore, acquiesce in the necessity which denounces our separation, and hold them, as we hold the rest of mankind, enemies in war; in peace, friends.

Freedom declared.

We, therefore, the representatives of the United States of America, in general congress assembled, appealing to the Supreme Judge of the World for the rectitude of our intentions, do, in the name and by the authority of the good people of these colonies solemnly publish and declare that these united colonies are, and of right ought to be, free and independent states; that they are absolved from all allegiance to the British crown, and that all political connection between them and the state of Great Britain is, and ought to be, totally dissolved; and that as free and independent states they have full power to levy war, conclude peace, contract alliances, establish commerce, and to do all other acts and things which independent states may of right do. And for the support of this declaration, with firm reliance on the protection of Divine Providence, we mutually pledge to each other our lives, our fortunes, and our sacred honor.

JOHN HANCOCK

NEW HAMPSHIRE:
Josiah Bartlett, Wm. Whipple, Matthew Thornton.

MASSACHUSETTS BAY:
Samuel Adams, John Adams, Robert Treat Paine, Elbridge Gerry.

RHODE ISLAND:
Stephen Hopkins, William Ellery.

CONNECTICUT:
Roger Sherman, Samuel Huntington, William Williams, Oliver Wolcott.

NEW YORK:
Wm. Floyd, Philip Livingston, Francis Lewis, Lewis Morris.

NEW JERSEY:
Richard Stockton, John Witherspoon, Francis Hopkinson, John Hart, Abraham Clarke.

PENNSYLVANIA:
Robert Morris, Benjamin Rush, Benjamin Franklin, John Morton, George Clymer, James Smith, George Taylor, James Wilson, George Ross.

DELAWARE:
Caesar Rodney, George Read, Thomas M'Kean.

MARYLAND:
Samuel Chase, William Paca, Thomas Stone, Charles Carroll of Carrollton.

VIRGINIA:
George Wythe, Richard Henry Lee, Thomas Jefferson, Benjamin Harrison, Thomas Nelson, Jun., Francis Lightfoot Lee, Carter Braxton.

NORTH CAROLINA:
William Hooper, Joseph Hewes, John Penn.

SOUTH CAROLINA:
Edward Rutledge, Thomas Heyward, Jun., Thomas Lynch, Jun., Arthur Middleton.

GEORGIA:
Button Gwinnett, Lyman Hall, George Walton.

THE CONSTITUTION OF THE UNITED STATES

Preamble

WE THE PEOPLE of the United States, in Order to form a more perfect Union, establish Justice, insure domestic Tranquillity, provide for the common defense, promote the general Welfare, and secure the Blessings of Liberty to ourselves and our Posterity, do ordain and establish this Constitution for the United States of America.

Article I. Legislative Department
Section 1. Congress
Legislative powers.

All legislative Powers herein granted shall be vested in a Congress of the United States, which shall consist of a Senate and House of Representatives.

Section 2. House of Representatives
1. Election of members.

The House of Representatives shall be composed of Members chosen every second Year by the People of the several States, and the Electors in each State shall have the Qualifications requisite for Electors of the most numerous Branch of the State Legislature.

2. Qualifications.

No Person shall be a Representative who shall not have attained to the Age of twenty-five Years, and been seven Years a Citizen of the United States, and who shall not, when elected, be an Inhabitant of that State in which he shall be chosen.

3. Apportionment.

Representatives and direct Taxes shall be apportioned among the several States which may be included within this Union, according to their respective Numbers, which shall be determined by adding to the whole Number of free Persons, including those bound to Service for a Term of Years, and excluding Indians not taxed, three fifths of all other Persons. The actual Enumeration shall be made within three Years after the first Meeting of the Congress of the United States, and within every subsequent Term of ten Years, in such Manner as they shall by Law direct. The Number of Representatives shall not exceed one for every thirty thousand, but each State shall have at least one Representative; and until such enumeration shall be made, the State of New Hampshire shall be entitled to choose three, Massachusetts eight, Rhode Island and Providence Plantations one, Connecticut five, New York six, New Jersey four, Pennsylvania eight, Delaware one, Maryland six, Virginia ten, North Carolina five,

South Carolina five and Georgia three.

4. Vacancies.

When vacancies happen in the Representation from any State, the Executive Authority thereof shall issue Writs of Election to fill such Vacancies.

5. Officers; impeachment.

The House of Representatives shall choose their Speaker and other Officers; and shall have the sole Power of Impeachment.

Section 3. The Senate
1. Number and election of Senators.

The Senate of the United States shall be composed of two Senators from each State, chosen by the Legislature thereof, for six Years; and each Senator shall have one Vote.

2. Classification.

Immediately after they shall be assembled in Consequence of the first Election, they shall be divided as equally as may be into three Classes. The Seats of the Senators of the first Class shall be vacated at the Expiration of the second Year, of the second Class at the Expiration of the fourth Year, and of the third Class at the Expiration of the sixth Year, so that one third may be chosen every second Year; and if vacancies happen by Resignation, or otherwise, during the Recess of the Legislature of any State, the Executive thereof may make temporary appointments until the next meeting of the Legislature, which shall then fill such Vacancies.

3. Qualifications.

No Person shall be a Senator who shall not have attained to the Age of thirty Years, and been nine Years a Citizen of the United States, and who shall not, when elected, be an inhabitant of that State for which he shall be chosen.

4. President of the Senate.

The Vice President of the United States shall be President of the Senate, but shall have no Vote, unless they be equally divided.

5. Officers of the Senate.

The Senate shall choose their other Officers, and also a President pro tempore, in the Absence of the Vice President, or when he shall exercise the Office of President of the United States.

6. Trial of Impeachments.

The Senate shall have the sole Power to try all Impeachments. When sitting for that Purpose, they shall be on Oath or Affirmation. When the President of the United States is tried, the Chief Justice shall preside: And no Person shall be convicted without the Concurrence of two thirds of the Members present.

7. Judgment on Conviction.

Judgment in Cases of Impeachment shall not extend further than to removal from Office, and disqualification to hold and enjoy any Office of honor, Trust, or Profit under the United States: but the Party convicted shall nevertheless be liable and subject to Indictment, Trial,

Judgment and Punishment, according to Law.

Section 4. Elections and Sessions

1. Elections.

The Times, Places and Manner of holding Elections for Senators and Representatives, shall be prescribed in each State by the Legislature thereof; but the Congress may at any time by Law make or alter such Regulations, except as to the Places of choosing Senators.

2. Meetings.

The Congress shall assemble at least once in every Year, and such Meeting shall be on the first Monday in December, unless they shall by Law appoint a different Day.

Section 5. Rules and Procedure

1. Conduct of business.

Each House shall be the Judge of the Elections, Returns and Qualifications of its own Members, and a Majority of each shall constitute a Quorum to do Business; but a smaller Number may adjourn from day to day and may be authorized to compel the Attendance of absent Members, in such Manner, and under such Penalties as each House may provide.

2. Proceedings.

Each House may determine the Rules of its Proceedings, punish its members for disorderly Behavior, and, with the Concurrence of two thirds, expel a Member.

3. Journal.

Each House shall keep a Journal of its Proceedings, and from time to time publish the same, excepting such Parts as may in their Judgment require Secrecy; and the Yeas and Nays of the Members of either House on any question shall, at the Desire of one fifth of those present, be entered on the Journal.

4. Adjournment.

Neither House, during the Session of Congress, shall, without the Consent of the other, adjourn for more than three days, nor to any other Place than that in which the two Houses shall be sitting.

Section 6. Privileges and Limitations on Members

1. Compensation and privileges of members.

The Senators and Representatives shall receive a Compensation for their Services, to be ascertained by Law, and paid out of the Treasury of the United States. They shall in all Cases, except Treason, Felony and Breach of the Peace, be privileged from Arrest during their Attendance at the Session of their respective Houses, and in going to and returning from the same; and for any Speech or Debate in either House, they shall not be questioned in any other Place.

2. Limitations upon members.

No Senator or Representative shall, during the time for which he was elected, be appointed to any civil Office under the authority of the United States, which shall have been created, or the Emoluments whereof shall have been increased during such time; and no Person holding any Office under the United States, shall be a Member of either House during his Continuance in Office.

Section 7. Method of Passing Laws

1. Revenue bills.

All Bills for raising Revenue shall originate in the House of Representatives; but the Senate may propose or concur with Amendments as on other Bills.

2. Passage of bills.

Every Bill which shall have passed the House of Representatives and the Senate, shall, before it become a Law, be presented to the President of the United States; if he approve he shall sign it, but if not he shall return it, with his Objections to that House in which it shall have originated, who shall enter the objections at large on their Journal and proceed to reconsider it. If after such Reconsideration two thirds of that House shall agree to pass the Bill, it shall be sent, together with the Objections, to the other House, by which it shall likewise be reconsidered, and if approved by two thirds of that House it shall become a Law. But in all such Cases the Votes of both Houses shall be determined by Yeas and Nays, and the Names of the Persons voting for and against the Bill shall be entered on the Journal of each House respectively. If any Bill shall not be returned by the President within ten days (Sundays excepted) after it shall have been presented to him, the Same shall be a law, in like Manner as if he had signed it, unless the Congress by their Adjournment prevent its Return, in which Case it shall not be a law.

3. Veto power of President.

Every Order, Resolution, or Vote to which the Concurrence of the Senate and House of Representatives may be necessary (except on a question of Adjournment) shall be presented to the President of the United States; and before the Same shall take Effect, shall be approved by him, or being disapproved by him, shall be repassed by two thirds of the Senate and House of Representatives, according to the Rules and Limitations prescribed in the Case of a bill.

Section 8. Powers of Congress

The Congress shall have the power:

1. To lay and collect Taxes, Duties, Imports and Excises, to pay the Debts and provide for the common Defense and general Welfare of the United States; but all Duties, Imports and Excises shall be uniform throughout the United States;

2. To borrow Money on the Credit of the United States;

3. To regulate Commerce with foreign Nations, and among the several States, and with the Indian Tribes;

4. To establish a uniform Rule of Naturalization, and uniform laws on

the subject of Bankruptcies throughout the United States;

5. To coin Money, regulate the Value thereof, and of foreign Coin, and fix the Standard of Weights and Measures;

6. To provide for the Punishment of counterfeiting the Securities and current Coin of the United States;

7. To establish Post Offices and post roads;

8. To promote the Progress of Science and useful Arts, by securing for limited Times to Authors and Inventors the exclusive Right to their respective Writings and Discoveries;

9. To constitute Tribunals inferior to the supreme Court;

10. To define and Punish Piracies and Felonies committed on the high seas, and Offences against the Law of Nations;

11. To declare War, grant Letters of Marque and Reprisal, and make Rules concerning Captures on Land and Water;

12. To raise and support Armies, but no Appropriation of Money to that Use shall be for a longer Term than two Years;

13. To provide and maintain a Navy;

14. To make Rules for the Government and Regulation of the land and naval Forces;

15. To provide for calling forth the Militia to execute the Laws of the Union, suppress Insurrections and repel Invasions;

16. To provide for organizing, arming, and disciplining the Militia, and for governing such Part of them as may be employed in the Service of the United States, reserving to the States respectively, the Appointment of the Officers, and the Authority of training the Militia according to the discipline prescribed by Congress;

17. To exercise exclusive Legislation in all Cases whatsoever, over such District (not exceeding ten Miles square) as may, by Cession of particular States, and the Acceptance of Congress, become the Seat of the Government of the United States, and to exercise like Authority over all Places purchased by the Consent of the Legislature of the States in which the Same shall be, for the Erection of Forts, Magazines, Arsenals, dock-Yards, and other needful Buildings;—And

18. To make all Laws which shall be necessary and proper for carrying into Execution the foregoing Powers, and all other Powers vested by this Constitution in the Government of the United States, or in any Department or Officer thereof.

Section 9. Powers Denied Congress

1. The Migration or Importation of such Persons as any of the States now existing shall think proper to admit, shall not be prohibited by the Congress, prior to the Year one thousand eight hundred and eight,

but a Tax or Duty may be imposed on such Importation, not exceeding ten dollars for each Person.

2. The Privilege of the Writ of Habeas Corpus shall not be suspended, unless when in Cases of Rebellion or Invasion the public Safety may require it.

3. No Bill of Attainder or ex post facto Law shall be passed.

4. No Capitation, or other direct, Tax shall be laid, unless in Proportion to the Census or Enumeration herein before directed to be taken.

5. No tax or Duty shall be laid on Articles exported from any State.

6. No Preference shall be given by any Regulation of Commerce or Revenue to the Ports of one State over those of another: nor shall Vessels bound to, or from one State, be obliged to enter, clear, or pay Duties in another.

7. No Money shall be drawn from the Treasury, but in Consequence of Appropriations made by Law; and a regular Statement and Account of the Receipts and Expenditures of all public Money shall be published from time to time.

8. No Title of Nobility shall be granted by the United States; And no Person holding any Office of Profit or Trust under them, shall, without the Consent of the Congress, accept of any present, Emolument, Office, or Title, of any kind whatever, from any King, Prince, or Foreign State.

Section 10. Powers Denied the States

1. General limitations.

No State shall enter into any Treaty, Alliance, or Confederation; grant Letters of Marque and Reprisal; coin Money; emit Bills of Credit; make any Thing but gold and silver Coin a Tender in Payment of Debts; pass any Bill of Attainder, ex post facto Law, or Law impairing the Obligation of Contracts, or grant any Title of Nobility.

2. Powers dependent upon Congress.

No State shall, without the Consent of the Congress, lay any Imposts or Duties on Imports or Exports, except what may be absolutely necessary for executing its inspection Laws: and the net Produce of all Duties and Imposts, laid by any State on Imports or Exports, shall be for the Use of the Treasury of the United States; and all such Laws shall be subject to the Revision and Control of the Congress.

No State shall, without the Consent of Congress, lay any Duty of Tonnage, keep Troops, or Ships of War in time of Peace, enter into any Agreement or Compact with another State, or with a foreign Power, or engage in War, unless actually invaded, or in such imminent Danger as will not admit of Delay.

Article II. Executive Department

Section 1. President and Vice-President

1. Terms of President and Vice-President.

The executive Power shall be vested in a President of the United

States of America. He shall hold his Office during the Term of four Years, and, together, with the Vice President chosen for the same term, be elected as follows:

2. Electors.

Each State shall appoint, in such Manner as the Legislature thereof may direct, a Number of Electors equal to the whole Number of Senators and Representatives to which the State may be entitled in the Congress: but no Senator or Representative, or Person holding an Office of Trust or Profit under the United States, shall be appointed an Elector.

3. Electoral procedure.

The electors shall meet in their respective States, and vote by ballot for two Persons, of whom one at least shall not be an Inhabitant of the same State with themselves. And they shall make a List of the Persons voted for, and of the Number of Votes for each; which List they shall sign and certify, and transmit sealed to the Seat of the Government of the United States, directed to the President of the Senate. The President of the Senate shall, in the presence of the Senate and House of Representatives, open all the Certificates, and the Votes shall then be counted. The Person having the greatest Number of Votes shall be President, if such Number be a Majority of the whole Number of Electors appointed; and if there be more than one who have such Majority and have an equal Number of Votes, then the House of Representatives shall immediately choose by Ballot one of them for President; and if no person have a Majority, then from the five highest on the List the said House shall in like Manner choose the President. But in choosing the President, the Votes shall be taken by States, the Representation from each State having one Vote; a quorum for this Purpose shall consist of a Member or Members from two-thirds of the States, and a Majority of all the States shall be necessary to a Choice. In every Case, after the Choice of the President, the person having the greatest Number of Votes of the Electors shall be the Vice President. But if there should remain two or more who have equal Votes, the Senate shall choose from them by Ballot the Vice President.

4. Date of choosing electors.

The Congress may determine the Time of choosing the electors and the Day on which they shall give their Votes; which Day shall be the same throughout the United States.

5. Qualifications of the President.

No Person except a natural born Citizen or a Citizen of the United States at the time of the Adoption of this Constitution, shall be eligible to the Office of President; neither shall any person be eligible to the Office who shall not have attained to the Age of thirty five Years, and been fourteen Years a Resident within the United States.

6. Vacancy.

In Case of the Removal of the President from Office, or of his Death, Resignation, or Inability to discharge the Powers and Duties of the said Office, the same shall devolve on the Vice President, and the Congress may by Law provide for the Case of Removal, Death, Resignation, or Inability, both of the President and Vice President, declaring what Officer shall then act as President, and such Officer shall act accordingly, until the Disability be removed, or a President shall be elected.

7. Compensation.

The President shall, at stated Times, receive for his Services, a Compensation, which shall neither be increased nor diminished during the Period for which he shall have been elected, and he shall not receive within that Period any other Emolument from the United States, or any of them.

8. Oath of office.

Before he enter on the execution of his Office, he shall take the following Oath or Affirmation: — "I do solemnly swear (or affirm) that I will faithfully execute the Office of President of the United States, and will to the best of my Ability, preserve, protect, and defend the Constitution of the United States."

Section 2. Powers of the President

1. Military and naval.

The President shall be Commander in Chief of the Army and Navy of the United States, and of the Militia of the several States, when called into the actual Service of the United States; he may require the Opinion, in writing, of the principal Officer in each of the executive Departments, upon any Subject relating to the Duties of their respective Offices, and he shall have Power to grant Reprieves and Pardons for Offenses against the United States, except in Cases of Impeachment.

2. Treaties and appointments.

He shall have Power, by and with the Advice and Consent of the Senate, to make Treaties, provided two thirds of the Senators present concur; and he shall nominate, and by and with the Advice and Consent of the Senate, shall appoint Ambassadors, other public Ministers and Consuls, Judges of the Supreme Court, and all other Officers of the United States, whose Appointments are not herein otherwise provided for, and which shall be established by Law; but the Congress may by Law vest the Appointment of such inferior Officers, as they think proper, in the President alone, in the Courts of Law, or in the heads of Departments.

3. Filling of vacancies.

The President shall have Power to fill up all Vacancies that may happen during the Recess of the Senate, by granting Commissions which shall expire at the End of their next Session.

Section 3. Duties of the President

He shall from time to time give to the Congress Information of the State of the Union, and recommend to their Consideration such Measures as he shall judge necessary and expedient; he may, on extraordinary Occasions, convene both Houses, or either of them, and in Case of Disagreement between them, with respect to the Time of Adjournment, he may adjourn them to such Time as he shall think proper; he shall receive Ambassadors and other public Ministers; he shall take Care that the Laws be faithfully executed, and shall Commission all the Officers of the United States.

Section 4. Impeachment

The President, Vice President, and all civil Officers of the United States shall be removed from office on Impeachment for, and Conviction of, Treason, Bribery, and other high Crimes and Misdemeanors.

Article III. The Judicial Department

Section 1. Courts

Supreme and inferior courts.

The judicial Power of the United States shall be vested in one supreme Court, and in such inferior Courts as the Congress may from time to time ordain and establish. The Judges, both of the supreme and inferior Courts, shall hold their Offices during good Behavior, and shall, at stated Times, receive for their Services a Compensation, which shall not be diminished during their Continuance in Office.

Section 2. Jurisdiction

1. Powers.

The judicial Power shall extend to all Cases, in Law and Equity, arising under this Constitution, the Laws of the United States, and Treaties made, or which shall be made, under their Authority; — to all Cases affecting Ambassadors, other public Ministers and Consuls; — to all Cases of admiralty and maritime Jurisdiction; — to Controversies to which the United States shall be a Party; — to Controversies between two or more States; — between a State and Citizens of another State; — between Citizens of different States; — between Citizens of the same State claiming Lands Under Grants of different States, and between a State, or the Citizens thereof, and foreign States, Citizens or Subjects.

2. Jurisdiction.

In all Cases affecting Ambassadors, other public Ministers and Consuls, and those in which a State shall be Party, the supreme Court shall have original Jurisdiction. In all the other Cases before mentioned, the Supreme Court shall have appellate Jurisdiction, both as to Law and Fact, with such exceptions, and under such Regulations as Congress shall make.

3. Trials.

The Trial of all Crimes, except in Cases of Impeachment, shall be by

Jury; and such Trial shall be held in the State where the said Crimes shall have been committed; but when not committed within any State, the Trial shall be at such Place or Places as the Congress may by Law have directed.

Section 3. Treason

1. Definition.

Treason against the United States, shall consist only in levying War against them, or in adhering to their Enemies, giving them Aid and Comfort. No Person shall be convicted of Treason unless on the Testimony of two Witnesses to the same overt Act, or on Confession in open Court.

2. Punishment.

The Congress shall have Power to declare the Punishment of Treason, but no Attainder of Treason shall work Corruption of Blood, or Forfeiture except during the Life of the Person Attained.

Article IV. The States

Section 1. Official Acts

Full Faith and Credit shall be given in each State to the public Acts, Records, and judicial Proceedings of every other State. And the Congress may by general Laws prescribe the Manner in which such Acts, Records and Proceedings shall be proved, and the Effect thereof.

Section 2. Privileges of Citizens

1. Privileges.

The Citizens of each State shall be entitled to all Privileges and Immunities of Citizens in the several States.

2. Fugitives.

A person charged in any State with Treason, Felony, or other Crime, who shall flee from Justice, and be found in another State, shall on Demand of the executive Authority of the State from which he fled, be delivered up to be removed to the State having Jurisdiction of the Crime.

3. Fugitives from labour.

No person held to Service or Labour in one State, under the Laws thereof, escaping into another, shall, in Consequence of any Law or Regulation therein, be discharged from such Service or Labour, but shall be delivered up on Claim of the Party to whom such Service or Labour may be due. (superseded by Amendment XIII.)

Section 3. New States and Territories

1. New States.

New States may be admitted by the Congress into this Union; but no new State shall be formed or erected within the Jurisdiction of any other States; nor any State be formed by the Junction of two or more States, or Parts of States, without the Consent of the Legislatures of the States concerned as well as of the Congress.

2. U. S. territory.

The Congress shall have Power to dispose of and make all needful Rules and Regulations respecting the Territory or other Property belonging to the United States; and nothing in this Constitution shall be so construed as to Prejudice any Claims of the United States, or of any particular State.

Section 4. Protection of the States

The United States shall guarantee to every State in this Union, a Republican Form of Government, and shall protect each of them against Invasion; and on Application of the Legislature, or of the Executive (when the Legislature cannot be convened) against domestic Violence.

Article V. Amendments to the Constitution

The Congress, whenever two thirds of both Houses shall deem it necessary, shall propose Amendments to this Constitution, or, on the Application of the Legislatures of two thirds of the several States, shall call a Convention for proposing Amendments, which, in either Case, shall be valid to all Intents and Purposes, as Part of this Constitution, when ratified by the Legislatures of three fourths of the several States, or by Conventions in three fourths thereof, as the one or the other mode of Ratification may be proposed by the Congress; Provided that no Amendment which may be made prior to the Year One thousand eight hundred and eight shall in any Manner affect the first and fourth Clauses in the Ninth Section of the first Article; and that no State, without its Consent shall be deprived of its equal Suffrage in the Senate.

Article VI. General Provisions

1. Validity of debts.

All Debts contracted and Engagements entered into, before the Adoption of this Constitution, shall be valid against the United States under this Constitution, as under the Confederation.

2. Supremacy of the Constitution.

This Constitution, and the Laws of the United States which shall be made in Pursuance thereof; and all Treaties made, or which shall be made, under the Authority of the United States, shall be the supreme Law of the Land; and the Judges in every State shall be bound thereby, any Thing in the Constitution or Laws of any State to the Contrary notwithstanding.

3. Oath.

The Senators and Representatives before mentioned, and the Members of the several State Legislatures, and all executive and judicial Officers, both of the United States and of the several States, shall be bound by Oath or Affirmation, to support this Constitution; but no religious Test shall ever be required as a Qualification to any Office or public Trust under the United States.

Article VII. Ratification of the Constitution

The Ratification of the Conventions of nine States, shall be sufficient for the Establishment of this Constitution between the States so ratifying the Same.

Done in Convention by the unanimous consent of the States present, the seventeenth day of September, in the year of our Lord one thousand seven hundred and eighty-seven, and of the Independence of the United States of America the twelfth.

In witness whereof, we have hereunto subscribed our names.

GEORGE WASHINGTON,
President and Deputy from Virginia.

NEW HAMPSHIRE:
John Langdon, Nicholas Gilman.

MASSACHUSETTS:
Nathaniel Gorham, Rufus King.

CONNECTICUT:
William Samuel Johnson,
Roger Sherman.

NEW YORK:
Alexander Hamilton.

NEW JERSEY:
William Livingston, David Brearly,
William Patterson,
Jonathan Dayton.

PENNSYLVANIA:
Benjamin Franklin,
Thomas Mifflin, Robert Morris,
George Clymer,
Thomas Fitzsimons,
Jared Ingersoll, James Wilson,
Gouverneur Morris.

DELAWARE:
George Read,
Gunning Bedford, Jr.,
John Dickinson,
Richard Bassett, Jacob Broom.

MARYLAND:
James McHenry,
Daniel of St. Thomas Jenifer,
Daniel Carroll.

VIRGINIA:
John Blair, James Madison, Jr.

NORTH CAROLINA:
William Blount,
Richard Dobbs Spaight,
Hugh Williamson.

SOUTH CAROLINA:
John Rutledge,
Charles Cotesworth Pinckney,
Charles Pinckney, Pierce Butler.

GEORGIA:
William Few, Abraham Baldwin.

Attest: WILLIAM JACKSON,
Secretary.

AMENDMENTS

I. Freedom of Religion, Speech, and the Press; Right of Assembly (1791)

Congress shall make no law respecting an establishment of religion or prohibiting the free exercise thereof; or abridging the freedom of speech or of the press; or the right of the people peaceably to assemble, and to petition the Government for a redress of grievances.

II. Right to Bear Arms (1791)

A well regulated Militia, being necessary to the security of a free State, the right of the people to keep and bear Arms, shall not be infringed.

III. Quartering of Troops (1791)

No Soldier shall, in time of peace be quartered in any house, without the consent of the owner, nor in time of war, but in a manner to be prescribed by law.

IV. Search (1791)

The right of the people to be secure in their persons, houses, papers, and effects, against unreasonable searches and seizures, shall not be violated, and no Warrants shall issue but upon probable cause, supported by Oath or affirmation, and particularly describing the place to be searched, and the persons or things to be seized.

V. Jury Trial (1791)

No person shall be held to answer for a capital, or otherwise infamous crime, unless on a presentment of indictment of a Grand Jury, except in cases arising in the land or naval forces, or in the Militia, when in actual service in time Of War or in public danger; nor shall any person be subject for the same offense to be twice put in jeopardy of life or limb; nor shall be compelled in any Criminal Case to be a witness against himself, nor be deprived of life, liberty, or property, without due process of law; nor shall private property be taken for public use, without just compensation.

VI. Rights of the Accused (1791)

In all criminal prosecutions, the accused shall enjoy the right to a speedy and public trial, by an impartial jury of the State and district wherein the crime shall have been committed, which district shall have been previously ascertained by law, and to be informed of the nature and cause of the accusation; to be confronted with the witnesses against him; to have compulsory process for obtaining Witnesses in his favor, and to have the Assistance of Counsel for his defense.

VII. Suits at Common Law (1791)

In suits at common law, where the value in controversy shall exceed twenty dollars, the right of trial by jury shall be preserved, and no fact tried by a jury shall be otherwise re-examined in any Court of the United States than according to the rules of the common law.

VIII. Excessive Bail and Punishments (1791)

Excessive bail shall not be required, nor excessive fines imposed, nor cruel and unusual punishments inflicted.

IX. Rights Reserved to the People (1791)

The enumeration in the Constitution, of certain rights, shall not be construed to deny or disparage others retained by the People.

X. Powers Reserved to States and People (1791)

The powers not delegated to the United States by the Constitution, nor prohibited by it to the States, are reserved to the States respectively, or to the people.

XI. Suits Against States (1798)

The Judicial power of the United States shall not be construed to extend to any suit in law or equity, commenced or prosecuted against one of the United States by Citizens of another State, or by Citizens or Subjects of any Foreign State.

XII. Election of President and Vice-President (1804)

The Electors shall meet in their respective states, and vote by ballot for President and Vice-President, one of whom, at least, shall not be an inhabitant of the same state with themselves; they shall name in their ballots the person voted for as President, and in distinct ballots the person voted for as Vice-President, and they shall make distinct lists of all persons voted for as President, and of all persons voted for as Vice-President, and of the number of votes for each, which lists they shall sign and certify, and transmit sealed to the seat of the government of the United States, directed to the President of the Senate; — The President of the Senate shall, in presence of the Senate and House of Representatives, open all the certificates and the votes shall then be counted; — The person having the greatest number of votes for President, shall be the President, if such a number be a majority of the whole number of Electors appointed; and if no person have such majority, then from the persons having the highest numbers not exceeding three on the list of those voted for as President, the House of Representatives shall choose immediately, by ballot, the President. But in choosing the President, the votes shall be taken by states, the representation from each state having one vote, a quorum for this purpose shall consist of a member or members from two-thirds of the states, and a majority of all the states shall be necessary to a choice. And if the House of Representatives shall not choose a President, whenever the right of choice shall devolve upon them, before the fourth day of March next following, then the Vice-President shall act as President, as in the case of the death or other constitutional disability of the President. The person having the greatest number of votes as Vice-President shall be the Vice-President, if such number be a majority of the whole number of Electors appointed, and if no person have a majority, then from the two highest numbers on the list the Senate shall choose the Vice-President; a quorum for the purpose shall consist of two-thirds of the whole number of Senators, and a majority of the whole number shall be necessary to a choice. But no person constitutionally ineligible to the office of President shall be eligible to that of Vice-President of the United States.

XIII. Abolishment of Slavery (1865)

Neither slavery nor involuntary servitude, except as punishment for crime whereof the party shall have been duly convicted, shall exist within the United States, or any place subject to their jurisdiction.

Section 2. Enforcement

Congress shall have power to enforce this article by appropriate legislation.

XIV. Citizenship (1868)

Section 1. Citizens

All persons born or naturalized in the United States, and subject to the jurisdiction thereof, are citizens of the United States and of the State wherein they reside. No State shall make or enforce any law which shall abridge the privileges or immunities of citizens of the United States; nor shall any State deprive any person of life, liberty, or property, without due process of law; nor deny to any person within its jurisdiction the equal protection of the laws.

Section 2. Representatives

Representatives shall be apportioned among the several States according to their respective numbers, counting the whole number of persons in each State, excluding Indians not taxed. But when the right to vote at any election for the choice of electors for President and Vice-President of the United States, Representatives in Congress, the Executive and Judicial officers of a State, or the members of the Legislature thereof, is denied to any of the male inhabitants of such State, being twenty-one years of age, and citizens of the United States, or in any way abridged, except for participation in rebellion, or other crime, the basis of representation therein shall be reduced in the proportion which the number of such male citizens shall bear to the whole number of male citizens twenty-one years of age in such State.

Section 3. Insurrection

No person shall be a Senator or Representative in Congress, or elector of President and Vice-President, or hold any office, civil or military, under the United States, or under any State, who, having previously taken an oath, as a member of Congress, or as an officer of the United States, or as a member of any State legislature, or as an executive or judicial officer of any State, to support the Constitution of the United States, shall have engaged in insurrection or rebellion against the same, or given aid or comfort to the enemies thereof. But Congress may by a vote of two-thirds of each House, remove such disability.

Section 4. Public Debt

The validity of the public debt of the United States, authorized by law, including debts incurred for payment of pensions and bounties for services in suppressing insurrection or rebellion, shall not be questioned. But neither the United States nor any State shall assume or pay any debt or obligation incurred in aid of insurrection or rebellion against the United States, or any claim for the loss or emancipation of any slave; but all such debts, obligations and claims shall be held illegal and void.

Section 5. Enforcement

The Congress shall have power to enforce, by appropriate legislation, the provisions of this article.

XV. Negro Suffrage (1870)

Section 1. Negro's Right to Vote

The right of citizens of the United States to vote shall not be denied or abridged by the United States or by any State on account of race, color, or previous condition of servitude.

Section 2. Enforcement

The Congress shall have power to enforce this article by appropriate legislation.

XVI. Income Tax (1913)

The Congress shall have power to lay and collect taxes on incomes, from whatever source derived, without apportionment among the several States, and without regard to any census or enumeration.

XVII. Election of Senators (1913)

The Senate of the United States shall be composed of two Senators from each State, elected by the people thereof, for six years; and each Senator shall have one vote. The electors in each State shall have the qualifications requisite for electors of the most numerous branch of the State Legislature.

When vacancies happen in the representation of any State in the Senate, the executive authority of such State shall issue writs of election to fill such vacancies; Provided, That the Legislature of any State may empower the executive thereof to make temporary appointment until the people fill the vacancies by election as the Legislature may direct.

This amendment shall not be so construed as to affect the election or term of any Senator chosen before it becomes valid as part of the Constitution.

XVIII. National Prohibition (1919)

After one year from the ratification of this article the manufacture, sale, or transportation of intoxicating liquors within, the Importation thereof into, or the exportation thereof from the United States and all territory subject to the jurisdiction thereof for beverage purposes is hereby prohibited.

The Congress and the several states shall have concurrent power to enforce this article by appropriate legislation.

This article shall be inoperative unless it shall have been ratified as an amendment to the Constitution by the legislatures of the several states, as provided in the Constitution, within seven years from the date of submission hereof to the states by the Congress.

XIX. Woman Suffrage (1920)

Section 1. Right of Women to Vote

The right of the citizens of the United States to vote shall not be denied or abridged by the United States or by any state on account of sex.

Section 2. Enforcement

Congress shall have power, by appropriate legislation, to enforce the provisions of this article.

XX. "Lame Duck" Amendment (1933)

Section 1. Terms of President, Vice-President, and Congressmen

The terms of the President and Vice-President shall end at noon on the 20th day of January, and the terms of Senators and Representatives at noon on the 3rd day of January, of the years in which such terms would have ended if this article had not been ratified; and the terms of their successors shall then begin.

Section 2. Sessions of Congress

The Congress shall assemble at least once in every year, and such meeting shall begin at noon on the 3rd day of January, unless they shall by law appoint a different day.

Section 3. Presidential Succession

If, at the time fixed for the beginning of the term of the President, the President elect shall have died, the Vice-President elect shall become President. If a President shall not have been chosen before the time fixed for the beginning of his term, or if the President elect shall have failed to qualify, then the Vice-President elect shall act as President until a President shall have qualified; and the Congress may by law provide for the case wherein neither a President elect nor a Vice-President elect shall have qualified, declaring who shall then act as President, or the manner in which one who is to act shall be selected, and such person shall act accordingly until a President or Vice-President shall have qualified.

Section 4. President Chosen by the House

The Congress may by law provide for the case of the death of any of the persons from whom the House of Representatives may choose a President whenever the right of choice shall have devolved upon them, and for the case of death of any of the persons from whom the Senate may choose a Vice-President whenever the right of choice shall have devolved upon them.

Section 5. Effective Date

Section 1 and 2 shall take effect on the 15th day of October following the ratification of this article.

Section 6. Ratification

This article shall be inoperative unless it shall have been ratified as an amendment to the Constitution by the legislatures of three-fourths of the several States within seven years from the date of its submission.

XXI. Repeal of Prohibition (1933)

Section 1. Repeal of Article XVIII

The eighteenth article of amendment to the Constitution of the United States is hereby repealed.

Section 2. Transportation of Liquor

The transportation or importation into any State, Territory or Possession of the United States for delivery or use therein of intoxicating liquors, in violation of the laws thereof, is hereby prohibited.

Section 3. Ratification

This article shall be inoperative unless it shall have been ratified as an amendment to the Constitution by conventions in the several States, as provided in the Constitution, within seven years from the date of the submission hereof to the States by the Congress.

XXII. Presidential Term of Office (1951)

No person shall be elected to the office of the President more than twice, and no person who has held the office of President, or acted as President for more than two years of a term to which some other person was elected President, shall be elected to the office of the President more than once. But this article shall not apply to any person holding the office of President when this article was proposed by the Congress, and shall not prevent any person who may be holding the office of President, or acting as President, during the term within which this article becomes effective, from holding the office of President or acting as President during the remainder of such term.

INDEX

atomic energy, 211-212,325-326
Atomic Energy Act, 212
Atomic Energy Commission, 212, 326
Augustinian Fathers, 188
aureomycin, 209
Austria, 225, 226, 245, 249, 257, 259, 292
authors, American, 194-195
automobile industry, 83, 88-89
Ave Maria, 193
Axis Powers, 257, 271

B

balance of power, 225
Balkan Peninsula, 260
Balkan states, 226
bank holiday, 127
banks, 89, 98, 99, 100, 127, 156
Bataan Peninsula, 276
Belgium, 227, 228, 229, 245, 259
Bell, Alexander, 84
Benedict XV, Pope, 227, 244, 245, 247
Benedictine Fathers, 188
Bering Sea dispute, 17-18
Bering, Vitus, 16
Berlin, 272, 275, 292
Berlin-Tokyo Pact, 263
"best sellers," religious, 194
"big business," 80-90, 91-95, 100-105, 148
"Big Four," 247
bigotry, 315
"big stick" policy, 53, 54
Bill of Rights, 174
Bishops' Program, 112, 113
Blaine, James G., 64
blitzkrieg, 259
blockade, British, 231

Bogota, 67, 311
Bolivar, Simon, 64
bonds, 98, 99
book clubs, 195
Book-of-the-Month Club, **195**
bootleggers, 177
Borglum, Gutzon, 196, 197
Boston College, 188
Boulder Dam, 162
Boxer Rebellion, 46-47
boycott, 119, 130
Boy Scouts, Catholic, 334
Boys Town, 335-336
Braille, 193
Bryan, William Jennings, 149
Bulge, Battle of, 275
Bureau of Air Commerce, 202
Burma Road, 277, 278
Butler, Dr. Nicholas Murray, 187
Byrd, Lieutenant Richard E., 203

C

Calles, Plutarco, 62
Canada, 51, 67, 99
capital, 86, 89, 119, 124, 131
captains of industry, 84
CARE. *See* Cooperative for American Remittances to Europe.
Caribbean area, U.S. possessions in, 53-54
Carnegie, Andrew, 81-82, 84-86
Carnegie Foundation for the Advancement of Teaching, 86
Carnegie Institution, 86
Carnegie Steel Company, 120
Carranza, General, 61, 62
Carroll, Bishop, 332
Carroll, Dr. James, 52
Casablanca, 280
"cash and carry" program, **258-259**

founding fathers, and world affairs, 14

Four Freedoms, 264

Four-H Clubs, 149, 150

France, 46, 49-50, 225, 227, 228, 229, 238, 240, 241, 245, 247, 259, 274, 276, 322

Franciscan Fathers, 188

freedom of the press, 192

French, Daniel Chester, 197

French influence, 201

Friars' lands in Philippines, 38

Frick, Henry Clay, 84, 85

Frost, Robert, 194

G

Garfield, President, 180

Garvan, Francis Patrick, 164

gasoline, 238

General Assembly of UN, 321, 322, 323, 324, 330

Geneva, 249

genocide treaty, 330

George, Lloyd, 246, 247

Georgetown University, 188, 189

German influence, 201

Germany, 22, 46, 225, 226, 227, 228, 229, 231, 232, 233, 234, 235, 240, 241, 242, 244, 245, 247, 249, 252, 253, 254, 255, 256, 257, 259, 260, 263, 265, 271, 276, 283, 292, 331

Gershwin, George, 199

GI Bill of Rights, 288

Gibbons, Cardinal, 37, 42, 47, 116, 189, 239

Girl Scouts, Catholic, 334

God, 39, 40, 91, 95, 165, 255, 309, 310, 330, 331, 339-340

Goethals, George, 57

gold, 17, 30, 51, 80, 99
  recall of, 127

Gompers, Samuel, 116, 117

"Good Neighbor Policy," 65-67, 68

Gorgas, Dr. William C., 52, 57

Grand Coulee Dam, 162

Grange, 148

Granger, Iowa, 163

Granger Laws, 101

Granger Plan, 163-164

Great Britain. See England.

Great Northern Railway, 101

Green, William, 117

Gregorian Chant, 200

Guadalcanal, 278

Guam, ceded to United States, 36

H

Hague, The, 48, 324

Haiti, 54, 66

Harding, Warren G., 249

Harlan, Justice, 104

Harriman, Edward H., 101

Hawaii, 24, 25
  annexation of, 26, 265

Hay, John, 46

Hay-Pauncefote Treaty, 57

Hayes, Patrick Cardinal, 239

H-bomb

health, public, 180
  in industry, 181
  services, 181-182

Hepburn Act, 102

Herbert, Victor, 200

heritage from Europe, 308-309

Hill, James J., 84, 101

Hiroshima, 279-280, 325

Hitler, Adolf, 253, 254, 255, 256, 257, 259, 272, 275, 330

Holland, 226, 259

New Zealand and Samoa, 23

Nicaragua, 56

Nieuwland, Father Julius, 83

NLRB. *See* National Labor Relations
    Board.

North Africa, 273

North Atlantic Pact, 331

North Pole, 203

North Sea, 229

Northern Securities Company,
    101-102

Noticias Catolicas, 67

Notre Dame University, 83, 188

NRA. *See* National Recovery
    Administration, 127

nylon, 210

O

Oahu, 26

Oblates of Mary Immaculate, 20

occupational diseases, 181

Office of Price Administration, 270

O'Hara, Bishop Edwin V., 150

oil, 82, 86-87, 121

oil pipe lines, 102

Okinawa, 278

old-age pensions, 182

Olney, Richard, 50

OPA. *See* Office of Price
    Administration.

open door policy in China, 46

open shop, 119

Oregon, 55

Oregon school case, 318

Organization of American States, 68

Orlando, Premier, 246, 247

Our Lady, devotions to, 337-338

Our Sunday Visitor, 193

owners, 91-92

P

Pagopago, 22, 23

Palestine, 283, 325

Panama, 57, 66

Panama Canal, 55-58

Panama Canal Zone, 57

Pan-American movement, **64, 65,**
    67-68

Pan-American Union, 68, 258

panics
   of 1873, 115-116
   of 1893, 98-99
   of 1929, 102

Papal Peace Plan, 284-285

parcel post, 155

Paris, 227, 228, 240, **283, 330**

parochial schools, 187, **317,** 318

partnership, 86

Patent Office, 154

Paulist Choristers, 200

Payne-Aldrich Tariff, 97

peace conference, 246-247

peace, world, 227-228
   proposals, 244, 245, 246, 285

peace treaty, 246-250; 283

Pearl Harbor, 26, 27, 264-265, 266, 276

Pendleton Act, 180

penicillin, 209

People's Party, 149

Perkins, Frances, 176

Perry, Commodore Matthew C., 45

Pershing, General John J., 62, 237

Peyton, C.S.C., Father Patrick, 338

Philippine Islands, 34, 36, 40, 237, 276

picketing, 119, 130

Pinchot, Gifford, 158

Pius X, Pope, 200, 337

Pius X School of Liturgical Music,
    201

Pius XI, Pope, 88, 94, 95, 113, 114, 131, 187, 190, 191, 209, 312
Pius XII, Pope, 68, 284, 285, 339, 340
plasma, blood, 209
plastics, 210-211
Platt Amendment, 53
Pledge of Allegiance, 313
Plenary Council of Baltimore, Third, 187
Poland, 257, 259
Polynesians, 23
Populist Party, 148-149
Portsmouth, treaty at, 48-49
postal savings banks, 149
postal service, rural, 155
poster painting, 197-198, 235, 238
Potsdam, 279
Powderly, Terence, 116
Presidential Succession Act, 290
press, Catholic, 192-193
press reporters, 191, 192
press services, 191
Pribilof Islands, 17, 18, 19
price controls, 287
private ownership, 95, 113
Pro, Father Miguel, 62-63
profit sharing, 130-131
prohibition, 177
propaganda, 192, 207
protective tariff, 97, 98
public health, 180
public health services, 181-182
public schools, 184-186
Public Works Administration, 128
Puerto Rico, 36, 54, 55
Pullman-car companies, 102
Pullman Strike, 120
Pure Food and Drug Act, 180

Q

Quadragesimo Anno, 113
Quebec, 280
Quezon, Manuel, 40

R

radar, 203-204
radio, 204, 206
R.A.F. *See* Royal Air Force.
railroads, 99, 101, 102, 120, 148
rationing, 269-270
raw materials, 44-45, 93
rayon, 210
rebates, 101
reciprocal trade agreements, 98
Reclamation Act, 159
Reconstruction Finance Corporation, 126
Red Cross, 35-36
Reed, Walter, 52
Register, 193
released time for teaching religion, 178-179, 318
religion, 186, 284, 285, 309, 310, 318 331, 339
religion and public schools, 186
religious liberty, 284, 285, 309
Remagen Bridge, Battle of, 275
repeal of amendment, 177-178
Republican Party, 97
Rerum Novarum, 111, 112
revenue, 96
rights, individual and national, 40-41, 165, 288
rights of workers, 112, 113, 115
Rio de Janeiro, 66; treaty at, 67
roads, 145, 155
Rockefeller, John D., 86-87
Romberg, Sigmund, 200
Roosevelt Dam, 159-160